Microsoft® Office

Excel 2007

Introductory Concepts and Techniques

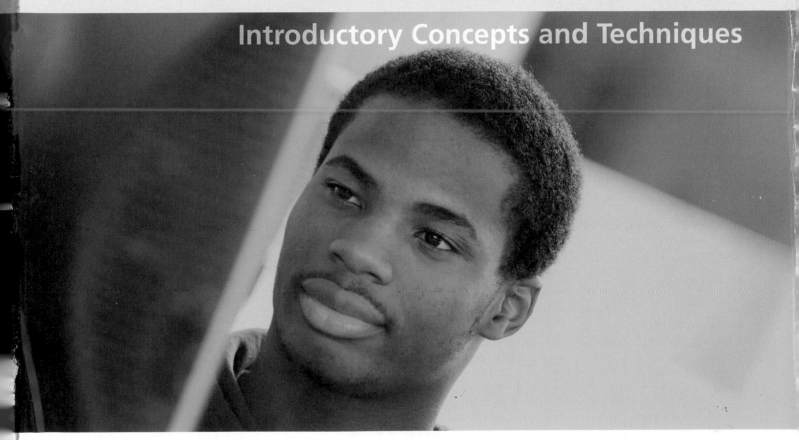

Gary B. Shelly

Thomas J. Cashman

Jeffrey J. Quasney

DAVID GLENN HUNT
MEMORIAL LIBRARY
GALVESTON COLLEGE

THOMSON
★
COURSE TECHNOLOGY™

SHELLY
CASHMAN
SERIES®

THOMSON COURSE TECHNOLOGY   25 THOMSON PLACE   BOSTON MA 02210

Australia • Canada • Denmark • Japan • Mexico • New Zealand • Philippines • Puerto Rico • Singapore • South Africa • Spain • United Kingdom • United States

THOMSON
COURSE TECHNOLOGY™

Microsoft Office Excel 2007
Introductory Concepts and Techniques

Gary B. Shelly

Thomas J. Cashman

Jeffrey J. Quasney

Executive Editor
Alexandra Arnold

Senior Product Manager
Mali Jones

Associate Product Manager
Klenda Martinez

Editorial Assistant
Jon Farnham

Senior Marketing Manager
Joy Stark-Vancs

Marketing Coordinator
Julie Schuster

Print Buyer
Julio Esperas

Director of Production
Patty Stephan

Senior Production Editor
Catherine G. DiMassa

Developmental Editor
Lyn Markowicz

Proofreader
Green Pen Quality Assurance

Indexer
Rich Carlson

QA Manuscript Reviewers
John Freitas, Serge Palladino,
Chris Scriver, Danielle Shaw,
Marianne Snow, Teresa Storch

Art Director
Bruce Bond

Cover and Text Design
Joel Sadagursky

Cover Photo
Jon Chomitz

Compositor
GEX Publishing Services

Printer
Banta Menasha

COPYRIGHT © 2008 Thomson Course Technology, a division of Thomson Learning, Inc. Thomson Learning™ is a trademark used herein under license.

Printed in the United States of America

1 2 3 4 5 6 7 8 9 10
BM 09 08 07

For more information, contact Thomson Course Technology 25 Thomson Place Boston, Massachusetts 02210

Or find us on the World Wide Web at: www.course.com

ALL RIGHTS RESERVED. No part of this work covered by the copyright hereon may be reproduced or used in any form or by any means — graphic, electronic, or mechanical, including photocopying, recording, taping, Web distribution, or information storage and retrieval systems — without the written permission of the publisher.

For permission to use material from this text or product, submit a request online at http://www.thomsonrights.com

Any additional questions about permissions can be submitted by email to thomsonrights@thomson.com

Thomson Course Technology, the Thomson Course Technology logo, the Shelly Cashman Series® are registered trademarks used under license. All other names used herein are for identification purposes only and are trademarks of their respective owners. Thomson Course Technology reserves the right to revise this publication and make changes from time to time in its content without notice.

softcover binding:
ISBN 13: 978-1-4188-4342-7
ISBN: 1-4188-4342-3

Microsoft® Office
Excel 2007
Introductory Concepts and Techniques

Contents

Preface

The Shelly Cashman Series® offers the finest textbooks in computer education. We are proud of the fact that our series of Microsoft Office 4.3, Microsoft Office 95, Microsoft Office 97, Microsoft Office 2000, Microsoft Office XP, and Microsoft Office 2003 textbooks have been the most widely used books in education. With each new edition of our Office books, we have made significant improvements based on the software and comments made by instructors and students.

Microsoft Office 2007 contains more changes in the user interface and feature set than all other previous versions combined. Recognizing that the new features and functionality of Microsoft Office 2007 would impact the way that students are taught skills, the Shelly Cashman Series development team carefully reviewed our pedagogy and analyzed its effectiveness in teaching today's Office student. An extensive customer survey produced results confirming what the series is best known for: its step-by-step, screen-by-screen instructions, its project-oriented approach, and the quality of its content.

We learned, though, that students entering computer courses today are different than students taking these classes just a few years ago. Students today read less, but need to retain more. They need not only to be able to perform skills, but to retain those skills and know how to apply them to different settings. Today's students need to be continually engaged and challenged to retain what they're learning.

As a result, we've renewed our commitment to focusing on the user and how they learn best. This commitment is reflected in every change we've made to our Office 2007 books.

Objectives of This Textbook

Microsoft Office Excel 2007: Introductory Concepts and Techniques is intended for a course that includes an introduction to Excel 2007. No experience with a computer is assumed, and no mathematics beyond the high school freshman level is required. The objectives of this book are:

- To teach the fundamentals of Microsoft Office Excel 2007
- To expose students to practical examples of the computer as a useful tool
- To acquaint students with the proper procedures to create workbooks and worksheets suitable for coursework, professional purposes, and personal use
- To help students discover the underlying functionality of Excel 2007 so they can become more productive
- To develop an exercise-oriented approach that allows learning by doing

The Shelly Cashman Approach

Features of the Shelly Cashman Series Microsoft Office Excel 2007 books include:

- **Project Orientation** Each chapter in the book presents a project with a practical problem and complete solution in an easy-to-understand approach.

- **Plan Ahead Boxes** The project orientation is enhanced by the inclusion of Plan Ahead boxes. These new features prepare students to create successful projects by encouraging them to think strategically about what they are trying to accomplish before they begin working.

- **Step-by-Step, Screen-by-Screen Instructions** Each of the tasks required to complete a project is clearly identified throughout the chapter. Now, the step-by-step instructions provide a context beyond point-and-click. Each step explains why students are performing a task, or the result of performing a certain action. Found on the screens accompanying each step, call-outs give students the information they need to know when they need to know it. Now, we've used color to distinguish the content in the call-outs. The Explanatory call-outs (in black) summarize what is happening on the screen and the Navigational call-outs (in red) show students where to click.

- **Q&A** Found within many of the step-by-step sequences, Q&As raise the kinds of questions students may ask when working through a step sequence and provide answers about what they are doing, why they are doing it, and how that task might be approached differently.

- **Experimental Steps** These new steps, within our step-by-step instructions, encourage students to explore, experiment, and take advantage of the features of the Office 2007 new user interface. These steps are not necessary to complete the projects, but are designed to increase the confidence with the software and build problem-solving skills.

- **Thoroughly Tested Projects** Unparalleled quality is ensured because every screen in the book is produced by the author only after performing a step, and then each project must pass Thomson Course Technology's Quality Assurance program.

- **Other Ways Boxes and Quick Reference Summary** The Other Ways boxes displayed at the end of most of the step-by-step sequences specify the other ways to do the task completed in the steps. Thus, the steps and the Other Ways box make a comprehensive reference unit. A Quick Reference Summary at the end of the book contains all of the tasks presented in the chapters, and all ways identified of accomplishing the tasks.

- **BTW** These marginal annotations provide background information, tips, and answers to common questions that complement the topics covered, adding depth and perspective to the learning process.

- **Integration of the World Wide Web** The World Wide Web is integrated into the Excel 2007 learning experience by (1) BTW annotations that send students to Web sites for up-to-date information and alternative approaches to tasks; (2) a Microsoft Business Certification Program Web page so students can prepare for the certification examinations; (3) a Quick Reference Summary Web page that summarizes the ways to complete tasks (mouse, Ribbon, shortcut menu, and keyboard); and (4) the Learn It Online section at the end of each chapter, which has chapter reinforcement exercises, learning games, and other types of student activities.

- **End-of-Chapter Student Activities** Extensive student activities at the end of each chapter provide the student with plenty of opportunities to reinforce the materials learned in the chapter through hands-on assignments. Several new types of activities have been added that challenge the student in new ways to expand their knowledge, and to apply their new skills to a project with personal relevance.

Q&A

What is a maximized window?

A maximized window fills the entire screen. When you maximize a window, the Maximize button changes to a Restore Down button.

Other Ways

1. Click Italic button on Mini toolbar

2. Right-click selected text, click Font on shortcut menu, click Font tab, click Italic in Font style list, click OK button

3. Click Font Dialog Box Launcher, click Font tab, click Italic in Font style list, click OK button

4. Press CTRL+I

BTW

Minimizing the Ribbon
If you want to minimize the Ribbon, right-click the Ribbon and then click Minimize the Ribbon on the shortcut menu, double-click the active tab, or press CTRL+F1. To restore a minimized Ribbon, right-click the Ribbon and then click Minimize the Ribbon on the shortcut menu, double-click any top-level tab, or press CTRL+F1. To use commands on a minimized Ribbon, click the top-level tab.

Organization of This Textbook

Microsoft Office Excel 2007: Introductory Concepts and Techniques consists of three chapters on Microsoft Office Excel 2007, one special feature emphasizing Web-related topics, seven appendices, and a Quick Reference Summary.

End-of-Chapter Student Activities

A notable strength of the Shelly Cashman Series Microsoft Office 2007 books is the extensive student activities at the end of each chapter. Well-structured student activities can make the difference between students merely participating in a class and students retaining the information they learn. The activities in the Shelly Cashman Series Office books include the following.

Figure 1-100

CHAPTER SUMMARY A concluding paragraph, followed by a listing of the tasks completed within a chapter together with the pages on which the step-by-step, screen-by-screen explanations appear.

LEARN IT ONLINE Every chapter features a Learn It Online section that is comprised of six exercises. These exercises include True/False, Multiple Choice, Short Answer, Flash Cards, Practice Test, and Learning Games.

APPLY YOUR KNOWLEDGE This exercise usually requires students to open and manipulate a file from the Data Files that parallels the activities learned in the chapter. To obtain a copy of the Data Files for Students, follow the instructions on the inside back cover of this text.

EXTEND YOUR KNOWLEDGE This exercise allows students to extend and expand on the skills learned within the chapter.

MAKE IT RIGHT This exercise requires students to analyze a document, identify errors and issues, and correct those errors and issues using skills learned in the chapter.

IN THE LAB Three all new in-depth assignments per chapter require students to utilize the chapter concepts and techniques to solve problems on a computer.

CASES AND PLACES Five unique real-world case-study situations, including Make It Personal, an open-ended project that relates to student's personal lives, and one small-group activity.

Instructor Resources CD-ROM

The Shelly Cashman Series is dedicated to providing you with all of the tools you need to make your class a success. Information about all supplementary materials is available through your Thomson Course Technology representative or by calling one of the following telephone numbers: Colleges, Universities, and Continuing Ed departments, 1-800-648-7450; High Schools, 1-800-824-5179; and Career Colleges, Business, Government, Library and Resellers, 1-800-477-3692.

The Instructor Resources CD-ROM for this textbook include both teaching and testing aids. The contents of each item on the Instructor Resources CD-ROM (ISBN 1-4239-1226-8) are described on the following pages.

INSTRUCTOR'S MANUAL The Instructor's Manual consists of Microsoft Word files, which include chapter objectives, lecture notes, teaching tips, classroom activities, lab activities, quick quizzes, figures and boxed elements summarized in the chapters, and a glossary page. The new format of the Instructor's Manual will allow you to map through every chapter easily.

LECTURE SUCCESS SYSTEM The Lecture Success System consists of intermediate files that correspond to certain figures in the book, allowing you to step through the creation of a project in a chapter during a lecture without entering large amounts of data.

SYLLABUS Sample syllabi, which can be customized easily to a course, are included. The syllabi cover policies, class and lab assignments and exams, and procedural information.

FIGURE FILES Illustrations for every figure in the textbook are available in electronic form. Use this ancillary to present a slide show in lecture or to print transparencies for use in lecture with an overhead projector. If you have a personal computer and LCD device, this ancillary can be an effective tool for presenting lectures.

POWERPOINT PRESENTATIONS PowerPoint Presentations is a multimedia lecture presentation system that provides slides for each chapter. Presentations are based on chapter objectives. Use this presentation system to present well-organized lectures that are both interesting and knowledge based. PowerPoint Presentations provides consistent coverage at schools that use multiple lecturers.

SOLUTIONS TO EXERCISES Solutions are included for the end-of-chapter exercises, as well as the Chapter Reinforcement exercises. Rubrics and annotated solution files, as described below, are also included.

RUBRICS AND ANNOTATED SOLUTION FILES The grading rubrics provide a customizable framework for assigning point values to the laboratory exercises. Annotated solution files that correspond to the grading rubrics make it easy for you to compare students' results with the correct solutions whether you receive their homework as hard copy or via e-mail.

TEST BANK & TEST ENGINE In the ExamView test bank, you will find our standard question types (40 multiple-choice, 25 true/false, 20 completion) and new objective-based question types (5 modified multiple-choice, 5 modified true/false and 10 matching). Critical Thinking questions are also included (3 essays and 2 cases with 2 questions each) totaling the test bank to 112 questions for every chapter with page number references, and when appropriate, figure references. A version of the test bank you can print also is included. The test bank comes with a copy of the test engine, ExamView, the ultimate tool for your objective-based testing needs. ExamView is a state-of-the-art test builder that is easy to use. ExamView enables you to create paper-, LAN-, or Web-based tests from test banks designed specifically for your Thomson Course Technology textbook. Utilize the ultra-efficient QuickTest Wizard to create tests in less than five minutes by taking advantage of Thomson Course Technology's question banks, or customize your own exams from scratch.

LAB TESTS/TEST OUT The Lab Tests/Test Out exercises parallel the In the Lab assignments and are supplied for the purpose of testing students in the laboratory on the material covered in the chapter or testing students out of the course.

DATA FILES FOR STUDENTS All the files that are required by students to complete the exercises are included. You can distribute the files on the Instructor Resources CD-ROM to your students over a network, or you can have them follow the instructions on the inside back cover of this book to obtain a copy of the Data Files for Students.

ADDITIONAL ACTIVITIES FOR STUDENTS These additional activities consist of Chapter Reinforcement Exercises, which are true/false, multiple-choice, and short answer questions that help students gain confidence in the material learned.

Assessment & Training Solutions
SAM 2007

SAM 2007 helps bridge the gap between the classroom and the real world by allowing students to train and test on important computer skills in an active, hands-on environment.

SAM 2007's easy-to-use system includes powerful interactive exams, training or projects on critical applications such as Word, Excel, Access, PowerPoint, Outlook, Windows, the Internet, and much more. SAM simulates the application environment, allowing students to demonstrate their knowledge and think through the skills by performing real-world tasks.

Designed to be used with the Shelly Cashman series, SAM 2007 includes built-in page references so students can print helpful study guides that match the Shelly Cashman series textbooks used in class. Powerful administrative options allow instructors to schedule exams and assignments, secure tests, and run reports with almost limitless flexibility.

Student Edition Labs

Our Web-based interactive labs help students master hundreds of computer concepts, including input and output devices, file management and desktop applications, computer ethics, virus protection, and much more. Featuring up-to-the-minute content, eye-popping graphics, and rich animation, the highly interactive Student Edition Labs offer students an alternative way to learn through dynamic observation, step-by-step practice, and challenging review questions.

Online Content

Blackboard is the leading distance learning solution provider and class-management platform today. Thomson Course Technology has partnered with Blackboard to bring you premium online content. Instructors: Content for use with *Microsoft Office 2007: Introductory Concepts and Techniques, Windows Vista Edition* is available in a Blackboard Course Cartridge and may include topic reviews, case projects, review questions, test banks, practice tests, custom syllabi, and more.

Thomson Course Technology also has solutions for several other learning management systems. Please visit http://www.course.com today to see what's available for this title.

Workbook for Microsoft Office 2007: Introductory Concepts and Techniques

This highly popular supplement (ISBN 1-4188-4335-0) includes a variety of activities that help students recall, review, and master the concepts presented. The Workbook complements the end-of-chapter material with an outline; a self-test consisting of true/false, multiple-choice, short answer, and matching questions; and activities calculated to help students develop a deeper understanding of the information presented.

CourseCasts Learning on the Go. Always Available...Always Relevant.

Want to keep up with the latest technology trends relevant to you? Visit our site to find a library of podcasts, CourseCasts, featuring a "CourseCast of the Week," and download them to your portable media player at http://coursecasts.course.com.

Our fast-paced world is driven by technology. You know because you are an active participant — always on the go, always keeping up with technological trends, and always learning new ways to embrace technology to power your life.

Ken Baldauf, a faculty member of the Florida State University (FSU) Computer Science Department, is responsible for teaching technology classes to thousands of FSU students each year. He knows what you know; he knows what you want to learn. He is also an expert in the latest technology and will sort through and aggregate the most pertinent news and information so you can spend your time enjoying technology, rather than trying to figure it out.

Visit us at http://coursecasts.course.com to learn on the go!

CourseNotes

Course Technology's CourseNotes are six-panel quick reference cards that reinforce the most important and widely used features of a software application in a visual and user-friendly format. CourseNotes will serve as a great reference tool during and after the student completes the course. CourseNotes for Microsoft Office 2007, Word 2007, Excel 2007, Access 2007, PowerPoint 2007, Windows Vista, and more are available now!

To the Student . . . Getting the Most Out of Your Book

Welcome to *Microsoft Office Excel 2007: Introductory Concepts and Techniques*. You can save yourself a lot of time and gain a better understanding of the Office 2007 programs if you spend a few minutes reviewing the figures and callouts in this section.

1 PROJECT ORIENTATION
Each chapter's project presents a practical problem and shows the solution in the first figure of the chapter. The project orientation lets you see firsthand how problems are solved from start to finish using application software and computers.

2 PROJECT PLANNING GUIDELINES AND PLAN AHEAD BOXES
Overall planning guidelines at the beginning of a chapter and Plan Ahead boxes throughout encourage you to think critically about how to accomplish the next goal before you actually begin working.

3 CONSISTENT STEP-BY-STEP, SCREEN-BY-SCREEN PRESENTATION
Chapter solutions are built using a step-by-step, screen-by-screen approach. This pedagogy allows you to build the solution on a computer as you read through the chapter. Generally, each step includes an explanation that indicates the result of the step.

4 MORE THAN JUST STEP-BY-STEP
BTW annotations in the margins of the book, Q&As in the steps, and substantive text in the paragraphs provide background information, tips, and answers to common questions that complement the topics covered, adding depth and perspective. When you finish with this book, you will be ready to use the Office programs to solve problems on your own. Experimental steps provide you with opportunities to step out on your own to try features of the programs, and pick up right where you left off in the chapter.

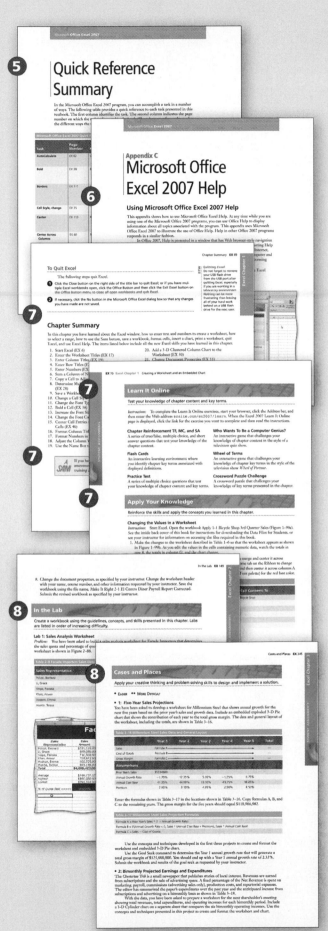

5 OTHER WAYS BOXES AND QUICK REFERENCE SUMMARY
Other Ways boxes that follow many of the step sequences and a Quick Reference Summary at the back of the book explain the other ways to complete the task presented, such as using the mouse, Ribbon, shortcut menu, and keyboard.

6 EMPHASIS ON GETTING HELP WHEN YOU NEED IT
The first project of each application and Appendix C show you how to use all the elements of Office Help. Being able to answer your own questions will increase your productivity and reduce your frustrations by minimizing the time it takes to learn how to complete a task.

7 REVIEW, REINFORCEMENT, AND EXTENSION
After you successfully step through a project in a chapter, a section titled Chapter Summary identifies the tasks with which you should be familiar. Terms you should know for test purposes are bold in the text. The SAM Training feature provides the opportunity for addional reinforcement on important skills covered in each chapter. The Learn It Online section at the end of each chapter offers reinforcement in the form of review questions, learning games, and practice tests. Also included are exercises that require you to extend your learning beyond the book.

8 LABORATORY EXERCISES
If you really want to learn how to use the programs, then you must design and implement solutions to problems on your own. Every chapter concludes with several carefully developed laboratory assignments that increase in complexity.

About Our New Cover Look

Learning styles of students have changed, but the
Shelly Cashman Series' dedication to their success has
remained steadfast for over 30 years. We are committed
to continually updating our approach and content to
reflect the way today's students learn and experience new
technology.

This focus on the user is reflected in our bold new cover
design, which features photographs of real students
using the Shelly Cashman Series in their courses. Each
book features a different user, reflecting the many ages,
experiences, and backgrounds of all of the students
learning with our books. When you use the Shelly
Cashman Series, you can be assured that you are learning
computer skills using the most effective courseware
available.

Microsoft Office Excel 2007

1 | Creating a Worksheet and an Embedded Chart

Objectives

You will have mastered the material in this chapter when you can:

- Start and quit Excel
- Describe the Excel worksheet
- Enter text and numbers
- Use the Sum button to sum a range of cells
- Copy the contents of a cell to a range of cells using the fill handle
- Save a workbook
- Format cells in a worksheet
- Create a 3-D Clustered Column chart

- Change document properties
- Save a workbook a second time using the same file name
- Print a worksheet
- Open a workbook
- Use the AutoCalculate area to determine statistics
- Correct errors on a worksheet
- Use Excel Help to answer questions

1 | Creating a Worksheet and an Embedded Chart

What Is Microsoft Office Excel 2007?

Microsoft Office Excel 2007 is a powerful spreadsheet program that allows users to organize data, complete calculations, make decisions, graph data, develop professional looking reports (Figure 1–1), publish organized data to the Web, and access real-time data from Web sites. The four major parts of Excel are:

- **Workbooks and Worksheets** Workbooks are a collection of worksheets. Worksheets allow users to enter, calculate, manipulate, and analyze data such as numbers and text. The terms worksheet and spreadsheet are interchangeable.

- **Charts** Excel can draw a variety of charts.

- **Tables** Tables organize and store data within worksheets. For example, once a user enters data into a worksheet, an Excel table can sort the data, search for specific data, and select data that satisfies defined criteria.

- **Web Support** Web support allows users to save Excel worksheets or parts of a worksheet in HTML format, so a user can view and manipulate the worksheet using a browser. Excel Web support also provides access to real-time data, such as stock quotes, using Web queries.

This latest version of Excel makes it much easier than in previous versions to perform common functions by introducing a new style of user interface. It also offers the capability of creating larger worksheets, improved formatting and printing, improved charting and table functionality, industry-standard XML support that simplifies the sharing of data within and outside an organization, improved business intelligence functionality, and the capability of performing complex tasks on a server.

In this chapter, you will create a worksheet that includes a chart. The data in the worksheet and chart includes sales data for several stores that a company owns and operates.

Project Planning Guidelines

The process of developing a worksheet that communicates specific information requires careful analysis and planning. As a starting point, establish why the worksheet is needed. Once the purpose is determined, analyze the intended users of the worksheet and their unique needs. Then, gather information about the topic and decide what to include in the worksheet. Finally, determine the worksheet design and style that will be most successful at delivering the message. Details of these guidelines are provided in Appendix A. In addition, each project developed in this book provides practical applications of these planning considerations.

Project — Worksheet with an Embedded Chart

The project in this chapter follows proper design guidelines and uses Excel to create the worksheet shown in Figure 1–1. The worksheet contains sales data for Walk and Rock Music stores. The Walk and Rock Music product line includes a variety of MP3 music players, called Rock-It MP3, including players that show pictures and video, as well as a complete line of headphones and other accessories. The company sells its products at kiosks in several malls throughout the United States. By concentrating its stores near colleges and universities and keeping the newest items in stock, the Walk and Rock Music stores quickly became trendy. As sales continued to grow in the past year, senior management requested an easy-to-read worksheet that shows product sales for the first quarter by region. In addition, they asked for a chart showing first quarter sales, because the president of the company likes to have a graphical representation of sales that allows him quickly to identify stronger and weaker product types by region.

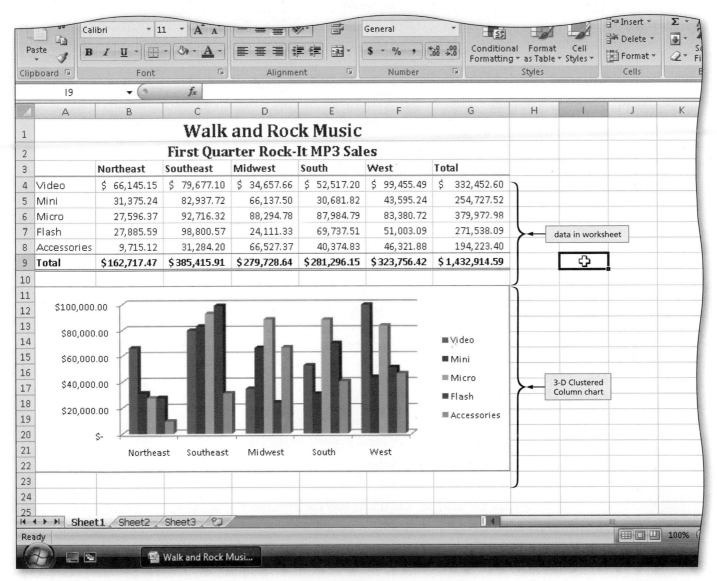

Figure 1–1

The first step in creating an effective worksheet is to make sure you understand what is required. The person or persons requesting the worksheet should supply their requirements in a requirements document. A **requirements document** includes a needs

BTW

Excel 2007 Features
With its what-if
analysis tools, research
capabilities, collaboration
tools, streamlined user
interface, smart tags,
charting features, Web
capabilities, hundreds of
functions, and enhanced
formatting capabilities,
Excel 2007 is one of the
easier and more powerful
spreadsheet packages
available.

statement, source of data, summary of calculations, and any other special requirements for the worksheet, such as charting and Web support. Figure 1–2 shows the requirements document for the new workbook to be created in this chapter.

requirements
document

REQUEST FOR NEW WORKBOOK

Date Submitted:	April 15, 2008
Submitted By:	Trisha Samuels
Worksheet Title:	Walk and Rock Music First Quarter Sales
Needs:	An easy-to-read worksheet that shows Walk and Rock Music's first quarter sales for each of our sales regions in which we operate (Northeast, Southeast, Midwest, South, West). The worksheet also should include total sales for each region, total sales for each product type, and total company sales for the first quarter.
Source of Data:	The data for the worksheet is available for the end of the first quarter from the chief financial officer (CFO) of Walk and Rock Music.
Calculations:	The following calculations must be made for the worksheet: (a) total first quarter sales for each of the five regions; (b) total first quarter sales for each of the five product types; and (c) total first quarter sales for the company.
Chart Requirements:	Below the data in the worksheet, construct a 3-D Clustered Column chart that compares the total sales for each region within each type of product.

Approvals

Approval Status:	X	Approved
		Rejected
Approved By:	Stan Maderbek	
Date:	April 22, 2008	
Assigned To:	J. Quasney, Spreadsheet Specialist	

Figure 1–2

BTW

Worksheet Development Cycle
Spreadsheet specialists
do not sit down and
start entering text,
formulas, and data into
a blank Excel worksheet
as soon as they have a
spreadsheet assignment.
Instead, they follow
an organized plan,
or methodology, that
breaks the development
cycle into a series of
tasks. The recommended
methodology for creating
worksheets includes:
(1) analyze requirements
(supplied in a requirements
document); (2) design
solution; (3) validate
design; (4) implement
design; (5) test solution;
and (6) document
solution.

Overview

As you read this chapter, you will learn how to create the worksheet shown in Figure 1–1 by performing these general tasks:

• Enter text in the worksheet

• Add totals to the worksheet

• Save the workbook that contains the worksheet

• Format the text in the worksheet

• Insert a chart in the worksheet

• Save the workbook a second time using the same file name

• Print the worksheet

Plan Ahead

General Project Guidelines

While creating an Excel worksheet, you need to make several decisions that will determine the appearance and characteristics of the finished worksheet. As you create the worksheet shown in Figure 1–1, you should follow these general guidelines:

1. **Select titles and subtitles for the worksheet.** Follow the *less is more* guideline. The less text in the titles and subtitles, the more impact the titles and subtitles will have. Use the fewest words possible to specify the information presented in the worksheet to the intended audience.

(continued)

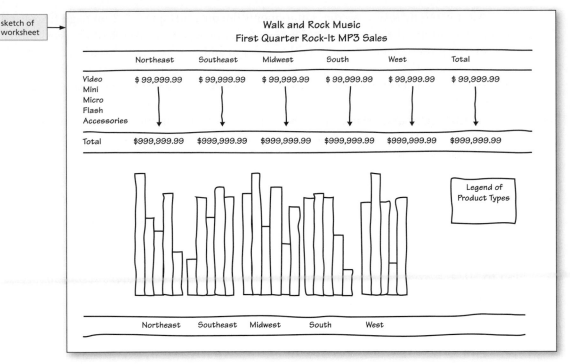

Figure 1–3

Plan
Ahead

(continued)

2. **Determine the contents for rows and columns.** Rows typically contain information that is analogous to items in a list, such as the products sold by a company. Columns typically contain descriptive information about items in rows or contain information that helps to group the data in the worksheet, such as company regions.

3. **Determine the calculations that are needed.** You can decide to total data in a variety of ways, such as across rows or in columns. You also can include a grand total.

4. **Determine where to save the workbook.** You can store a workbook permanently, or **save** it, on a variety of storage media including a hard disk, USB flash drive, or CD. You also can indicate a specific location on the storage media for saving the workbook.

5. **Identify how to format various elements of the worksheet.** The overall appearance of a worksheet significantly affects its ability to communicate clearly. Examples of how you can modify the appearance, or **format**, of text include changing its shape, size, color, and position on the worksheet.

6. **Decide on the type of chart needed.** Excel includes the capability of creating many different types of charts, such as bar charts and pie charts. Each chart type relays a different message about the data in the worksheet. Choose a chart type that relays the message that you want to convey.

7. **Establish where to position and how to format the chart.** The position and format of the chart should command the attention of the intended audience. If possible, position the chart so that it prints with the worksheet data on a single page.

When necessary, more specific details concerning the above guidelines are presented at appropriate points in the chapter. The chapter also will identify the actions performed and decisions made regarding these guidelines during the creation of the worksheet shown in Figure 1–1 on page EX 3.

After carefully reviewing the requirements document (Figure 1–2 on page EX 4) and necessary decisions, the next step is to design a solution or draw a sketch of the worksheet based on the requirements, including titles, column and row headings, location of data values, and the 3-D Clustered Column chart, as shown in Figure 1–3 on page EX 5. The dollar signs, 9s, and commas that you see in the sketch of the worksheet indicate formatted numeric values.

With a good understanding of the requirements document, an understanding of the necessary decisions, and a sketch of the worksheet, the next step is to use Excel to create the worksheet and chart.

Starting Excel

If you are using a computer to step through the project in this chapter and you want your screen to match the figures in this book, you should change your computer's resolution to 1024 × 768. For information about how to change a computer's resolution, read Appendix E.

To Start Excel

The following steps, which assume Windows Vista is running, start Excel based on a typical installation of Microsoft Office on your computer. You may need to ask your instructor how to start Excel for your computer.

Note: If you are using Windows XP, see Appendix F for alternate steps.

1

- Click the Start button on the Windows Vista taskbar to display the Start menu.

- Click All Programs at the bottom of left pane on the the Start menu to display the All Programs list.

- Click Microsoft Office in the All Programs list to display the Microsoft Office list (Figure 1–4).

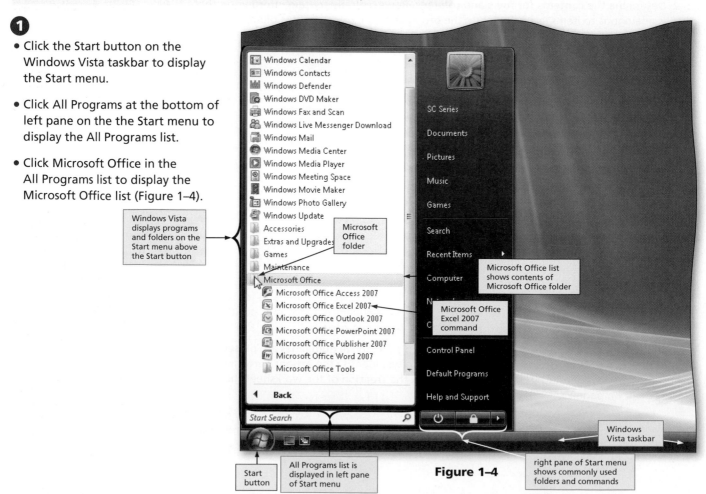

Figure 1–4

2

- Click Microsoft Office Excel 2007 to start Excel and display a new blank workbook titled Book1 in the Excel window (Figure 1–5).

- If the Excel window is not maximized, click the Maximize button next to the Close button on its title bar to maximize the window.

- If the worksheet window in Excel is not maximized, click the Maximize button next to the Close button on its title bar to maximize the worksheet window within Excel.

Q&A

What is a maximized window?

A maximized window fills the entire screen. When you maximize a window, the Maximize button changes to a Restore Down button. When you restore a maximized window, the window returns to its previous size and the Restore Down button changes to a Maximize button.

Figure 1–5

Other Ways

1. Double-click Excel 2007 icon on desktop, if one is present

2. Click Microsoft Office Excel 2007 on Start menu

The Excel Workbook

The Excel window consists of a variety of components to make your work more efficient and worksheets more professional. These include the document window, Ribbon, Mini toolbar and shortcut menus, Quick Access Toolbar, and Office Button. Some of these components are common to other Microsoft Office 2007 programs; others are unique to Excel.

When Excel starts, it creates a new blank workbook, called Book1. The **workbook** (Figure 1–6) is like a notebook. Inside the workbook are sheets, each of which is called a **worksheet**. Excel opens a new workbook with three worksheets.

If necessary, you can add additional worksheets as long as your computer has enough memory to accommodate them. Each worksheet has a sheet name that appears on a **sheet tab** at the bottom of the workbook. For example, Sheet1 is the name of the active worksheet displayed in the Book1 workbook. If you click the sheet tab labeled Sheet2, Excel displays the Sheet2 worksheet. The project in this chapter uses only the Sheet1 worksheet.

The Worksheet

The worksheet is organized into a rectangular grid containing vertical columns and horizontal rows. A column letter above the grid, also called the **column heading**, identifies each column. A row number on the left side of the grid, also called the **row heading**, identifies

BTW

Excel Help

Help with Excel is no further away than the Help button on the right side of the Ribbon. Click the Help button, type help in the 'Type words to search for' box, and then press the ENTER key. Excel responds with a list of topics you can click to learn about obtaining Help on any Excel-related topic. To find out what is new in Excel 2007, type what is new in Excel in the 'Type words to search for' box.

each row. With the screen resolution set to 1024 × 768 and the Excel window maximized, Excel displays 15 columns (A through O) and 25 rows (1 through 25) of the worksheet on the screen, as shown in Figure 1–6.

Figure 1–6

BTW

Worksheet Development
The key to developing a useful worksheet is careful planning. Careful planning can reduce your effort significantly and result in a worksheet that is accurate, easy to read, flexible, and useful. When analyzing a problem and designing a worksheet solution, you should follow these steps: (1) define the problem, including need, source of data, calculations, charting, and Web or special requirements; (2) design the worksheet; (3) enter the data and formulas; and (4) test the worksheet.

The intersection of each column and row is a cell. A **cell** is the basic unit of a worksheet into which you enter data. Each worksheet in a workbook has 16,384 columns and 1,048,576 rows for a total of 17,179,869,180 cells. Only a small fraction of the active worksheet appears on the screen at one time.

A cell is referred to by its unique address, or **cell reference**, which is the coordinates of the intersection of a column and a row. To identify a cell, specify the column letter first, followed by the row number. For example, cell reference D11 refers to the cell located at the intersection of column D and row 11 (Figure 1–6).

One cell on the worksheet, designated the **active cell**, is the one into which you can enter data. The active cell in Figure 1–6 is A1. The active cell is identified in three ways. First, a heavy border surrounds the cell; second, the active cell reference shows immediately above column A in the Name box; and third, the column heading A and row heading 1 are highlighted so it is easy to see which cell is active (Figure 1–6).

The horizontal and vertical lines on the worksheet itself are called **gridlines**. Gridlines make it easier to see and identify each cell in the worksheet. If desired, you can turn the gridlines off so they do not show on the worksheet, but it is recommended that you leave them on for now.

The mouse pointer in Figure 1–6 has the shape of a block plus sign. The mouse pointer appears as a block plus sign whenever it is located in a cell on the worksheet. Another common shape of the mouse pointer is the block arrow. The mouse pointer turns into the block arrow whenever you move it outside the worksheet or when you drag cell contents between rows or columns. The other mouse pointer shapes are described when they appear on the screen.

Worksheet Window

You view the portion of the worksheet displayed on the screen through a **worksheet window** (Figure 1–6). The default (preset) view is **normal view**. Below and to the right of the worksheet window are **scroll bars**, **scroll arrows**, and **scroll boxes** that you can use to move the worksheet window around to view different parts of the active worksheet. To the right of the sheet tabs at the bottom of the screen is the tab split box. You can drag the **tab split box** to increase or decrease the view of the sheet tabs (Figure 1–6). When you decrease the view of the sheet tabs, you increase the length of the horizontal scroll bar, and vice versa.

Status Bar

The status bar is located immediately above the Windows Vista taskbar at the bottom of the screen (Figure 1–6). The **status bar** presents information about the worksheet, the function of the button the mouse pointer is pointing to, or the mode of Excel. **Mode indicators**, such as Enter and Ready, appear on the status bar and specify the current mode of Excel. When the mode is **Ready**, Excel is ready to accept the next command or data entry. When the mode indicator reads **Enter**, Excel is in the process of accepting data through the keyboard into the active cell.

Keyboard indicators, such as Scroll Lock, show which toggle keys are engaged. Keyboard indicators appear to the right of the mode indicator. Toward the right edge of the status bar are buttons and controls you can use to change the view of a document and adjust the size of the displayed document.

Ribbon

The **Ribbon**, located near the top of the Excel window, is the control center in Excel (Figure 1–7a). The Ribbon provides easy, central access to the tasks you perform while creating a worksheet. The Ribbon consists of tabs, groups, and commands. Each **tab** surrounds a collection of groups, and each **group** contains related commands.

BTW

The Worksheet Size and Window
Excel's 16,384 columns and 1,048,576 rows make for a huge worksheet that – if you could imagine – takes up the entire side of a building to display in its entirety. Your computer screen, by comparison, is a small window that allows you to view only a minute area of the worksheet at one time. While you cannot see the entire worksheet, you can move the window over the worksheet to view any part of it.

BTW

Increasing the Viewing Area
You can increase the size of the Excel window or viewing area to show more of the worksheet. Two ways exist to increase what you can see in the viewing area: (1) on the View tab on the Ribbon, click Full Screen; and (2) change to a higher resolution. See Appendix E for information about how to change to a higher resolution.

(a) The Excel Ribbon

(b) The Excel Ribbon Minimized

Figure 1–7

BTW

Minimizing the Ribbon
If you want to minimize the Ribbon, right-click the Ribbon and then click Minimize the Ribbon on the shortcut menu, double-click the active tab, or press CTRL+F1. To restore a minimized Ribbon, right-click the Ribbon and then click Minimize the Ribbon on the shortcut menu, double-click any top-level tab, or press CTRL+F1. To use commands on a minimized Ribbon, click the top-level tab.

When you start Excel, the Ribbon displays seven top-level tabs: Home, Insert, Page Layout, Formulas, Data, Review, and View. The **Home tab**, called the primary tab, contains groups with the more frequently used commands. To display a different tab on the Ribbon, click the top-level tab. That is, to display the Insert tab, click Insert on the Ribbon. To return to the Home tab, click Home on the Ribbon. The tab currently displayed is called the **active tab**.

To display more of the document in the document window, some users prefer to minimize the Ribbon, which hides the groups on the Ribbon and displays only the top-level tabs (Figure 1–7b). To use commands on a minimized Ribbon, click the top-level tab.

Each time you start Excel, the Ribbon appears the same way it did the last time you used Excel. The chapters in this book, however, begin with the Ribbon appearing as it did at the initial installation of the software. If you are stepping through this chapter on a computer and you want your Ribbon to match the figures in this book, read Appendix E.

In addition to the top-level tabs, Excel displays other tabs, called **contextual tabs**, when you perform certain tasks or work with objects such as charts or tables. If you insert a chart in the worksheet, for example, the Chart Tools tab and its related subordinate Design tab appear (Figure 1–8). When you are finished working with the chart, the Chart Tools and Design tabs disappear from the Ribbon. Excel determines when contextual tabs should appear and disappear, based on the tasks you perform.

Figure 1–8

Ribbon commands include buttons, boxes (text boxes, check boxes, etc.), and galleries (Figure 1–8). A **gallery** is a set of choices, often graphical, arranged in a grid or in a list. You can scroll through choices on an in-Ribbon gallery by clicking the gallery's scroll arrows. An **in-Ribbon** gallery shows common gallery choices on the Ribbon rather than in a dropdown list. Or, you can click a gallery's More button to view more gallery options on the screen at a time. Some buttons and boxes have arrows that, when clicked, also display a gallery; others always cause a gallery to be displayed when clicked. Most galleries support **live preview**, which is a feature that allows you to point to a gallery choice and see its effect in the worksheet without actually selecting the choice (Figure 1–9).

Some commands on the Ribbon display an image to help you remember their function. When you point to a command on the Ribbon, all or part of the command glows in shades of yellow and orange, and an Enhanced ScreenTip appears on the screen. An **Enhanced ScreenTip** is an on-screen note that provides the name of the command, available keyboard shortcut(s), a description of the command, and sometimes instructions for how to obtain Help about the command (Figure 1–10). Enhanced ScreenTips are more detailed than a typical **ScreenTip**, which usually displays only the name of the command.

The lower-right corner of some groups on the Ribbon has a small arrow, called a **Dialog Box Launcher**, that when clicked displays a dialog box or a task pane (Figure 1–11). A **dialog box** contains additional commands and options for the group. When presented with a dialog box, you make selections and must close the dialog box before returning to the worksheet. A **task pane**, by contrast, is a window that contains additional commands and can stay open and visible while you work on the worksheet.

clicking Themes button displays gallery

as you move mouse pointer from one gallery option to next, Excel shows preview of style in document, so you can decide whether you want to select option

worksheet style changes to Foundry as you point to that style in the gallery

Figure 1–9

mouse pointer on Paste button arrow

Enhanced ScreenTip for Paste button arrow

image of clipboard helps to identify Paste button

Figure 1–10

clicking Dialog Box Launcher in Clipboard group displays Clipboard task pane

clicking Dialog Box Launcher in Font group displays Format Cells dialog box

Format Cells dialog box

Clipboard task pane

Figure 1–11

Formula Bar

The formula bar appears below the Ribbon (Figure 1–12a). As you type, Excel displays the entry in the **formula bar**. You can make the formula bar larger by dragging the sizing handle (Figure 1–7) on the formula bar or clicking the expand button to the right of the formula bar. Excel also displays the active cell reference in the **Name box** on the left side of the formula bar.

Mini Toolbar and Shortcut Menus

The **Mini toolbar**, which appears automatically based on tasks you perform (such as selecting text), contains commands related to changing the appearance of text in a worksheet. All commands on the Mini toolbar also exist on the Ribbon. The purpose of the Mini toolbar is to minimize mouse movement. For example, if you want to format text using a command that currently is not displayed on the active tab, you can use the command on the Mini toolbar — instead of switching to a different tab to use the command.

When the Mini toolbar appears, it initially is transparent (Figure 1–12a). If you do not use the transparent Mini toolbar, it disappears from the screen. To use the Mini toolbar, move the mouse pointer into the toolbar, which causes the Mini toolbar to change from a transparent to bright appearance (Figure 1–12b).

(a) Transparent Mini Toolbar

(b) Bright Mini Toolbar

Figure 1–12

A **shortcut menu**, which appears when you right-click an object, is a list of frequently used commands that relate to the right-clicked object. If you right-click an item in the document window such as a cell, Excel displays both the Mini toolbar and a shortcut menu (Figure 1–13).

Figure 1–13

Quick Access Toolbar

The **Quick Access Toolbar**, located by default above the Ribbon, provides easy access to frequently used commands (Figure 1–14a). The commands on the Quick Access Toolbar always are available, regardless of the task you are performing. Initially, the Quick Access Toolbar contains the Save, Undo, and Redo buttons. If you click the Customize Quick Access Toolbar button, Excel provides a list of commands you quickly can add to and remove from the Quick Access Toolbar (Figure 1–14b).

You also can add other commands to or delete commands from the Quick Access Toolbar so that it contains the commands you use most often. As you add commands to the Quick Access Toolbar, its commands may interfere with the workbook title on the title bar. For this reason, Excel provides an option of displaying the Quick Access Toolbar below the Ribbon (Figure 1–14c).

BTW

Quick Access Toolbar Commands
To add a Ribbon command as a button to the Quick Access Toolbar, right-click the command on the Ribbon and then click Add to Quick Access Toolbar on the shortcut menu. To delete a button from the Quick Access Toolbar, right-click the button on the Quick Access Toolbar and then click Remove from Quick Access Toolbar on the shortcut menu. To display the Quick Access Toolbar below the Ribbon, right-click the Quick Access Toolbar and then click Show Quick Access Toolbar Below the Ribbon on the shortcut menu.

(a) Quick Access Toolbar above Ribbon

(c) Quick Access Toolbar below Ribbon

(b) Customize Quick Access Toolbar Menu

Figure 1–14

Each time you start Excel, the Quick Access Toolbar appears the same way it did the last time you used Excel. The chapters in this book, however, begin with the Quick Access Toolbar appearing as it did at the initial installation of the software. If you are stepping through this chapter on a computer and you want your Quick Access Toolbar to match the figures in this book, you should reset your Quick Access Toolbar. For more information about how to reset the Quick Access Toolbar, read Appendix E.

Office Button

While the Ribbon is a control center for creating worksheets, the **Office Button** is a central location for managing and sharing workbooks. When you click the Office Button, located in the upper-left corner of the window, Excel displays the Office Button menu (Figure 1–15). A **menu** contains a list of commands.

Figure 1–15

When you click the New, Open, Save As, and Print commands on the Office Button menu, Excel displays a dialog box with additional options. The Save As, Print, Prepare, Send, and Publish commands have an arrow to their right. If you point to a button that includes an arrow, Excel displays a **submenu**, which is a list of additional commands associated with the selected command (Figure 1–16). For the Prepare, Send, and Publish commands that do not display a dialog box when clicked, you can point either to the command or the arrow to display the submenu.

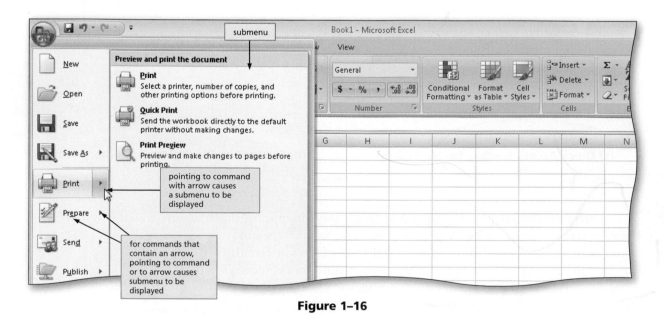

Figure 1–16

Key Tips

If you prefer using the keyboard, instead of the mouse, you can press the ALT key on the keyboard to display a **Key Tip badge**, or keyboard code icon, for certain commands (Figure 1–17). To select a command using the keyboard, press its displayed code letter, or **Key Tip**. When you press a Key Tip, additional Key Tips related to the selected command appear. For example, to select the New command on the Office Button menu, press the ALT key, then press the F key, then press the N key.

Figure 1–17

To remove the Key Tip badges from the screen, press the ALT key or the ESC key on the keyboard until all Key Tip badges disappear or click the mouse anywhere in the Excel window.

Selecting a Cell

To enter data into a cell, you first must select it. The easiest way **to select a cell** (make it active) is to use the mouse to move the block plus sign mouse pointer to the cell and then click.

An alternative method is to use the arrow keys that are located just to the right of the typewriter keys on the keyboard. An arrow key selects the cell adjacent to the active cell in the direction of the arrow on the key.

You know a cell is selected, or active, when a heavy border surrounds the cell and the active cell reference appears in the Name box on the left side of the formula bar. Excel also changes the active cell's column heading and row heading to a gold color.

Entering Text

In Excel, any set of characters containing a letter, hyphen (as in a telephone number), or space is considered text. **Text** is used to place titles, such as worksheet titles, column titles, and row titles, on the worksheet.

BTW

Selecting a Cell
You can select any cell by entering its cell reference, such as b4, in the Name box on the left side of the formula bar.

Plan Ahead

Select titles and subtitles for the worksheet.

As previously stated, worksheet titles and subtitles should be as brief and meaningful as possible. As shown in Figure 1–18, the worksheet title, Walk and Rock Music, identifies the company for whom the worksheet is being created in Chapter 1. The worksheet subtitle, First Quarter Rock-It MP3 Sales, identifies the type of report.

Plan Ahead

Determine the contents of rows and columns.

As previously mentioned, rows typically contain information that is similar to items in a list. For the Walk and Rock Music sales data, the list of product types meets this criterion. It is more likely that in the future, the company will add more product types as opposed to more regions. Each product type, therefore, should be placed in its own row. The row titles in column A (Video, Mini, Micro, Flash, Accessories, and Total) identify the numbers in each row.

Columns typically contain descriptive information about items in rows or contain information that helps to group the data in the worksheet. In the case of the Walk and Rock Music sales data, the regions classify the sales of each product type. The regions, therefore, are placed in columns. The column titles in row 3 (Northeast, Southeast, Midwest, South, West, and Total) identify the numbers in each column.

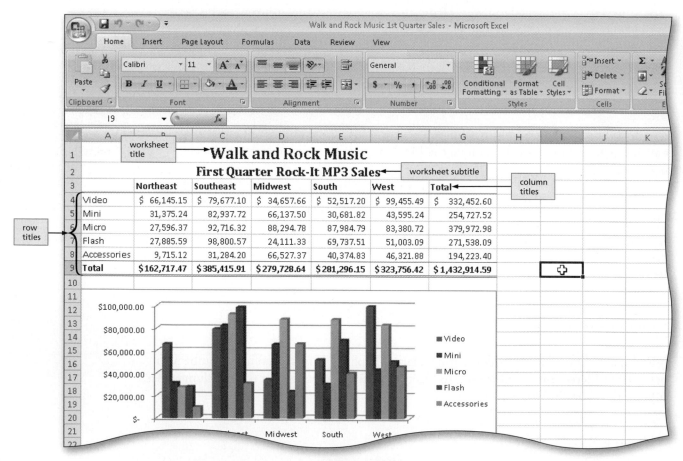

Figure 1–18

To Enter the Worksheet Titles

The following steps show how to enter the worksheet titles in cells A1 and A2. Later in this chapter, the worksheet titles will be formatted so they appear as shown in Figure 1–18.

1

- Click cell A1 to make cell A1 the active cell (Figure 1–19).

Figure 1–19

2

- Type Walk and Rock Music in cell A1, and then point to the Enter box in the formula bar.

Q&A Why did the appearance of the formula bar change?

Excel displays the title in the formula bar and in cell A1. When you begin typing a cell entry, Excel displays two additional boxes in the formula bar: the Cancel box and the Enter box. Clicking the **Enter box** completes an entry. Clicking the **Cancel box** cancels an entry.

Q&A What is the vertical line in cell A1?

In Figure 1–20, the text in cell A1 is followed by the insertion point. The **insertion point** is a blinking vertical line that indicates where the next typed character will appear.

Figure 1–20

3

- Click the Enter box to complete the entry and enter the worksheet title in cell A1 (Figure 1–21).

Figure 1–21

4

- Click cell A2 to select it.

- Type First Quarter Rock-It MP3 Sales as the cell entry.

- Click the Enter box to complete the entry and enter the worksheet subtitle in cell A2 (Figure 1–22).

Figure 1–22

Other Ways

1. To complete entry, click any cell other than active cell

2. To complete entry, press ENTER key

3. To complete entry, press HOME, PAGE UP, PAGE DOWN, or END key

4. To complete entry, press UP, DOWN, LEFT, or RIGHT key.

Entering Text in a Cell

When you complete a text entry into a cell, a series of events occurs. First, Excel positions the text left-aligned in the cell. **Left-aligned** means the cell entry is positioned at the far left in the cell. Therefore, the W in the worksheet title, Walk and Rock Music, begins in the leftmost position of cell A1.

Second, when the text is longer than the width of a column, Excel displays the overflow characters in adjacent cells to the right as long as these adjacent cells contain no data. In Figure 1–22, the width of cell A1 is approximately nine characters. The text consists of 19 characters. Therefore, Excel displays the overflow characters from cell A1 in cells B1 and C1, because cells B1 and C1 are empty. If cell B1 contained data, Excel would hide the overflow characters, so that only the first nine characters in cell A1 would appear on the worksheet. Excel stores the overflow characters in cell A1 and displays them in the formula bar whenever cell A1 is the active cell.

Third, when you complete an entry by clicking the Enter box, the cell in which the text is entered remains the active cell.

Correcting a Mistake while Typing

If you type the wrong letter and notice the error before clicking the Enter box or pressing the ENTER key, use the BACKSPACE key to delete all the characters back to and including the incorrect letter. To cancel the entire entry before entering it into the cell, click the Cancel box in the formula bar or press the ESC key. If you see an error in a cell after entering the text, select the cell and retype the entry. Later in this chapter, additional error-correction techniques are discussed.

AutoCorrect

The **AutoCorrect feature** of Excel works behind the scenes, correcting common mistakes when you complete a text entry in a cell. AutoCorrect makes three types of corrections for you:

1. Corrects two initial capital letters by changing the second letter to lowercase.

2. Capitalizes the first letter in the names of days.

3. Replaces commonly misspelled words with their correct spelling. For example, it will change the misspelled word *recieve* to *receive* when you complete the entry. AutoCorrect will correct the spelling of hundreds of commonly misspelled words automatically.

BTW

The ENTER Key
When you first install Excel, the ENTER key not only completes the entry, but it also moves the selection to an adjacent cell. You can instruct Excel not to move the selection after pressing the ENTER key by clicking the Excel Options button on the Office Button menu, clicking the Advanced option, removing the checkmark from the 'After pressing Enter, move selection' check box, and then clicking the OK button.

To Enter Column Titles

To enter the column titles in row 3, select the appropriate cell and then enter the text. The following steps enter the column titles in row 3.

*   Click cell B3 to make cell B3 the active cell (Figure 1–23).

Figure 1–23

2

- Type Northeast in cell B3 (Figure 1–24).

Figure 1–24

3

- Press the RIGHT ARROW key to enter the column title, Northeast, in cell B3 and make cell C3 the active cell (Figure 1–25).

 Why is the RIGHT ARROW key used to complete the entry in the cell?

If the next entry is in an adjacent cell, use the arrow keys to complete the entry in a cell. When you press an arrow key to complete an entry, the adjacent cell in the direction of the arrow (up, down, left, or right) becomes the active cell. If the next entry is in a nonadjacent cell, complete an entry by clicking the next cell in which you plan to enter data. You also can click the Enter box or press the ENTER key and then click the appropriate cell for the next entry.

Figure 1–25

4

- Repeat Steps 2 and 3 to enter the remaining column titles in row 3; that is, enter Southeast in cell C3, Midwest in cell D3, South in cell E3, West in cell F3, and Total in cell G3 (complete the last entry in cell G3 by clicking the Enter box in the formula bar) (Figure 1–26).

Figure 1–26

To Enter Row Titles

The next step in developing the worksheet for this project is to enter the row titles in column A. This process is similar to entering the column titles. The following steps enter the row titles in the worksheet.

1

- Click cell A4 to select it.

- Type Video and then press the DOWN ARROW key to enter the row title and make cell A5 the active cell (Figure 1–27).

Figure 1–27

2

- Repeat Step 1 to enter the remaining row titles in column A; that is, enter `Mini` in cell A5, `Micro` in cell A6, `Flash` in cell A7, `Accessories` in cell A8, and `Total` in cell A9 (Figure 1–28).

Q&A

Why is the text left-aligned in the cells?

When you enter text, Excel automatically left-aligns the text in the cell. Excel treats any combination of numbers, spaces, and nonnumeric characters as text. For example, the following entries are text:

401AX21, 921-231, 619 321, 883XTY

You can change the text alignment in a cell by realigning it. Several alignment techniques are discussed later in the chapter.

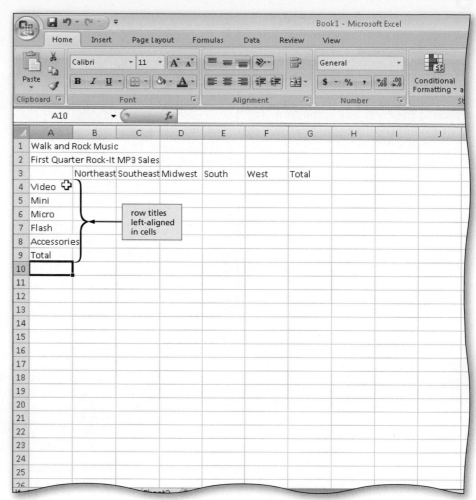

Figure 1–28

BTW

Numeric Limitations
In Excel, a number can be between approximately -1×10^{308} and 1×10^{308}, that is, between a negative 1 followed by 308 zeros and a positive 1 followed by 308 zeros. To enter a number such as 6,000,000,000,000,000, you can type 6,000,000,000,000,000, or you can type 6E15, which stands for 6×10^{15}.

Entering Numbers

In Excel, you can enter numbers into cells to represent amounts. A **number** can contain only the following characters:

    0 1 2 3 4 5 6 7 8 9 + - ( ) , / . $ % E e

If a cell entry contains any other keyboard character (including spaces), Excel interprets the entry as text and treats it accordingly. The use of the special characters is explained when they are used in this book.

To Enter Numbers

The Walk and Rock Music First Quarter Rock-It MP3 Sales numbers used in Chapter 1 are summarized in Table 1–1. These numbers, which represent sales revenue for each of the product types and regions, must be entered in rows 4, 5, 6, 7, and 8.

Table 1–1 Walk and Rock Music First Quarter Rock-It MP3 Sales					
	Northeast	**Southeast**	**Midwest**	**South**	**West**
Video	66145.15	79677.10	34657.66	52517.20	99455.49
Mini	31375.24	82937.72	66137.50	30681.82	43595.24
Micro	27596.37	92716.32	88294.78	87984.79	83380.72
Flash	27885.59	98800.57	24111.33	69737.51	51003.09
Accessories	9715.12	31284.20	66527.37	40374.83	46321.88

The following steps enter the numbers in Table 1–1 one row at a time.

1

- Click cell B4.

- Type 66145.15 and then press the RIGHT ARROW key to enter the data in cell B4 and make cell C4 the active cell (Figure 1–29).

Do I need to enter dollar signs, commas, or trailing zeros for the quarterly sales numbers?

You are not required to type dollar signs, commas, or trailing zeros. When you enter a dollar value that has cents, however, you must add the decimal point and the numbers representing the cents. Later in this chapter, the numbers will be formatted to use dollar signs, commas, and trailing zeros to improve the appearance and readability of the numbers.

Figure 1–29

2

- Enter 79677.1 in cell C4, 34657.66 in cell D4, 52517.2 in cell E4, and 99455.49 in cell F4 (Figure 1–30).

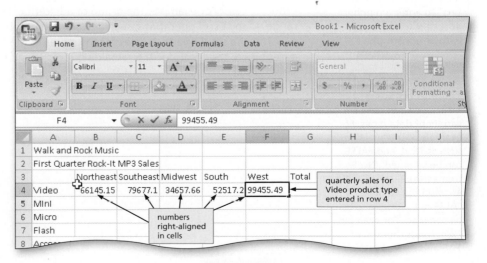

Figure 1–30

3

- Click cell B5.

- Enter the remaining first quarter sales numbers provided in Table 1–1 for each of the four remaining offerings in rows 5, 6, 7, and 8 to display the quarterly sales in the worksheet (Figure 1–31).

Figure 1–31

Calculating a Sum

The next step in creating the worksheet is to perform any necessary calculations, such as calculating the column and row totals.

Plan Ahead

Determine calculations that are needed.

As stated in the requirements document in Figure 1–2 on page EX 4, totals are required for each region, each product type, and the company. The first calculation is to determine the quarterly sales for the stores in the Northeast region in column B. To calculate this value in cell B9, Excel must add, or sum, the numbers in cells B4, B5, B6, B7, and B8. Excel's **SUM function**, which adds all of the numbers in a range of cells, provides a convenient means to accomplish this task.

A **range** is a series of two or more adjacent cells in a column or row or a rectangular group of cells. For example, the group of adjacent cells B4, B5, B6, B7, and B8 is called a range. Many Excel operations, such as summing numbers, take place on a range of cells.

After the total quarterly sales for the stores in the Northeast region in column B is determined, the totals for the remaining regions and totals for each product type will be determined.

BTW

Entering Numbers as Text
Sometimes, you will want Excel to treat numbers, such as Zip codes and telephone numbers, as text. To enter a number as text, start the entry with an apostrophe (').

BTW

Calculating Sums
Excel calculates sums for a variety of data types. For example, Boolean values, such as TRUE and FALSE, can be summed. Excel treats the value of TRUE as 1 and the value of FALSE as 0. Times also can be summed. For example, Excel treats the sum of 1:15 and 2:45 as 4:00.

To Sum a Column of Numbers

The following steps sum the numbers in column B.

1

- Click cell B9 to make it the active cell and then point to the Sum button on the Ribbon (Figure 1–32).

Figure 1–32

2

- Click the Sum button on the Ribbon to display =SUM(B4: B8) in the formula bar and in the active cell B9 (Figure 1–33).

Q&A

How does Excel know which cells to sum?

When you enter the SUM function using the Sum button, Excel automatically selects what it considers to be your choice of the range to sum. When proposing the range to sum, Excel first looks for a range of cells with numbers above the active cell and then to the left. If Excel proposes the wrong range, you can correct it by dragging through the correct range before pressing the ENTER key. You also can enter the correct range by typing the beginning cell reference, a colon (:), and the ending cell reference.

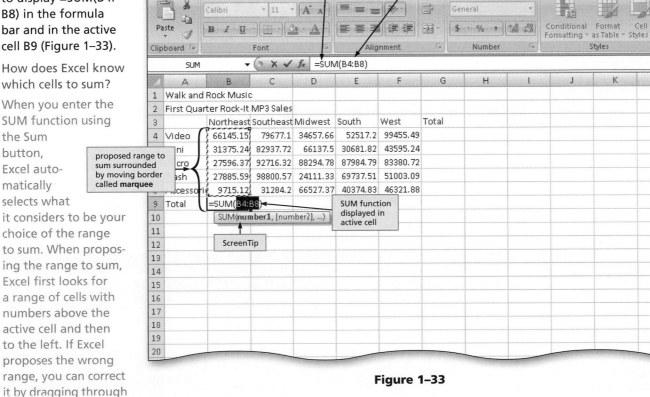

Figure 1–33

❸

• Click the Enter box in the formula bar to enter the sum of the first quarter sales for the five product types for the Northeast region in cell B9 (Figure 1-34).

Q&A

What is the purpose of the Sum button arrow?

If you click the Sum button arrow on the right side of the Sum button (Figure 1–34), Excel displays a list of often-used functions from which you can choose. The list includes functions that allow you to determine the average, the number of items in the selected range, the minimum value, or the maximum value of a range of numbers.

Figure 1–34

Other Ways

1. Click Insert Function button in formula bar, select SUM in Select a function list, click OK button, select range, click OK button

2. Click Sum button arrow on Ribbon, click More Functions, select SUM in Select a function list, click OK button, select range, click OK button

3. Type = s in cell, select SUM from list, select range

4. Press ALT + EQUAL SIGN (=) twice

Using the Fill Handle to Copy a Cell to Adjacent Cells

Excel also must calculate the totals for the Southeast in cell C9, the Midwest in cell D9, the South in cell E9, and for the West in cell F9. Table 1–2 illustrates the similarities between the entry in cell B9 and the entries required to sum the totals in cells C9, D9, E9, and F9.

Table 1–2 Sum Function Entries in Row 9		
Cell	**Sum Function Entries**	**Remark**
B9	=SUM(B4:B8)	Sums cells B4, B5, B6, B7, and B8
C9	=SUM(C4:C8)	Sums cells C4, C5, C6, C7, and C8
D9	=SUM(D4:D8)	Sums cells D4, D5, D6, D7, and D8
E9	=SUM(E4:E8)	Sums cells E4, E5, E6, E7, and E8
F9	=SUM(F4:F8)	Sums cells F4, F5, F6, F7, and F8

To place the SUM functions in cells C9, D9, E9, and F9, you could follow the same steps shown previously in Figures 1–32 through 1–34. A second, more efficient method is to copy the SUM function from cell B9 to the range C9:F9. The cell being copied is called the **source area** or **copy area**. The range of cells receiving the copy is called the **destination area** or **paste area**.

Although the SUM function entries in Table 1–2 are similar, they are not exact copies. The range in each SUM function entry uses cell references that are one column to the right of the previous column. When you copy cell references, Excel automatically adjusts them for each new position, resulting in the SUM function entries illustrated in Table 1–2. Each adjusted cell reference is called a **relative reference**.

To Copy a Cell to Adjacent Cells in a Row

The easiest way to copy the SUM formula from cell B9 to cells C9, D9, E9, and F9 is to use the fill handle. The **fill handle** is the small black square located in the lower-right corner of the heavy border around the active cell. The following steps use the fill handle to copy cell B9 to the adjacent cells C9:F9.

- With cell B9 active, point to the fill handle (Figure 1–35).

Figure 1–35

- Drag the fill handle to select the destination area, range C9:F9, to display a shaded border around the destination area, range C9:F9, and the source area, cell B9 (Figure 1–36). Do not release the mouse button.

Figure 1–36

- Release the mouse button to copy the SUM function in cell B9 to the range C9:F9 (Figure 1–37) and calculate the sums in cells C9, D9, E9, and F9.

Q&A

What is the purpose of the Auto Fill Options button?

When you copy one range to another, Excel displays an Auto Fill Options button (Figure 1–37). The Auto Fill Options button allows you to choose whether you want to copy the values from the source area to the destination area with formatting, without formatting, or copy only the format. To view the available fill options, click the Auto Fill Options button. The Auto Fill Options button disappears when you begin another activity.

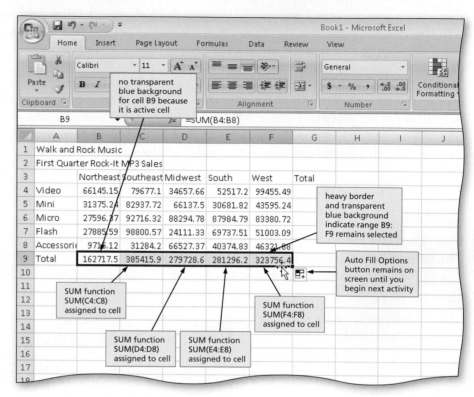

Figure 1–37

Other Ways
1. Select source area, click Copy button on Ribbon, select destination area, click Paste button on Ribbon	2. Right-click source area, click Copy on shortcut menu, right-click destination area, click Paste on shortcut menu	3. Select source area and then point to border of range; while holding down CTRL key, drag source area to destination area

To Determine Multiple Totals at the Same Time

The next step in building the worksheet is to determine the quarterly sales for each product type and total quarterly sales for the company in column G. To calculate these totals, you can use the SUM function much as it was used to total the quarterly sales by region in row 9. In this example, however, Excel will determine totals for all of the rows at the same time. The following steps illustrate this process.

- Click cell G4 to make it the active cell (Figure 1–38).

Figure 1–38

②

- With the mouse pointer in cell G4 and in the shape of a block plus sign, drag the mouse pointer down to cell G9 to highlight the range G4:G9 with a transparent view (Figure 1–39).

Figure 1–39

③

- Click the Sum button on the Ribbon to calculate and display the sums of the corresponding rows of sales in cells G4, G5, G6, G7, G8, and G9 (Figure 1–40).

④

- Select cell A10 to deselect the range G4:G9.

Q&A

Why does Excel create totals for each row?

If each cell in a selected range is next to a row of numbers, Excel assigns the SUM function to each cell when you click the Sum button.

Figure 1–40

Saving the Project

While you are building a worksheet in a workbook, the computer stores it in memory. When you save a workbook, the computer places it on a storage medium such as a USB flash drive, CD, or hard disk. A saved workbook is referred to as a **file**. A **file name** is the name assigned to a file when it is saved. It is important to save the workbook frequently for the following reasons:

- The worksheet in memory will be lost if the computer is turned off or you lose electrical power while Excel is open.
- If you run out of time before completing your workbook, you may finish your worksheet at a future time without starting over.

BTW

Saving

Excel allows you to save a workbook in more than 30 different file formats. Choose the file format by clicking the 'Save as type' box arrow at the bottom of the Save As dialog box (Figure 1–41 on the next page). Excel Workbook is the default file format.

<table>
<tr><td>**Plan
Ahead**</td><td>**Determine where to save the workbook.**
When saving a workbook, you must decide which storage medium to use.

• If you always work on the same computer and have no need to transport your projects to a different location, then your computer's hard drive will suffice as a storage location. It is a good idea, however, to save a backup copy of your projects on a separate medium in case the file becomes corrupted or the computer's hard drive fails.

• If you plan to work on your workbooks in various locations or on multiple computers, then you should save your workbooks on a portable medium, such as a USB flash drive or CD. The workbooks used in this book are saved to a USB flash drive, which saves files quickly and reliably and can be reused. CDs are easily portable and serve as good backups for the final versions of workbooks because they generally can save files only one time.</td></tr>
</table>

To Save a Workbook

You have performed many tasks while creating this project and do not want to risk losing the work completed thus far. Accordingly, you should save the workbook. The following steps save a workbook on a USB flash drive using the file name, Walk and Rock Music 1st Quarter Sales.

Note: If you are using Windows XP, see Appendix F for alternate steps.

1
• With a USB flash drive connected to one of the computer's USB ports, click the Save button on the Quick Access Toolbar to display the Save As dialog box (Figure 1–41).

• If the Navigation pane is not displayed in the Save As dialog box, click the Browse Folders button to expand the dialog box.

• If a Folders list is displayed below the Folders button, click the Folders button to remove the Folders list.

Q&A Do I have to save to a USB flash drive?

No. You can save to any device or folder. A **folder** is a specific location on a storage medium. You can save to the default folder or a different folder. You also can create your own folders, which is explained later in this book.

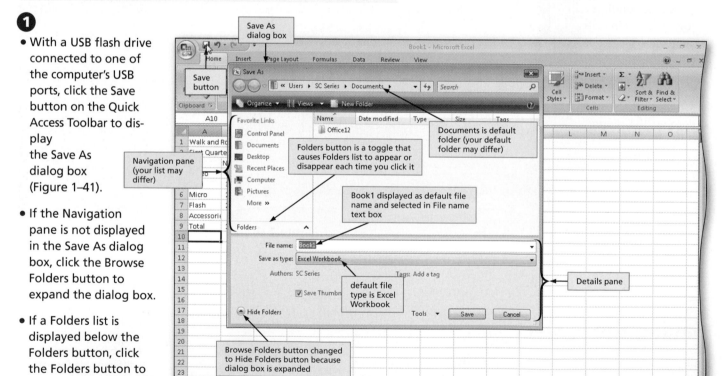

Figure 1–41

2

- Type `Walk and Rock Music 1st Quarter Sales` in the File name text box to change the file name. Do not press the ENTER key after typing the file name (Figure 1–42).

Q&A

What characters can I use in a file name?

A file name can have a maximum of 255 characters, including spaces. The only invalid characters are the backslash (\), slash (/), colon (:), asterisk (*), question mark (?), quotation mark ("), less than symbol (<), greater than symbol (>), and vertical bar (|).

Figure 1–42

3

- If Computer is not displayed in the Favorite Links section, drag the top or bottom edge of the Save As dialog box until Computer is displayed.

- Click Computer in the Favorite Links section to display a list of available drives (Figure 1–43).

- If necessary, scroll until UDISK 2.0 (E :) appears in the list of available drives.

Q&A

Why is my list of files, folders, and drives arranged and named differently from those shown in the figure?

Figure 1–43

Your computer's configuration determines how the list of files and folders is displayed and how drives are named. You can change the save location by clicking links on the **Favorite Links section**.

Q&A

How do I save the file if I am not using a USB flash drive?

Use the same process, but be certain to select your device in the list of available drives.

4

- Double-click UDISK 2.0 (E:) in the Save in list to select the USB flash drive, Drive E in this case, as the new save location (Figure 1–44).

What if my USB flash drive has a different name or letter?

It is very likely that your USB flash drive will have a different name and drive letter and be connected to a different port.

Figure 1–44

5

- Click the Save button in the Save As dialog box to save the workbook on the USB flash drive with the file name, Walk and Rock Music 1st Quarter Sales (Figure 1–45).

How do I know that Excel saved the workbook?

While Excel is saving your file, it briefly displays a message on the status bar indicating the amount of the file saved. In addition, your USB drive may have a light that flashes during the save process.

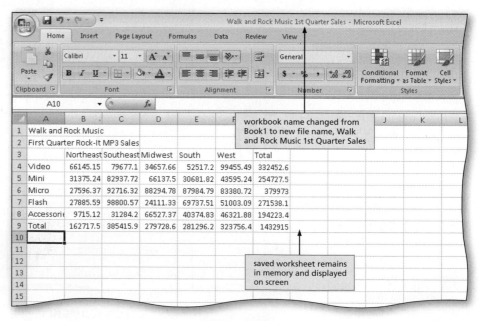

Figure 1–45

Other Ways

1. Click Office Button, click Save, type file name, select drive or folder, click Save button
2. Press CTRL+S or press SHIFT+F12, type file name, select drive or folder, click Save button

Formatting the Worksheet

The text, numeric entries, and functions for the worksheet now are complete. The next step is to format the worksheet. You **format** a worksheet to emphasize certain entries and make the worksheet easier to read and understand.

Figure 1–46a shows the worksheet before formatting. Figure 1–46b shows the worksheet after formatting. As you can see from the two figures, a worksheet that is formatted not only is easier to read but also looks more professional.

(a) Before Formatting

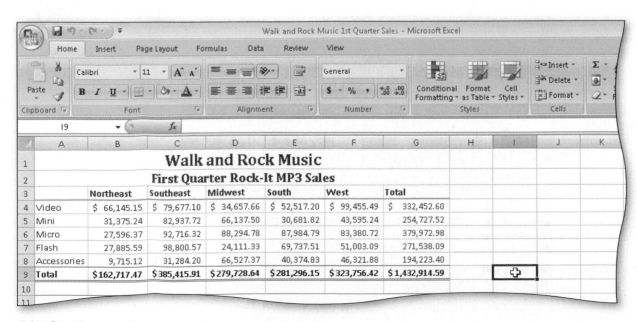

(b) After Formatting

Figure 1–46

<table>
<tr><td>Plan
Ahead</td><td>

Identify how to format various elements of the worksheet.

To change the unformatted worksheet in Figure 1–46a to the formatted worksheet in Figure 1–46b, the following tasks must be completed:

1. Change the font type, change the font style to bold, increase the font size, and change the font color of the worksheet titles in cells A1 and A2. These changes make the worksheet title prominently display to the user and inform the user of the purpose of the worksheet.

2. Center the worksheet titles in cells A1 and A2 across columns A through G.

3. Format the body of the worksheet. The body of the worksheet, range A3:G9, includes the column titles, row titles, and numbers. Formatting the body of the worksheet changes the numbers to use a dollars-and-cents format, with dollar signs in the first row (row 4) and the total row (row 9); adds underlining that emphasizes portions of the worksheet; and modifies the column widths to make the text and numbers readable.

</td></tr>
</table>

The remainder of this section explains the process required to format the worksheet. Although the format procedures are explained in the order described above, you should be aware that you could make these format changes in any order. Modifying the column widths, however, usually is done last.

Font Type, Style, Size, and Color

The characters that Excel displays on the screen are a specific font type, style, size, and color. The **font type**, or font face, defines the appearance and shape of the letters, numbers, and special characters. Examples of font types include Calibri, Cambria, Times New Roman, Arial, and Courier. **Font style** indicates how the characters are emphasized. Common font styles include regular, bold, underline, or italic. The **font size** specifies the size of the characters on the screen. Font size is gauged by a measurement system called points. A single point is about 1/72 of one inch in height. Thus, a character with a **point size** of 10 is about 10/72 of one inch in height. The **font color** defines the color of the characters. Excel can display characters in a wide variety of colors, including black, red, orange, and blue.

When Excel begins, the preset font type for the entire workbook is Calibri, with a font size, font style, and font color of 11-point regular black. Excel allows you to change the font characteristics in a single cell, a range of cells, the entire worksheet, or the entire workbook.

BTW

Fonts
In general, use no more than two font types in a worksheet.

BTW

Fonts and Themes
Excel uses default recommended fonts based on the workbook's theme. A theme is a collection of fonts and color schemes. The default theme is named Office, and the two recommended fonts for the Office theme are Calibri and Cambria. Excel, however, allows you to apply any font to a cell or range as long as the font is installed on your computer.

To Change a Cell Style

Excel includes the capability of changing several characteristics of a cell, such as font type, font size, and font color, all at once by assigning a predefined cell style to a cell. The following steps assign the Title cell style to the worksheet title in cell A1.

1

- Click cell A1 to make cell A1 the active cell.

- Click the Cell Styles button on the Ribbon to display the Cell Styles gallery (Figure 1–47).

Figure 1–47

2

- Point to the Title cell style in the Titles and Headings area of the Cell Styles gallery to see a live preview of the cell style in cell A1 (Figure 1–48).

 Experiment

- Point to several other cell styles in the Cell Styles gallery to see a live preview of other cell styles in cell A1.

Q&A

Why does the font type, font size, and font color change in cell A1 when I point to it?

The change in cell A1 is a result of live preview. Live preview is a feature of Excel 2007 that allows you to preview cell styles as you point to them in the Cell Styles gallery.

Figure 1–48

3

- Click the Title cell style to apply the cell style to cell A1 (Figure 1–49).

Q&A

Why do several items in the Font group on the Ribbon change?

The changes to the Font box, Bold button, and Font Size box indicate the font changes applied to the active cell, cell A1, as a result of applying the Title cell style.

Figure 1–49

To Change the Font Type

Different font types often are used in a worksheet to make it more appealing to the reader. The following steps show how to change the worksheet subtitle's font type from Calibri to Cambria.

1

- Click cell A2 to make cell A2 the active cell.

- Click the Font box arrow on the Ribbon to display the Font gallery (Figure 1–50).

Q&A

Which fonts are displayed in the Font gallery?

Because many applications supply additional font types beyond what comes with the Windows Vista operating system, the number of font types available on your computer will depend on the applications installed. This book uses only font types that come with the Windows Vista operating system and Microsoft Office.

Figure 1–50

2
- Point to Cambria in the Theme Fonts area of the Font gallery to see a live preview of the Cambria font in cell A2 (Figure 1–51).

🔎 **Experiment**
- Point to several other fonts in the Font gallery to see a live preview of other fonts in cell A2.

Q&A

What is the Theme Fonts area?

Excel applies the same default theme to any new workbook that you start. A **theme** is a collection of cell styles and other styles that have common characteristics, such as a color scheme and font type. The default theme for an Excel workbook is the Office theme. The Theme Fonts area of the Font gallery includes the fonts included in the default Office theme. Cambria is recommended for headings and Calibri is recommended for cells in the body of the worksheet (Figure 1–51).

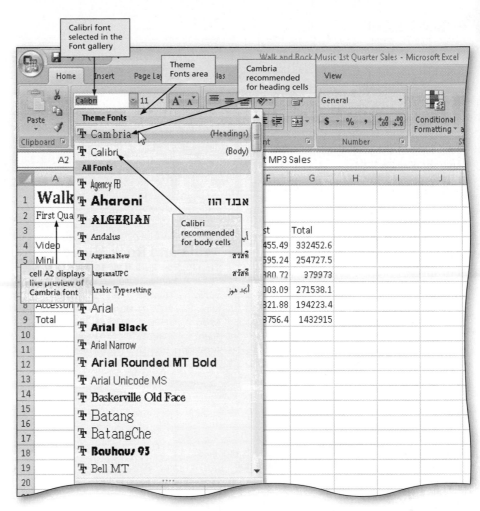

Figure 1–51

3
- Click Cambria in the Theme Fonts area to change the font type of the worksheet subtitle in cell A2 from Calibri to Cambria (Figure 1–52).

Figure 1–52

Other Ways

1. Select font type from Font list on Mini toolbar
2. Right-click cell, click Format Cells on shortcut menu, click Font tab, click desired font type, click OK button

To Bold a Cell

You **bold** an entry in a cell to emphasize it or make it stand out from the rest of the worksheet. The following step shows how to bold the worksheet subtitle in cell A2.

1

• With cell A2 active, click the Bold button on the Ribbon to change the font style of the worksheet subtitle to bold (Figure 1–53).

Q&A

What if a cell already includes a bold style?

If you point to the Bold button and the active cell already is bold, then Excel displays the button with a transparent orange background.

Q&A

How do I remove the bold style from a cell?

Clicking the Bold button a second time removes the bold font style.

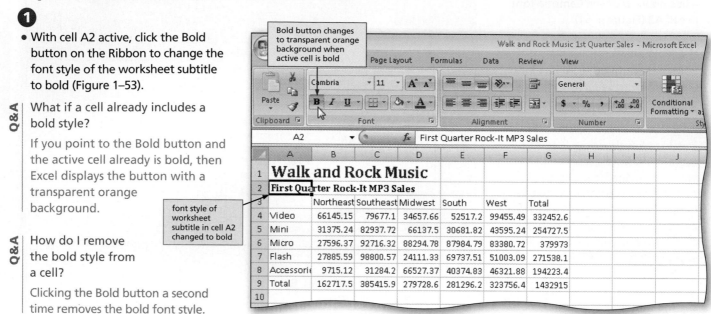

Figure 1–53

Other Ways

1. Click Bold button on Mini toolbar

2. Right-click cell, click Format Cells on shortcut menu, click Font tab, click Bold, click OK button

3. Press CTRL+B

To Increase the Font Size of a Cell Entry

Increasing the font size is the next step in formatting the worksheet subtitle. You increase the font size of a cell so the entry stands out and is easier to read. The following steps increase the font size of the worksheet subtitle in cell A2.

1

• With cell A2 selected, click the Font Size box arrow on the Ribbon to display the Font Size list.

• Point to 14 in the Font Size list to see a live preview of cell A2 with a font size of 14 (Figure 1–54).

Experiment

• Point to several other font sizes in the Font Size list to see a live preview of other font sizes in cell A2.

Figure 1–54

2

- Click 14 in the Font Size list to change the font in cell A2 from 11 point to 14 point (Figure 1–55).

Q&A

Can I assign a font size that is not in the Font Size list?

Yes. An alternative to clicking a font size in the Font Size list is to click the Font Size box, type the font size, and then press the ENTER key. This procedure allows you to assign a font size not available in the Font Size list to a selected cell entry.

font in active cell A2 is 14-point Cambria bold

font changes from 11 point to 14 point

Figure 1–55

Other Ways

1. Click Increase Font Size button or Decrease Font Size button on Ribbon

2. Select font size from Font Size list on Mini toolbar

3. Right-click cell, click Format Cells on shortcut menu, click Font tab, select font size in Size box, click OK button

To Change the Font Color of a Cell Entry

The next step is to change the color of the font in cell A2 from black to dark blue. The following steps change the font color of a cell entry.

1

- With cell A2 selected, click the Font Color button arrow on the Ribbon to display the Font Color palette.

- Point to Dark Blue, Text 2 (dark blue color in column 4, row 1) in the Theme Colors area of the Font Color palette to see a live preview of the font color in cell A2 (Figure 1–56).

Experiment

- Point to several other colors in the Font Color palette to see a live preview of other font colors in cell A2.

Q&A

Which colors does Excel make available on the Font Color palette?

Figure 1–56

You can choose from more than 60 different font colors on the Font Color palette (Figure 1–56). Your Font Color palette may have more or fewer colors, depending on color settings of your operating system. The Theme Colors area includes colors that are included in the current workbook's theme.

2

- Click Dark Blue, Text 2 (column 4, row 1) on the Font Color palette to change the font of the worksheet subtitle in cell A2 from black to dark blue (Figure 1–57).

Q&A

Why does the Font Color button change after I select the new font color?

When you choose a color on the Font Color palette, Excel changes the Font Color button on the Formatting toolbar to the chosen color. Thus, to change the font color of the cell entry in another cell to the same color, you need only to select the cell and then click the Font Color button.

Figure 1–57

Other Ways

1. Select font color from Font Color list on Mini toolbar
2. Right-click cell, click Format Cells on shortcut menu, click Font tab, select color on Font Color palette, click OK button

To Center Cell Entries across Columns by Merging Cells

The final step in formatting the worksheet title and subtitle is to center them across columns A through G. Centering a title across the columns used in the body of the worksheet improves the worksheet's appearance. To do this, the seven cells in the range A1:G1 are combined, or merged, into a single cell that is the width of the columns in the body of the worksheet. The seven cells in the range A2:G2 also are merged in a similar manner. **Merging cells** involves creating a single cell by combining two or more selected cells. The following steps center the worksheet title and subtitle across columns by merging cells.

1

- Select cell A1 and then drag to cell G1 to highlight the range A1:G1 (Figure 1–58).

Q&A

What if a cell in the range B1:G1 contained data?

For the Merge & Center button to work properly, all the cells except the leftmost cell in the selected range must be empty.

Figure 1–58

- Click the Merge & Center button on the Ribbon to merge cells A1 through G1 and center the contents of cell A1 across columns A through G (Figure 1–59).

Q&A What happened to cells B1 through G1?

After the merge, cells B1 through G1 no longer exist. Cell A1 now extends across columns A through G.

Figure 1–59

❸

- Repeat Steps 1 and 2 to merge and center the worksheet subtitle across cells A2 through G2 (Figure 1–60).

Q&A Are cells B1 through G1 and B2 through G2 lost forever?

No. The opposite of merging cells is **splitting a merged cell**. After you have merged multiple cells to create one merged cell, you can unmerge, or split, the merged cell to display the original cells on the worksheet. You split a merged cell by

Figure 1–60

selecting it and clicking the Merge & Center button. For example, if you click the Merge & Center button a second time in Step 2, it will split the merged cell A1 to cells A1, B1, C1, D1, E1, F1, and G1.

Other Ways

1. Right-click selection, click Merge & Center button on Mini toolbar

2. Right-click selection, click Format Cells on shortcut menu, click Alignment tab, select Center Across Selection in Horizontal list, click OK button

To Format Column Titles and the Total Row

The next step to format the worksheet is to format the column titles in row 3 and the total row, row 9. Column titles and the total row should be formatted so anyone who views the worksheet can quickly distinguish the column titles and total row from the data in the body of the worksheet. The following steps format the column titles and total row using cell styles in the default worksheet theme.

1

- Click cell A3 and then drag the mouse pointer to cell G3 to select the range A3:G3.

- Point to the Cell Styles button on the Ribbon (Figure 1–61).

Q&A

Why is cell A3 selected in the range for the column headings?

The style to be applied to the column headings includes an underline that will help to distinguish the column headings from the rest of the worksheet. Including cell A3 in the range

Figure 1–61

ensures that the cell will include the underline, which is visually appealing and further helps to separate the data in the worksheet.

2

- Click the Cell Styles button to display the Cell Styles gallery.

- Point to the Heading 3 cell style in the Titles and Headings area of the Cell Styles gallery to see a live preview of the cell style in the range A3:G3 (Figure 1–62).

Experiment

- Point to other cell styles in the Titles and Headings area of the Cell Styles gallery to see a live preview of other cell styles in the range A3:G3.

Figure 1–62

3

- Click the Heading 3 cell style to apply the cell style to the range A3:G3.

- Click cell A9 and then drag the mouse pointer to cell G9 to select the range A9:G9.

- Point to the Cell Styles button on the Ribbon (Figure 1–63).

Q&A

Why should I choose Heading 3 instead of another heading cell style?

Excel includes many types of headings, such as Heading 1 and Heading 2, because worksheets often include many levels of headings above columns. In the case of the worksheet created for this project, the Heading 3 title includes formatting that makes the column titles' font size smaller than the title and subtitle and makes the column titles stand out from the data in the body of the worksheet.

Figure 1–63

4

- Click the Cell Styles button on the Ribbon to display the Cell Styles gallery and then click the Total cell style in the Titles and Headings area to apply the Total cell style to the cells in the range A9:G9.

- Click cell A11 to select the cell (Figure 1–64).

Figure 1–64

To Format Numbers in the Worksheet

As previously noted, the numbers in the worksheet should be formatted to use a dollar-and-cents format, with dollar signs in the first row (row 4) and the total row (row 9). Excel allows you to format numbers in a variety of ways, and these methods are discussed in other chapters in this book. The following steps use buttons on the Ribbon to format the numbers in the worksheet.

 1

- Select cell B4 and drag the mouse pointer to cell G4 to select the range B4:G4.

- Point to the Accounting Number Format button on the Ribbon to display the Enhanced ScreenTip (Figure 1–65).

Figure 1–65

2

- Click the Accounting Number Format button on the Ribbon to apply the Accounting Number format to the cells in the range B4:G4.

- Select the range B5:G8 (Figure 1–66).

Q&A

What effect does the Accounting Number format have on the selected cells?

The Accounting Number format causes the cells to display with two decimal places so that decimal places in cells below the selected cells align vertically. Cell widths are automatically adjusted to accommodate the new formatting.

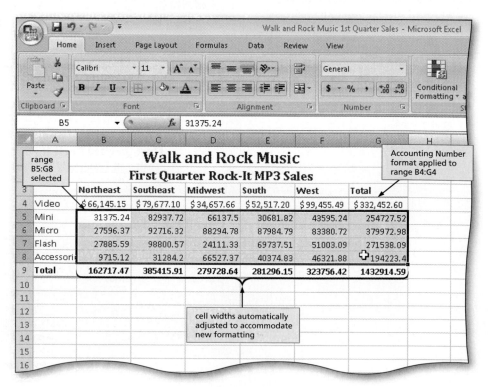

Figure 1–66

3

- Click the Comma Style button on the Ribbon to apply the Comma Style to the range B5:G8.

- Select the range B9:G9 (Figure 1–67).

Q&A

What effect does the Comma Style format have on the selected cells?

The Comma Style format causes the cells to display with two decimal places and commas as thousands separators.

Figure 1–67

4

- Click the Accounting Number Format button on the Ribbon to apply the Accounting Number format to the cells in the range B9:G9.

- Select cell A11 (Figure 1-68).

Figure 1–68

Other Ways	
1. Click Accounting Number Format or Comma button on Mini toolbar	2. Right-click selection, click Format Cells on the shortcut menu, click Number tab, select Accounting in Category list or select Number and click Use 1000 Separator, click OK button

To Adjust the Column Width

The last step in formatting the worksheet is to adjust the width of column A so that the word Accessories in cell A8 is shown in its entirety in the cell. Excel includes several methods for adjusting cell widths and row heights, and these methods are discussed later in this book. The following steps adjust the width of column A so that the contents of cell A8 are displayed in the cell.

1

- Point to the boundary on the right side of the column A heading above row 1 to change the mouse pointer to a split double arrow (Figure 1–69).

Figure 1–69

2

- Double-click on the boundary to adjust the width of column A to the width of the largest item in the column (Figure 1–70).

Q&A

What if none of the items in column A extended through the entire width of the column?

If all of the items in column A were shorter in length than the width of the column when you double-click the right side of the column A heading, then Excel still would adjust the column width to the largest item in the column. That is, Excel would reduce the width of the column to the largest item.

Figure 1–70

Using the Name Box to Select a Cell

The next step is to chart the quarterly sales for the five product types sold by the company. To create the chart, you must select the cell in the upper-left corner of the range to chart (cell A3). Rather than clicking cell A3 to select it, the next section describes how to use the Name box to select the cell.

To Use the Name Box to Select a Cell

As previously noted, the Name box is located on the left side of the formula bar. To select any cell, click the Name box and enter the cell reference of the cell you want to select. The following steps select cell A3.

1

• Click the Name box in the formula bar and then type a3 as the cell to select (Figure 1–71).

Q&A

Why is cell A11 still selected?

Even though cell A11 is the active cell, Excel displays the typed cell reference a3 in the Name box until you press the ENTER key.

Figure 1–71

2

• Press the ENTER key to change the active cell from A11 to cell A3 (Figure 1–72).

Figure 1–72

Other Ways to Select Cells

As you will see in later chapters, in addition to using the Name box to select any cell in a worksheet, you also can use it to assign names to a cell or range of cells. Excel supports several additional ways to select a cell, as summarized in Table 1–3.

BTW

Find & Select
You can find and select cells based on their content. Click the Find & Select button on the Home tab on the Ribbon. Then, click the Go To Special command. Choose your desired option in the Select area of the Go To Special dialog box and then click the OK button.

Table 1–3 Selecting Cells in Excel	
Key, Box, or Command	**Function**
ALT+PAGE DOWN	Selects the cell one worksheet window to the right and moves the worksheet window accordingly.
ALT+PAGE UP	Selects the cell one worksheet window to the left and moves the worksheet window accordingly.
ARROW	Selects the adjacent cell in the direction of the arrow on the key.
CTRL+ARROW	Selects the border cell of the worksheet in combination with the arrow keys and moves the worksheet window accordingly. For example, to select the rightmost cell in the row that contains the active cell, press CTRL+RIGHT ARROW. You also can press the END key, release it, and then press the appropriate arrow key to accomplish the same task.
CTRL+HOME	Selects cell A1 or the cell one column and one row below and to the right of frozen titles and moves the worksheet window accordingly.
Find command on Find and Select menu or SHIFT+F5	Finds and selects a cell that contains specific contents that you enter in the Find dialog box. If necessary, Excel moves the worksheet window to display the cell. You also can press CTRL+F to display the Find dialog box.
Go To command on Find and Select menu or F5	Selects the cell that corresponds to the cell reference you enter in the Go To dialog box and moves the worksheet window accordingly. You also can press CTRL+G to display the Go To dialog box.
HOME	Selects the cell at the beginning of the row that contains the active cell and moves the worksheet window accordingly.
Name box	Selects the cell in the workbook that corresponds to the cell reference you enter in the Name box.
PAGE DOWN	Selects the cell down one worksheet window from the active cell and moves the worksheet window accordingly.
PAGE UP	Selects the cell up one worksheet window from the active cell and moves the worksheet window accordingly.

Plan Ahead

Decide on the type of chart needed.
Excel includes 11 chart types from which you can choose including column, line, pie, bar, area, X Y (scatter), stock, surface, doughnut, bubble, and radar. The type of chart you choose depends on the type of data that you have, how much data you have, and the message you want to convey.

A column chart is a good way to compare values side-by-side. A Clustered Column chart can go even further in comparing values across categories. In the case of the Walk and Rock Music quarterly sales data, comparisons of product types within each region can be made side-by-side with a Clustered Column chart.

Establish where to position and how to format the chart.

- When possible, try to position charts so that both the data and chart appear on the screen on the worksheet together and so that the data and chart can be printed in the most readable manner possible. By placing the chart below the data on the Walk and Rock Music 1st Quarter Sales worksheet, both of these goals are accomplished.

- When choosing/selecting colors for a chart, consider the color scheme of the rest of the worksheet. The chart should not present colors that are in stark contrast to the rest of the worksheet. If the chart will be printed in color, minimize the amount of dark colors on the chart so that the chart both prints quickly and preserves ink.

Adding a 3-D Clustered Column Chart to the Worksheet

As outlined in the requirements document in Figure 1–2 on page EX 4, the worksheet should include a 3-D Clustered Column chart to graphically represent quarterly sales for each product type that the company sells. The 3-D Clustered Column chart shown in Figure 1–73 is called an **embedded chart** because it is drawn on the same worksheet as the data.

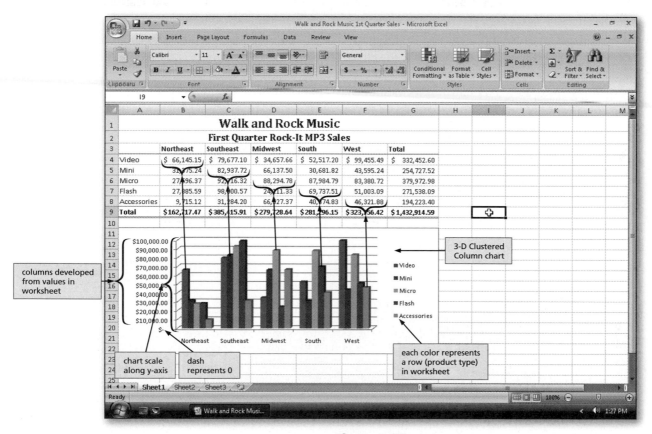

Figure 1–73

The chart uses different colored columns to represent sales for different product types. Each region uses the same color scheme for identifying product types, which allows for easy identification and comparison. For the Northeast sales region, for example, the dark blue column representing Video products shows quarterly sales of $66,145.15; for the Southeast sales region, the maroon column representing Mini products shows quarterly sales of $82,937.72; for the Midwest sales region, the pale green column representing Micro products shows quarterly sales of $88,294.78; for the South sales region, the violet column representing Flash products shows quarterly sales of $69,737.51; and for the West sales region, the light blue column representing Accessories shows quarterly sales of $46,321.88. Because the same color scheme is used in each region to represent the five product types, you easily can compare sales of product types among the sales regions. The totals from the worksheet are not represented, because the totals are not in the range specified for charting.

BTW

Cell Values and Charting
When you change a cell value on which a chart is dependent, Excel redraws the chart instantaneously, unless automatic recalculation is disabled. If automatic recalculation is disabled, then you must press the F9 key to redraw the chart. To enable or disable automatic recalculation, click the Calculations Options button on the Formulas tab on the Ribbon.

Excel derives the chart scale based on the values in the worksheet and then displays the scale along the vertical axis (also called the **y-axis** or **value axis**) of the chart. For example, no value in the range B4:F8 is less than 0 or greater than $100,000.00, so the scale ranges from 0 to $100,000.00. Excel also determines the $10,000.00 increments of the scale automatically. For the numbers along the y-axis, Excel uses a format that includes representing the 0 value with a dash (Figure 1–73 on the previous page).

To Add a 3-D Clustered Column Chart to the Worksheet

The commands to insert a chart are located on the Insert tab. With the range to chart selected, you click the Column button on the Ribbon to initiate drawing the chart. The area on the worksheet where the chart appears is called the chart location. As shown in Figure 1–73, the chart location in this worksheet is the range A11:G22, immediately below the worksheet data.

The following steps draw a 3-D Clustered Column chart that compares the quarterly sales by product type for the five sales regions.

- Click cell A3 and then drag the mouse pointer to the cell F8 to select the range A3:F8 (Figure 1–74).

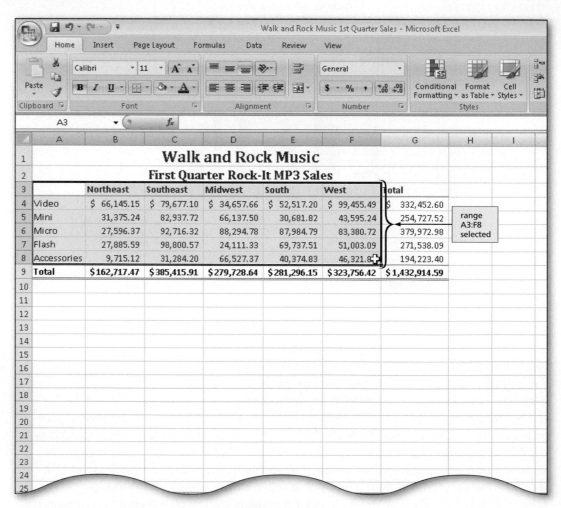

Figure 1–74

2

- Click the Insert tab to make the Insert tab the active tab (Figure 1–75).

Q&A What tasks can I perform with the Insert tab?

The Insert tab includes commands that allow you to insert various objects, such as shapes, tables, illustrations, and charts, into a worksheet. These objects will be discussed as they are used throughout this book.

Figure 1–75

3

- Click the Column button on the Ribbon to display the Column gallery.

- Point to the 3-D Clustered Column chart type in the 3-D Column area of the Column gallery (Figure 1–76).

Figure 1–76

4

- Click the 3-D Clustered Column chart type in the 3-D Column area of the Column gallery to add a 3-D Clustered Column chart to the middle of the worksheet in a selection rectangle.

- Click the top-right edge of the selection rectangle but do not release the mouse to grab the chart and change the mouse pointer to a crosshair with four arrowheads (Figure 1–77).

Q&A

Why is a new tab displayed on the Ribbon?

When you select objects such as shapes or charts, Excel displays contextual tabs that include special commands that are used to work with the type of object selected. Because a chart is selected, Excel displays the Chart Tools contextual tab. The three tabs below the Chart Tools contextual tab, Design, Layout, and Format, are tabs that include commands to work with charts.

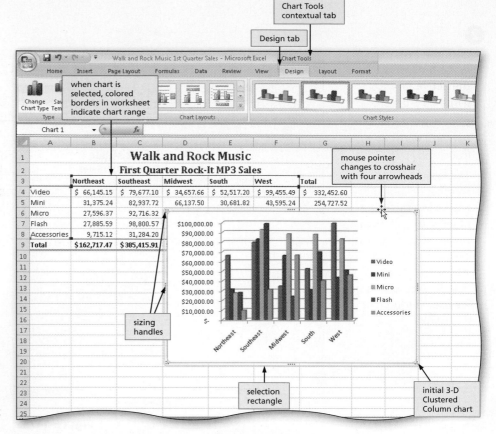

Figure 1–77

5

- Continue holding down the left mouse button while dragging the chart down and to the left to position the upper-left corner of the dotted line rectangle over the upper-left corner of cell A11. Release the mouse button to complete the move of the chart.

- Click the middle sizing handle on the right edge of the chart and do not release the mouse button (Figure 1–78).

Q&A

How does Excel know how to create the chart?

Excel automatically selects the entries in the topmost row of the chart range (row 3) as the titles for the horizontal axis (also called the **x-axis** or **category axis**) and draws a column for each of the 25 cells in the range containing numbers.

Figure 1–78

6

- While continuing to hold down the mouse button, press the ALT key and drag the right edge of the chart to the right edge of column G and then release the mouse button to resize the chart.

- Point to the middle sizing handle on the bottom edge of the selection rectangle and do not release the mouse button (Figure 1–79).

Why should I hold the ALT key down while I resize a chart?

Holding down the ALT key while you drag a chart **snaps** (aligns) the edge of the chart area to the worksheet gridlines. If you do not hold down the ALT key, then you can place an edge of a chart in the middle of a column or row.

Figure 1–79

7

- While continuing to hold down the mouse button, press the ALT key and drag the bottom edge of the chart up to the bottom edge of row 22 and then release the mouse button to resize the chart.

- Click the More button in the Chart Styles gallery to expand the gallery and point to Style 2 in the gallery (column 2, row 1) (Figure 1–80).

Figure 1–80

8

- Click Style 2 in the Chart Styles gallery to apply the chart style Style 2 to the chart.

Experiment

- Select other chart styles in the Chart Styles gallery to apply other chart styles to the chart, but select Style 2 as your final choice.

- Click cell I9 to deselect the chart and complete the worksheet (Figure 1–81).

Q&A

What is the purpose of the items on the right side of the chart?

The items to the right of the column chart in Figure 1–81 are the **legend**, which identifies the colors assigned to each bar in the chart. Excel automatically selects the entries in the leftmost column of the chart range (column A) as titles within the legend.

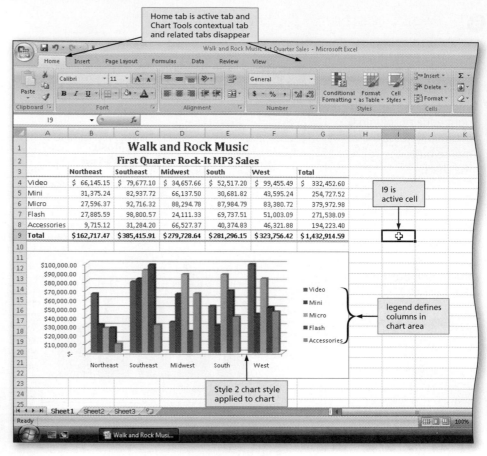

Figure 1–81

Changing Document Properties and Saving Again

BTW

Document Properties
Excel allows you to assign additional document properties by clicking the Document Properties button arrow in the Document Information Panel and then clicking Advanced Properties. You can assign custom properties, such as Department, Purpose, and Editor. Or, you can create your own document properties.

Excel helps you organize and identify your files by using **document properties**, which are the details about a file. Document properties, also known as **metadata**, can include such information as the project author, title, or subject. **Keywords** are words or phrases that further describe the document. For example, a class name or worksheet topic can describe the file's purpose or content. Document properties are valuable for a variety of reasons:

- Users can save time locating a particular file because they can view a document's properties without opening the workbook.

- By creating consistent properties for files having similar content, users can better organize their workbooks.

- Some organizations require Excel users to add document properties so that other employees can view details about these files.

Five different types of document properties exist, but the more common ones used in this book are standard and automatically updated properties. **Standard properties** are associated with all Microsoft Office documents and include author, title, and subject. **Automatically updated properties** include file system properties, such as the date you create or change a file, and statistics, such as the file size.

To Change Document Properties

The **Document Information Panel** contains areas where you can view and enter document properties. You can view and change information in this panel at any time while you are creating your workbook. Before saving the workbook again, you want to add your name and class name as document properties. The following steps use the Document Information Panel to change document properties.

- Click the Office Button to display the Office Button menu.

- Point to Prepare on the Office Button menu to display the Prepare submenu (Figure 1–82).

Q&A

What other types of actions besides changing properties can you take to prepare a document for distribution?

The Prepare submenu provides commands related to sharing a document with others, such as allowing or restricting people to view and modify your document, checking to see if your worksheet will work in earlier versions of Excel, and searching for hidden personal information.

Figure 1–82

- Click Properties on the Prepare submenu to display the Document Information Panel (Figure 1–83).

Q&A

Why are some of the document properties in my Document Information Panel already filled in?

The person who installed Microsoft Office 2007 on your computer or network may have set or customized the properties.

Figure 1–83

- Click the Author text box and then type your name as the Author property. If a name already is displayed in the Author text box, delete it before typing your name.

- Click the Subject text box, if necessary delete any existing text, and then type your course and section as the Subject property.

- Click the Keywords text box, if necessary delete any existing text, and then type First Quarter Rock-It MP3 Sales (Figure 1-84).

 What types of document properties does Excel collect automatically?

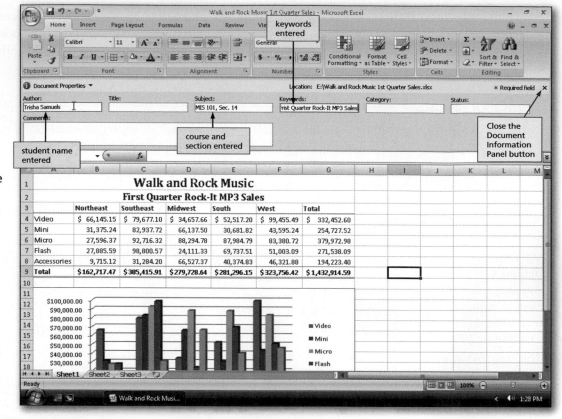

Figure 1–84

Excel records such details as how long you worked at creating your project, how many times you revised the document, and what fonts and themes are used.

4

- Click the Close the Document Information Panel button so that the Document Information Panel no longer is displayed.

To Save an Existing Workbook with the Same File Name

Saving frequently cannot be overemphasized. Several modifications have been made to the workbook since it was saved earlier in the chapter. Earlier in this chapter, the Save button on the Quick Access Toolbar caused the Save As dialog box to appear, and the file name, Walk and Rock Music 1st Quarter Sales, was entered. Clicking the Save button on the Quick Access Toolbar causes Excel to save the changes made to the workbook since the last time it was saved. The following step saves the workbook again.

1

- With your USB flash drive connected to one of the computer's USB ports, click the Save button on the Quick Access Toolbar to overwrite the previous Walk and Rock Music 1st Quarter Sales file on the USB flash drive (Figure 1–85).

Q&A

Why did the Save As dialog box not appear?

Excel overwrites the document using the settings specified the first time the document was saved. To save the file with a different file name or on different media, display the Save As dialog box by clicking the Office Button and then clicking Save As on the Office Button menu. Then, fill in the Save As dialog box as described in Steps 2 through 5 on pages EX 31 and EX 32.

Figure 1–85

Other Ways

1. Press CTRL+S or press SHIFT+F12, press ENTER

Printing a Worksheet

After you create a worksheet, you often want to print it. A printed version of the worksheet is called a **hard copy** or **printout**. Printed copies of your worksheet can be useful for the following reasons:

- Many people prefer proofreading a hard copy of the worksheet rather than viewing the worksheet on the screen to check for errors and readability.

- Someone without computer access can view the worksheet's content.

- Copies can be distributed as handouts to people during a meeting or presentation.

- Hard copies can serve as reference material if your storage medium is lost or becomes corrupted and you need to recreate the worksheet.

It is a good practice to save a workbook before printing it, in the event you experience difficulties with the printer.

BTW

Conserving Ink and Toner
You can print a presentation in black and white to conserve ink or toner by clicking the Office Button, pointing to Print on the Office Button menu, and then clicking Print Preview on the Print submenu. Click the Page Setup button on the Print Preview tab, click the Sheet tab, and then click the Black and White check box in the Print area. Click the OK button to close the Page Setup dialog box. Click the Office Button, point to Print, and then click Quick Print.

To Print a Worksheet

With the completed worksheet saved, you may want to print it. The following steps print the worksheet in the saved Walk and Rock Music 1st Quarter Sales workbook.

1

- Click the Office Button to display the Office Button menu.

- Point to Print on the Office Button menu to display the Print submenu (Figure 1–86).

Figure 1–86

2

- Click Quick Print on the Print submenu to print the document (Figure 1–87).

Q&A Can I print my document in black and white to conserve ink or toner?

Yes. Click the Office Button and then click the Excel Options button on the Office Button menu. When the Excel Options dialog box is displayed, click Advanced, scroll to the Print area, place a check mark in the Use draft quality check box if it is displayed, and then click the OK button. Click the Office Button, point to Print, and then click Quick Print.

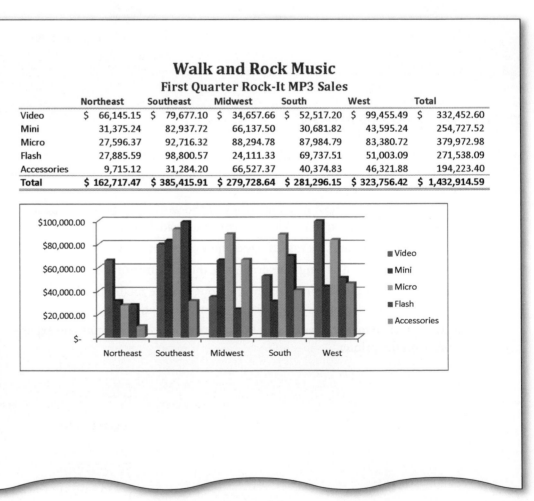

Walk and Rock Music
First Quarter Rock-It MP3 Sales

	Northeast	Southeast	Midwest	South	West	Total
Video	$ 66,145.15	$ 79,677.10	$ 34,657.66	$ 52,517.20	$ 99,455.49	$ 332,452.60
Mini	31,375.24	82,937.72	66,137.50	30,681.82	43,595.24	254,727.52
Micro	27,596.37	92,716.32	88,294.78	87,984.79	83,380.72	379,972.98
Flash	27,885.59	98,800.57	24,111.33	69,737.51	51,003.09	271,538.09
Accessories	9,715.12	31,284.20	66,527.37	40,374.83	46,321.88	194,223.40
Total	$ 162,717.47	$ 385,415.91	$ 279,728.64	$ 281,296.15	$ 323,756.42	$ 1,432,914.59

Figure 1–87

Other Ways

1. Press CTRL+P, press ENTER

Quitting Excel

When you quit Excel, if you have made changes to a workbook since the last time the file was saved, Excel displays a dialog box asking if you want to save the changes you made to the file before it closes that window. The dialog box contains three buttons with these resulting actions:

- Yes button — Saves the changes and then quits Excel
- No button — Quits Excel without saving changes
- Cancel button — Closes the dialog box and redisplays the worksheet without saving the changes

If no changes have been made to an open workbook since the last time the file was saved, Excel will close the window without displaying a dialog box.

To Quit Excel with One Workbook Open

The Walk and Rock 1st Quarter Sales worksheet is complete. The following steps quit Excel if only one workbook is open.

1

- Point to the Close button on the right side of the Excel title bar (Figure 1–88).

2

- Click the Close button to quit Excel.

Q&A

What if I have more than one Excel workbook open?

You would click the Close button on the Excel title bar for each open workbook. When you click the Close button with the last workbook open, Excel also quits. As an alternative, you could click the Office Button and then click the Exit Excel button on the Office Button menu, which closes all open workbooks and then quits Excel.

Figure 1–88

Other Ways

1. Double-click Office Button

2. With multiple workbooks open, click Office Button, click Exit Excel on Office Button menu

3. Right-click Microsoft Excel button on Windows Vista taskbar, click Close on shortcut menu

4. Press ALT+F4

BTW

Print Preview
You can preview the printout on your screen using the Print Preview command on the Print submenu (Figure 1–86 on page EX 58), make adjustments to the worksheet, and then print it only when it appears exactly as you want. Each time you preview rather than print, you save both ink and paper.

Starting Excel and Opening a Workbook

Once you have created and saved a workbook, you may need to retrieve it from your storage medium. For example, you might want to revise a worksheet or reprint it. Opening a workbook requires that Excel is running on your computer.

To Start Excel

The following steps, which assume Windows Vista is running, start Excel.

Note: If you are using Windows XP, please see Appendix F for alternate steps.

1 Click the Start button on the Windows Vista taskbar to display the Start menu.

2 Click All Programs at the bottom of the left pane on the Start menu to display the All Programs list and then click Microsoft Office in the All Programs list to display the Microsoft Office list.

3 Click Microsoft Office Excel 2007 in the Microsoft Office list to start Excel and display a new blank worksheet in the Excel window.

4 If the Excel window is not maximized, click the Maximize button on its title bar to maximize the window.

To Open a Workbook from Excel

Earlier in this chapter, the workbook was saved on a USB flash drive using the file name, Walk and Rock Music 1st Quarter Sales. The following steps open the Walk and Rock Music 1st Quarter Sales file from the USB flash drive.

1

- With your USB flash drive connected to one of the computer's USB ports, click the Office Button to display the Office Button menu (Figure 1–89).

Q&A

What files are shown in the Recent Documents list?

Excel displays the most recently opened document file names in this list. If the name of the file you want to open appears in the Recent Documents list, you could double-click it to open the file.

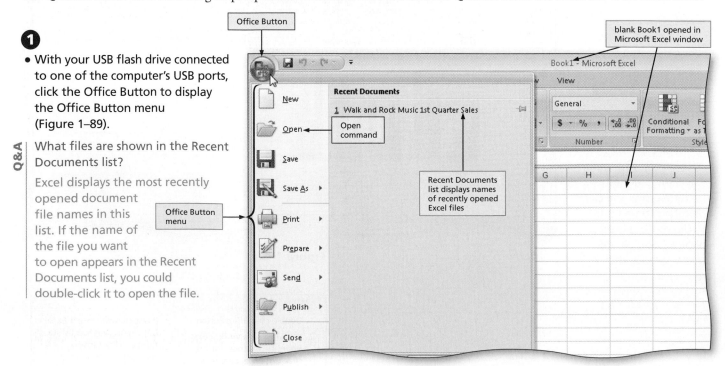

Figure 1–89

2

- Click Open on the Office Button menu to display the Open dialog box.

- If the Folders list is displayed below the Folders button, click the Folders button to remove the Folders list.

- If necessary, click Computer in the Favorite Links section and then scroll until UDISK 2.0 (E:) appears in the list of available drives.

- Double-click UDISK 2.0 (E:) to select the USB flash drive, Drive E in this case, as the new open location.

- Click Walk and Rock Music 1st Quarter Sales to select the file name (Figure 1–90).

Q&A

How do I open the file if I am not using a USB flash drive?

Use the same process, but be certain to select your device in the Computer list.

Figure 1–90

3

- Click the Open button to open the selected file and display the worksheet in the Excel window (Figure 1–91).

Q&A

Why do I see the Microsoft Excel icon and name on the Windows Vista taskbar?

When you open an Excel file, the application name (Microsoft Excel) is displayed on a selected button on the Windows Vista taskbar. If you point to this button, the file name also appears in a ScreenTip.

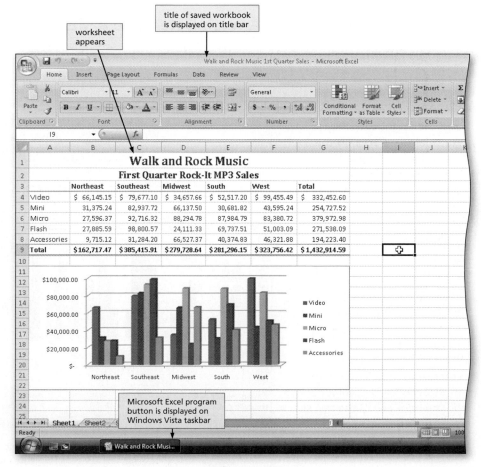

Figure 1–91

Other Ways

1. Click Office Button, double-click file name in Recent Documents list

2. Press CTRL+O, select file name, press ENTER

BTW

AutoCalculate
Use the AutoCalculate area on the status bar to check your work as you enter data in a worksheet. If you enter large amounts of data, you select a range of data and then check the AutoCalculate area to provide insight into statistics about the data you entered. Often, you will have an intuitive feel for whether the numbers are accurate or if you may have made a mistake while entering the data.

AutoCalculate

You easily can obtain a total, an average, or other information about the numbers in a range by using the **AutoCalculate area** on the status bar. First, select the range of cells containing the numbers you want to check. Next, right-click the AutoCalculate area to display the Status Bar Configuration shortcut menu (Figure 1–92). The check mark to the left of the active functions (Average, Count, and Sum) indicates that the sum, count, and average of the selected range are displayed in the AutoCalculate area on the status bar. The functions of the AutoCalculate commands on the Status Bar Configuration shortcut menu are described in Table 1–4.

Table 1–4 AutoCalculate Shortcut Menu Commands	
Command	**Function**
Average	AutoCalculate area displays the average of the numbers in the selected range
Count	AutoCalculate area displays the number of nonblank cells in the selected range
Numerical Count	AutoCalculate area displays the number of cells containing numbers in the selected range
Minimum	AutoCalculate area displays the lowest value in the selected range
Maximum	AutoCalculate area displays the highest value in the selected range
Sum	AutoCalculate area displays the sum of the numbers in the selected range

To Use the AutoCalculate Area to Determine a Maximum

The following steps show how to display the largest quarterly sales for any region for the Micro product type.

1

• Select the range B6:F6 and then right-click the AutoCalculate area on the status bar to display the Status Bar Configuration shortcut menu (Figure 1–92).

Q&A

What is displayed on the Status Bar Configuration shortcut menu?

This shortcut menu includes several commands that allow you to control the items displayed on the Customize Status Bar shortcut menu. The AutoCalculate area of the shortcut menu includes six commands as well as the result of the associated calculation on the right side of the menu.

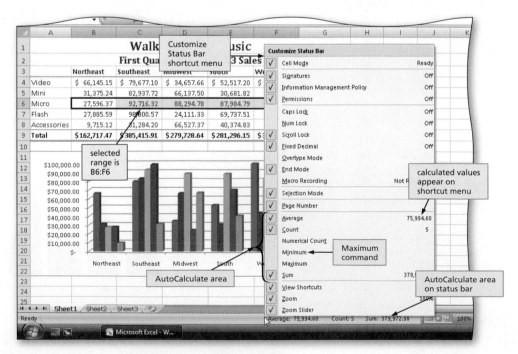

Figure 1–92

2
- Click Maximum on the shortcut menu to display the Maximum value in the range B6:F6 in the AutoCalculate area of the status bar.

- Click anywhere on the worksheet to cause the shortcut menu to disappear (Figure 1–93).

3
- Right-click the AutoCalculate area and then click Maximum on the shortcut menu to cause the Maximum value to no longer appear in the AutoCalculate area.

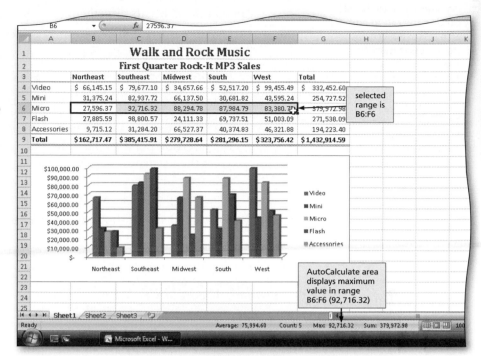

Figure 1–93

Correcting Errors

You can correct errors on a worksheet using one of several methods. The method you choose will depend on the extent of the error and whether you notice it while typing the data or after you have entered the incorrect data into the cell.

Correcting Errors while You Are Typing Data into a Cell

If you notice an error while you are typing data into a cell, press the BACKSPACE key to erase the incorrect characters and then type the correct characters. If the error is a major one, click the Cancel box in the formula bar or press the ESC key to erase the entire entry and then reenter the data from the beginning.

Correcting Errors after Entering Data into a Cell

If you find an error in the worksheet after entering the data, you can correct the error in one of two ways:

1. If the entry is short, select the cell, retype the entry correctly, and then click the Enter box or press the ENTER key. The new entry will replace the old entry.

2. If the entry in the cell is long and the errors are minor, using Edit mode may be a better choice than retyping the cell entry. Use the Edit mode as described below.

   a. Double-click the cell containing the error to switch Excel to Edit mode. In **Edit mode**, Excel displays the active cell entry in the formula bar and a flashing

BTW

In-Cell Editing
An alternative to double-clicking the cell to edit it is to select the cell and then press the F2 key.

insertion point in the active cell (Figure 1–94). With Excel in Edit mode, you can edit the contents directly in the cell — a procedure called **in-cell editing**.

b. Make changes using in-cell editing, as indicated below.

(1) To insert new characters between two characters, place the insertion point between the two characters and begin typing. Excel inserts the new characters at the location of the insertion point.

(2) To delete a character in the cell, move the insertion point to the left of the character you want to delete and then press the DELETE key or place the insertion point to the right of the character you want to delete and then press the BACKSPACE key. You also can use the mouse to drag through the character or adjacent characters you want to delete and then press the DELETE key or click the Cut button on the Home tab on the Ribbon.

(3) When you are finished editing an entry, click the Enter box or press the ENTER key.

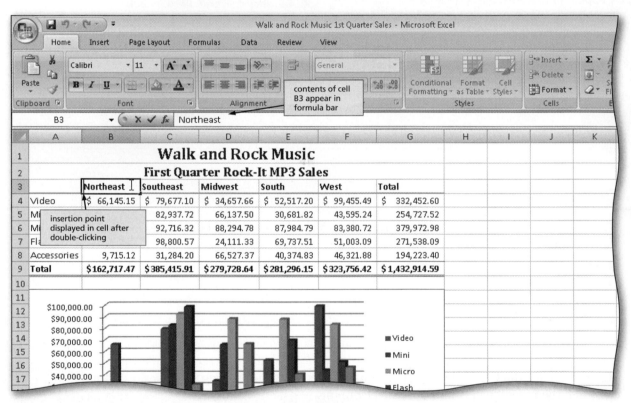

Figure 1–94

When Excel enters the Edit mode, the keyboard usually is in Insert mode. In **Insert mode**, as you type a character, Excel inserts the character and moves all characters to the right of the typed character one position to the right. You can change to Overtype mode by pressing the INSERT key. In **Overtype mode**, Excel overtypes, or replaces, the character to the right of the insertion point. The INSERT key toggles the keyboard between Insert mode and Overtype mode.

While in Edit mode, you may have reason to move the insertion point to various points in the cell, select portions of the data in the cell, or switch from inserting characters to overtyping characters. Table 1–5 summarizes the more common tasks used during in-cell editing.

BTW

Editing the Contents of a Cell
Rather than using in-cell editing, you can select the cell and then click the formula bar to edit the contents.

Table 1–5 Summary of In-Cell Editing Tasks

	Task	Mouse	Keyboard
1	Move the insertion point to the beginning of data in a cell.	Point to the left of the first character and click.	Press HOME
2	Move the insertion point to the end of data in a cell.	Point to the right of the last character and click.	Press END
3	Move the insertion point anywhere in a cell.	Point to the appropriate position and click the character.	Press RIGHT ARROW or LEFT ARROW
4	Highlight one or more adjacent characters.	Drag the mouse pointer through adjacent characters.	Press SHIFT+RIGHT ARROW or SHIFT+LEFT ARROW
5	Select all data in a cell.	Double-click the cell with the insertion point in the cell if there are no spaces in the data in the cell.	
6	Delete selected characters.	Click the Cut button on the Home tab on the Ribbon.	Press DELETE
7	Delete characters to the left of the insertion point.		Press BACKSPACE
8	Delete characters to the right of the insertion point.		Press DELETE
9	Toggle between Insert and Overtype modes.		Press INSERT

Undoing the Last Cell Entry

Excel provides the Undo command on the Quick Access Toolbar (Figure 1–95), which allows you to erase recent cell entries. Thus, if you enter incorrect data in a cell and notice it immediately, click the Undo button and Excel changes the cell entry to what it was prior to the incorrect data entry.

Figure 1–95

Excel remembers the last 100 actions you have completed. Thus, you can undo up to 100 previous actions by clicking the Undo button arrow to display the Undo list and then clicking the action to be undone (Figure 1–95). You can drag through several actions in the Undo list to undo all of them at once. If no actions are available for Excel to undo, then the Undo button is dimmed and inoperative.

The Redo button, next to the Undo button on the Quick Access Toolbar, allows you to repeat previous actions.

BTW

Quick Reference
For a table that lists how to complete the tasks covered in this book using the mouse, Ribbon, shortcut menu, and keyboard, see the Quick Reference Summary at the back of this book, or visit the Excel 2007 Quick Reference Web page (scsite.com/ex2007/qr).

BTW

Certification
The Microsoft Certified Application Specialist (MCAS) program provides an opportunity for you to obtain a valuable industry credential – proof that you have the Excel 2007 skills required by employers. For more information, see Appendix G or visit the Excel 2007 Certification Web page (scsite.com/ex2007/cert).

BTW

Getting Back to Normal
If you accidentally assign unwanted formats to a range of cells, you can use the Normal cell style selection in the Cell Styles gallery. Click Cell Styles on the Home tab on the Ribbon and then click Normal. Doing so changes the format to Normal style. To view the characteristics of the Normal style, right-click the style in the Cell Styles gallery and then click Modify, or press ALT+APOSTROPHE (').

Clearing a Cell or Range of Cells

If you enter data into the wrong cell or range of cells, you can erase, or clear, the data using one of the first four methods listed below. The fifth method clears the formatting from the selected cells.

To Clear Cell Entries Using the Fill Handle

1. Select the cell or range of cells and then point to the fill handle so the mouse pointer changes to a crosshair.
2. Drag the fill handle back into the selected cell or range until a shadow covers the cell or cells you want to erase. Release the mouse button.

To Clear Cell Entries Using the Shortcut Menu

1. Select the cell or range of cells to be cleared.
2. Right-click the selection.
3. Click Clear Contents on the shortcut menu.

To Clear Cell Entries Using the delete Key

1. Select the cell or range of cells to be cleared.
2. Press the DELETE key.

To Clear Cell Entries and Formatting Using the Clear Button

1. Select the cell or range of cells to be cleared.
2. Click the Clear button on the Home tab (Figure 1–95 on the previous page).
3. Click Clear Contents on the menu.

To Clear Formatting Using the Cell Styles Button

1. Select the cell or range of cells from which you want to remove the formatting.
2. Click the Cell Styles button on the Home tab and point to Normal.
3. Click Normal in the Live Preview Gallery.

The Clear button on the Home tab is the only command that clears both the cell entry and the cell formatting. As you are clearing cell entries, always remember that you should *never press the* SPACEBAR *to clear a cell*. Pressing the SPACEBAR enters a blank character. A blank character is text and is different from an empty cell, even though the cell may appear empty.

Clearing the Entire Worksheet

If required worksheet edits are extremely extensive, you may want to clear the entire worksheet and start over. To clear the worksheet or delete an embedded chart, use the following steps.

To Clear the Entire Worksheet

1. Click the Select All button on the worksheet (Figure 1–95).
2. Click the Clear button on the Home tab to delete both the entries and formats.

The Select All button selects the entire worksheet. Instead of clicking the Select All button, you also can press CTRL+A. To clear an unsaved workbook, click the workbook's Close Window button or click the Close command on the Office Button menu. Click the No button if the Microsoft Excel dialog box asks if you want to save changes. To start a new, blank workbook, click the New command on the Office Button menu.

To delete an embedded chart, complete the following steps.

BTW

Excel Help
The best way to become familiar with Excel Help is to use it. Appendix C includes detailed information about Excel Help and exercises that will help you gain confidence in using it.

To Delete an Embedded Chart

1. Click the chart to select it.
2. Press the DELETE key.

Excel Help

At any time while using Excel, you can find answers to questions and display information about various topics through **Excel Help**. This section introduces you to Excel Help.

To Search for Excel Help

Using Excel Help, you can search for information based on phrases such as save a workbook or format a chart, or key terms such as copy, save, or format. Excel Help responds with a list of search results displayed as links to a variety of resources. The following steps, which use Excel Help to search for information about formatting a chart, assume you are connected to the Internet.

- Click the Microsoft Office Excel Help button near the upper-right corner of the Excel window to open the Excel Help window.

- Type format a chart in the Type words to search for text box at the top of the Excel Help window (Figure 1–96).

Figure 1–96

2

- Press the ENTER key to display the search results.

- Click the Maximize button on the Excel Help window title bar to maximize the Help window (Figure 1–97).

Q&A

Where is the Excel window with the Walk and Rock Music 1st Quarter Sales worksheet?

Excel is open in the background, but the Excel Help window is overlaid on top of the Microsoft Excel window. When the Excel Help window is closed, the worksheet will reappear.

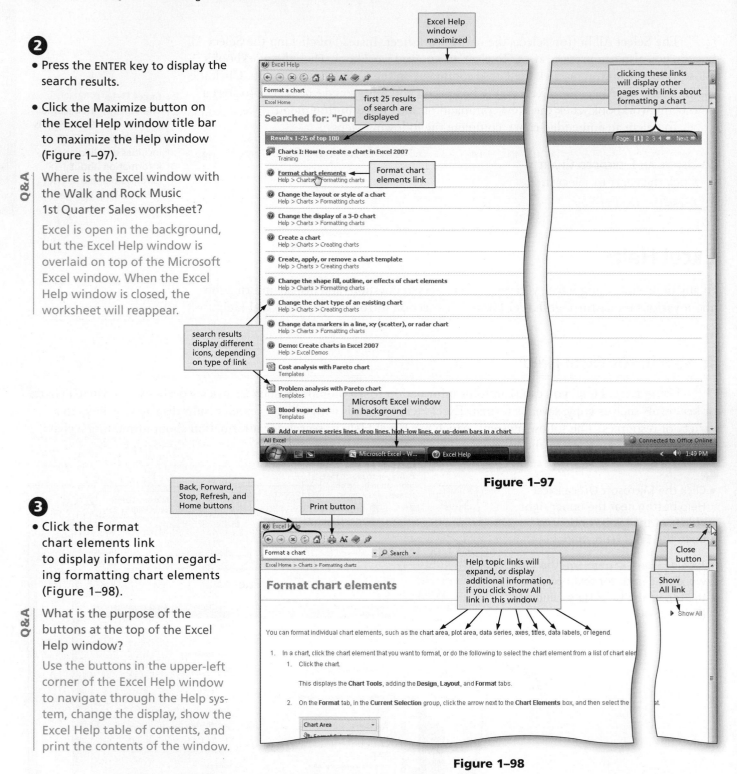

Figure 1–97

3

- Click the Format chart elements link to display information regarding formatting chart elements (Figure 1–98).

Q&A

What is the purpose of the buttons at the top of the Excel Help window?

Use the buttons in the upper-left corner of the Excel Help window to navigate through the Help system, change the display, show the Excel Help table of contents, and print the contents of the window.

Figure 1–98

4

- Click the Close button on the Excel Help window title bar to close the Excel Help window and make Excel active.

Other Ways
1. Press F1

To Quit Excel

The following steps quit Excel.

1 Click the Close button on the right side of the title bar to quit Excel; or if you have multiple Excel workbooks open, click the Office Button and then click the Exit Excel button on the Office Button menu to close all open workbooks and quit Excel.

2 If necessary, click the No button in the Microsoft Office Excel dialog box so that any changes you have made are not saved.

BTW

Quitting Excel
Do not forget to remove your USB flash drive from the USB port after quitting Excel, especially if you are working in a laboratory environment. Nothing can be more frustrating than leaving all of your hard work behind on a USB flash drive for the next user.

Chapter Summary

In this chapter you have learned about the Excel window, how to enter text and numbers to create a worksheet, how to select a range, how to use the Sum button, save a workbook, format cells, insert a chart, print a worksheet, quit Excel, and use Excel Help. The items listed below include all the new Excel skills you have learned in this chapter.

1. Start Excel (EX 6)
2. Enter the Worksheet Titles (EX 17)
3. Enter Column Titles (EX 19)
4. Enter Row Titles (EX 21)
5. Enter Numbers (EX 23)
6. Sum a Column of Numbers (EX 25)
7. Copy a Cell to Adjacent Cells in a Row (EX 27)
8. Determine Multiple Totals at the Same Time (EX 28)
9. Save a Workbook (EX 30)
10. Change a Cell Style (EX 35)
11. Change the Font Type (EX 36)
12. Bold a Cell (EX 38)
13. Increase the Font Size of a Cell Entry (EX 38)
14. Change the Font Color of a Cell Entry (EX 39)
15. Center Cell Entries across Columns by Merging Cells (EX 40)
16. Format Column Titles and the Total Row (EX 42)
17. Format Numbers in the Worksheet (EX 44)
18. Adjust the Column Width (EX 46)
19. Use the Name Box to Select a Cell (EX 47)
20. Add a 3-D Clustered Column Chart to the Worksheet (EX 50)
21. Change Document Properties (EX 55)
22. Save an Existing Workbook with the Same File Name (EX 58)
23. Print a Worksheet (EX 58)
24. Quit Excel with One Workbook Open (EX 59)
25. Open a Workbook from Excel (EX 60)
26. Use the AutoCalculate Area to Determine a Maximum (EX 62)
27. Clear Cell Entries Using the Fill Handle (EX 66)
28. Clear Cell Entries Using the Shortcut Menu (EX 66)
29. Clear Cell Entries Using the DELETE Key (EX 66)
30. Clear Cell Entries and Formatting Using the Clear Button (EX 66)
31. Clear Formatting Using the Cell Styles Button (EX 66)
32. Clear the Entire Worksheet (EX 66)
33. Delete an Embedded Chart (EX 67)
34. Search for Excel Help (EX 67)

If you have a SAM user profile, you may have access to hands-on instruction, practice, and assessment. Log in to your SAM account (http://sam2007.course.com) to launch any assigned training activities or exams that relate to the skills covered in this chapter.

Learn It Online

Test your knowledge of chapter content and key terms.

Instructions: To complete the Learn It Online exercises, start your browser, click the Address bar, and then enter the Web address scsite.com/ex2007/learn. When the Excel 2007 Learn It Online page is displayed, click the link for the exercise you want to complete and then read the instructions.

Chapter Reinforcement TF, MC, and SA

A series of true/false, multiple choice, and short answer questions that test your knowledge of the chapter content.

Flash Cards

An interactive learning environment where you identify chapter key terms associated with displayed definitions.

Practice Test

A series of multiple choice questions that test your knowledge of chapter content and key terms.

Who Wants To Be a Computer Genius?

An interactive game that challenges your knowledge of chapter content in the style of a television quiz show.

Wheel of Terms

An interactive game that challenges your knowledge of chapter key terms in the style of the television show *Wheel of Fortune*.

Crossword Puzzle Challenge

A crossword puzzle that challenges your knowledge of key terms presented in the chapter.

Apply Your Knowledge

Reinforce the skills and apply the concepts you learned in this chapter.

Changing the Values in a Worksheet

Instructions: Start Excel. Open the workbook Apply 1-1 Bicycle Shop 3rd Quarter Sales (Figure 1–99a). See the inside back cover of this book for instructions for downloading the Data Files for Students, or see your instructor for information on accessing the files required in this book.

1. Make the changes to the worksheet described in Table 1–6 so that the worksheet appears as shown in Figure 1–99b. As you edit the values in the cells containing numeric data, watch the totals in row 8, the totals in column G, and the chart change.

2. Change the worksheet title in cell A1 to the Title cell style and then merge and center it across columns A through G. Use commands in the Font group on the Home tab on the Ribbon to change the worksheet subtitle in cell A2 to 16-point Corbel red, bold font and then center it across columns A through G. Use the Accent 1 theme color (column 5, row 1 on the Font palette) for the red font color.

3. Update the document properties with your name, course number, and name for the workbook. Save the workbook using the file name, Apply 1-1 Spoke-Up Bicycle Shop 3rd Quarter Sales. Submit the assignment as requested by your instructor.

Table 1–6 New Worksheet Data	
Cell	**Change Cell Contents To**
A1	Spoke-Up Bicycle Shop
B4	11869.2
E4	9157.83
D6	5217.92
F6	6239.46
B7	3437.64

(a) Before

(b) After

Figure 1–99

Extend Your Knowledge

Extend the skills you learned in this chapter and experiment with new skills. You may need to use Help to complete the assignment.

Formatting Cells and Inserting Multiple Charts

Instructions: Start Excel. Open the workbook Extend 1-1 Pack-n-Away Shipping. See the inside back cover of this book for instructions for downloading the Data Files for Students, or see your instructor for information on accessing the files required in this book. Perform the following tasks to format cells in the worksheet and to add two charts to the worksheet.

1. Use the commands in the Font group on the Home tab on the Ribbon to change the font of the title in cell A1 to 24-point Arial, red; bold and subtitle of the worksheet to 16-point Arial Narrow, blue, bold.

2. Select the range A3:E8, click the Insert tab on the Ribbon, and then click the Dialog Box Launcher in the Charts group on the Ribbon to open the Insert Chart dialog box (Figure 1–100).

Figure 1–100

3. Insert a Stacked Line chart by clicking the Stacked Line chart in the gallery and then clicking the OK button. Move the chart either below or to the right of the data in the worksheet. Click the Design tab and apply a chart style to the chart.

4. With the same range selected, follow Step 3 above to insert a 3-D Area chart in the worksheet. You may need to use the scroll box on the right side of the Insert Chart dialog box to view the Area charts in the gallery. Move the chart either below or to the right of the data so that each chart does not overlap the Stacked Line chart. Choose a different chart style for this chart than the one you selected for the Stacked Line chart.

5. Resize each chart so that each snaps to the worksheet gridlines. Make certain that both charts are visible with the worksheet data without the need to scroll the worksheet.

6. Update the document properties with your name, course number, and name for the workbook.

7. Save the workbook using the file name, Extend 1-1 Pack-n-Away Shipping Charts. Submit the assignment as requested by your instructor.

Make It Right

Analyze a workbook and correct all errors and/or improve the design.

Correcting Formatting and Values in a Worksheet

Instructions: Start Excel. Open the workbook Make It Right 1-1 Book Sales. See the inside back cover of this book for instructions for downloading the Data Files for Students, or see your instructor for information on accessing the files required for this book. Correct the following formatting problems and data errors (Figure 1–101) in the worksheet, while keeping in mind the guidelines presented in this chapter.

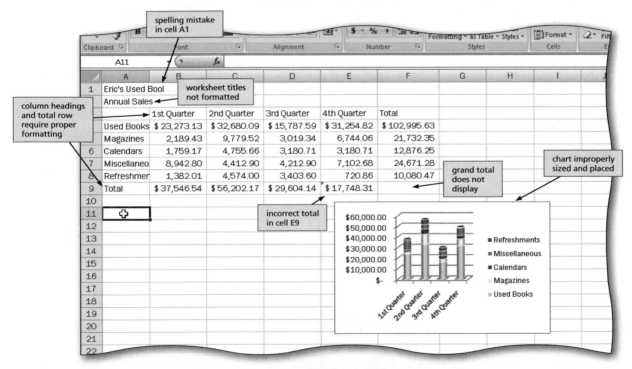

Figure 1–101

1. Merge and center the worksheet title and subtitle appropriately.

2. Format the worksheet title with a cell style appropriate for a worksheet title.

3. Format the subtitle using commands in the Font group on the Ribbon.

4. Correct the spelling mistake in cell A1 by changing Bool to Books.

5. Apply proper formatting to the column headers and total row.

Continued >

Make It Right *continued*

6. Adjust column sizes so that all data in each column is visible.

7. Use the SUM function to create the grand total for annual sales.

8. The SUM function in cell E9 does not sum all of the numbers in the column. Correct this error by editing the range for the SUM function in the cell.

9. Resize and move the chart so that it is below the worksheet data and does not extend past the right edge of the worksheet data. Be certain to snap the chart to the worksheet gridlines by holding down the ALT key as you resize the chart.

10. Update the document properties with your name, course number, and name for the workbook. Save the workbook using the file name, Make It Right 1-1 Eric's Used Books Annual Sales. Submit the assignment as requested by your instructor.

In the Lab

Design and/or create a workbook using the guidelines, concepts, and skills presented in this chapter. Labs 1, 2, and 3 are listed in order of increasing difficulty.

Lab 1: Annual Cost of Goods Worksheet

Problem: You work part-time as a spreadsheet specialist for Kona's Expresso Coffee, one of the up-and-coming coffee franchises in the United States. Your manager has asked you to develop an annual cost of goods analysis worksheet similar to the one shown in Figure 1–102.

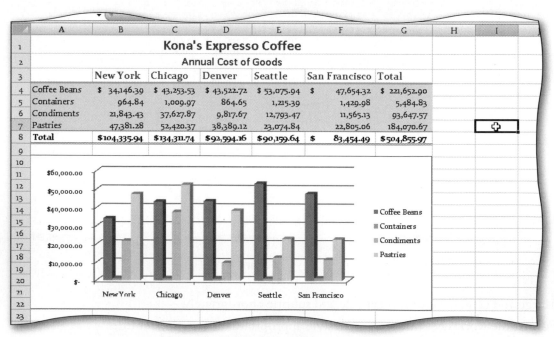

Figure 1–102

Instructions: Perform the following tasks.

1. Start Excel. Enter the worksheet title, Kona's Expresso Coffee, in cell A1 and the worksheet subtitle, Annual Cost of Goods, in cell A2. Beginning in row 3, enter the store locations, costs of goods, and supplies categories shown in Table 1–7.

Table 1–7 Kona's Expresso Coffee Annual Cost of Goods

	New York	Chicago	Denver	Seattle	San Franscisco
Coffee Beans	34146.39	43253.53	43522.72	53075.94	47654.32
Containers	964.84	1009.97	864.65	1215.39	1429.98
Condiments	21843.43	37627.87	9817.67	12793.47	11565.13
Pastries	47381.28	52420.37	38389.12	23074.84	22805.06

2. Use the SUM function to determine the totals for each store location, type of supply, and company grand total.

3. Use Cell Styles in the Styles group on the Home tab on the Ribbon to format the worksheet title with the Title cell style. Center the title across columns A through G. Do not be concerned if the edges of the worksheet title are not displayed.

4. Use buttons in the Font group on the Home tab on the Ribbon to format the worksheet subtitle to 14-point Calibri dark blue, bold font, and center it across columns A through G.

5. Use Cell Styles in the Styles group on the Home tab on the Ribbon to format the range A3:G3 with the Heading 2 cell style, the range A4:G7 with the 20% - Accent1 cell style, and the range A8:G8 with the Total cell style. Use the buttons in the Number group on the Home tab on the Ribbon to apply the Accounting Number format to the range B4:G4 and the range B8:G8. Use the buttons in the Number group on the Home tab on the Ribbon to apply the Comma Style to the range B5:G7. Adjust any column widths to the widest text entry in each column.

6. Select the range A3:F7 and then insert a 3-D Clustered Column chart. Apply the Style 8 chart style to the chart. Move and resize the chart so that it appears in the range A10:G22. If the labels along the horizontal axis (x-axis) do not appear as shown in Figure 1-102, then drag the right side of the chart so that it is displayed in the range A10:H22.

7. Update the document properties with your name, course number, and name for the workbook.

8. Save the workbook using the file name Lab 1-1 Konas Expresso Coffee Annual Cost of Goods.

9. Print the worksheet.

10. Make the following two corrections to the sales amounts: $9,648.12 for Seattle Condiments (cell E6), $12,844.79 for Chicago Pastries (cell C7). After you enter the corrections, the company totals in cell G8 should equal $462,135.04.

11. Print the revised worksheet. Close the workbook without saving the changes. Submit the assignment as requested by your instructor.

In the Lab

Lab 2: Annual Sales Analysis Worksheet

Problem: As the chief accountant for Scissors Office Supply, Inc., you have been asked by the sales manager to create a worksheet to analyze the annual sales for the company by location and customer type category (Figure 1–103). The office locations and corresponding sales by customer type for the year are shown in Table 1–8.

Continued >

In the Lab *continued*

Instructions: Perform the following tasks.

1. Create the worksheet shown in Figure 1–103 using the data in Table 1–8.

2. Use the SUM function to determine totals sales for the four offices, the totals for each customer type, and the company total. Add column and row headings for the totals row and totals column, as appropriate.

Table 1–8 Scissors Office Supply Annual Sales				
	Boston	**Miami**	**St. Louis**	**Santa Fe**
Consumer	206348.81	113861.40	69854.13	242286.82
Small Business	235573.28	133511.24	199158.35	228365.51
Large Business	237317.55	234036.08	126519.10	111773.38
Government	178798.04	144548.80	135470.86	132599.75
Nonprofit	15180.63	28837.75	63924.48	21361.42

3. Format the worksheet title with the Title cell style and center it across columns A through F. Use the Font group on the Ribbon to format the worksheet subtitle to 16-point Cambria green, and bold font. Center the title across columns A through F.

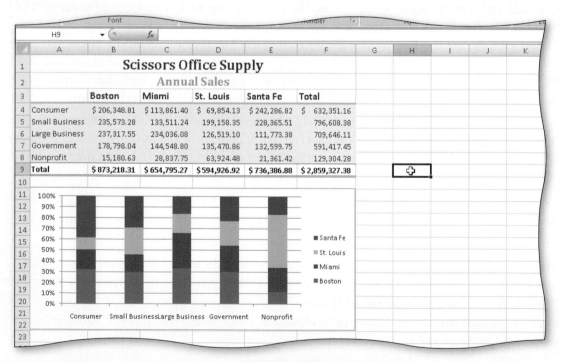

Figure 1–103

4. Format the range A3:F3 with the Heading 2 cell style, the range A4:F8 with the 20% - Accent3 cell style, and the range B9:F9 with the Total cell style. Use the Number group on the Ribbon to format cells B4:F4 and B9:F9 with the Accounting Number Format and cells B5:F8 with the Comma Style numeric format.

5. Chart the range A3:E8. Insert a 100% Stacked Column chart for the range A3:E8, as shown in Figure 1–103, by using the Column button on the Insert tab on the Ribbon. Use the chart location A11:F22.

6. Update the document properties with your name, course number, and name for the workbook.

7. Save the workbook using the file name, Lab 1-2 Scissors Office Supply Annual Sales. Print the worksheet.

8. Two corrections to the figures were sent in from the accounting department. The correct sales are $98,342.16 for Miami's annual Small Business sales (cell C5) and $48,933.75 for St. Louis's annual Nonprofit sales (cell D8). After you enter the two corrections, the company total in cell F9 should equal $2,809,167.57. Print the revised worksheet.

9. Use the Undo button to change the worksheet back to the original numbers in Table 1–8. Use the Redo button to change the worksheet back to the revised state.

10. Close Excel without saving the latest changes. Start Excel and open the workbook saved in Step 7. Double-click cell E6 and use in-cell editing to change the Santa Fe annual Large Business sales (cell E6) to $154,108.49. Write the company total in cell F9 at the top of the first printout. Click the Undo button.

11. Click cell A1 and then click the Merge & Center button to split cell A1 into cells A1, B1, C1, D1, E1, and F1. To merge the cells into one again, select the range A1:F1 and then click the Merge & Center button on the Home tab on the Ribbon.

12. Close the workbook without saving the changes. Submit the assignment as requested by your instructor.

In the Lab

Lab 3: College Cost and Financial Support Worksheet

Problem: Attending college is an expensive proposition and your resources are limited. To plan for your four-year college career, you have decided to organize your anticipated resources and costs in a worksheet. The data required to prepare your worksheet is shown in Table 1–9.

Table 1–9 College Cost and Resources				
Cost	**Freshman**	**Sophomore**	**Junior**	**Senior**
Books	450.00	477.00	505.62	535.95
Room & Board	7500.00	7950.00	8427.00	8932.62
Tuition	8200.00	8692.00	9213.52	9766.33
Entertainment	1325.00	1404.50	1488.77	1578.10
Miscellaneous	950.00	1007.00	1067.42	1131.47
Clothes	725.00	768.50	814.61	863.49
Financial Support	**Freshman**	**Sophomore**	**Junior**	**Senior**
Job	3400.00	3604.00	3820.24	4049.45
Savings	4350.00	4611.00	4887.66	5180.92
Parents	4700.00	4982.00	5280.92	5597.78
Financial Aid	5500.00	5830.00	6179.80	6550.59
Other	1200.00	1272.00	1348.32	1429.22

Continued >

In the Lab *continued*

Instructions Part 1: Using the numbers in Table 1–9, create the worksheet shown in columns A through F in Figure 1–104. Format the worksheet title as Calibri 24-point bold red. Merge and center the worksheet title in cell A1 across columns A through F. Format the worksheet subtitles in cells A2 and A11 as Calibri 16-point bold green. Format the ranges A3:F3 and A12:F12 with the Heading 2 cell style, the ranges A4:F9 and A13:F17 with the 20% - Accent cell style, and the ranges A10:F10 and A18:F18 with the Total cell style.

Update the document properties, including the addition of at least one keyword to the properties, and save the workbook using the file name, Lab 1-3 Part 1 College Cost and Financial Support. Print the worksheet. Submit the assignment as requested by your instructor.

Figure 1–104

After reviewing the numbers, you realize you need to increase manually each of the Junior-year expenses in column D by $600. Change the Junior-year expenses to reflect this change. Manually change the financial aid for the Junior year by the amount required to cover the increase in costs. The totals in cells F10 and F18 should equal $87,373.90. Print the worksheet. Close the workbook without saving changes.

Instructions Part 2: Open the workbook Lab 1-3 Part 1 College Cost and Financial Support and then save the workbook using the file name, Lab 1-3 Part 2 College Cost and Financial Support. Insert an Exploded pie in 3-D chart in the range G3:K10 to show the contribution of each category of cost for the Freshman year. Chart the range A4:B9 and apply the Style 8 chart style to the chart. Add the Pie chart title as shown in cell G2 in Figure 1–104. Insert an Exploded pie in 3-D chart in the range G12:K18 to show the contribution of each category of financial support for the Freshman year. Chart the range A13:B17 and apply the Style 8 chart style to the chart. Add the Pie chart title shown in cell G11 in Figure 1–104. Update the identification area with the exercise part number and save the workbook. Print the worksheet. Submit the assignment as requested by your instructor.

Instructions Part 3: Open the workbook Lab 1-3 Part 2 College Cost and Financial Support. Do not save the workbook in this part. A close inspection of Table 1–9 shows that both cost and financial support figures increase 6% each year. Use Excel Help to learn how to enter the data for the last three years using a formula and the Copy and Paste buttons on the Home tab on the Ribbon. For example, the formula to enter in cell C4 is =B4*1.06. Enter formulas to replace all the numbers in the range C4:E9 and C13:E17. If necessary, reformat the tables, as described in Part 1. The worksheet should appear as shown in Figure 1–104, except that some of the totals will be off by 0.01 due to rounding errors. Save the worksheet using the file name, Lab 1-3 Part 3 College Cost and Financial Support. Print the worksheet. Press CTRL+ACCENT MARK (`) to display the formulas. Print the formulas version. Submit the assignment as requested by your instructor. Close the workbook without saving changes.

Cases and Places

Apply your creative thinking and problem solving skills to design and implement a solution.

● EASIER　●● MORE DIFFICULT

● 1: Design and Create a Workbook to Analyze Yearly Sales

You are working as a summer intern for Hit-the-Road Mobile Services. Your manager has asked you to prepare a worksheet to help her analyze historical yearly sales by type of product (Table 1–10). Use the concepts and techniques presented in this chapter to create the worksheet and an embedded 3-D Clustered Column chart.

Table 1–10 Hit-the-Road Mobile Services Sales				
	2005	**2006**	**2007**	**2008**
Standard Mobile Phones	87598	99087	129791	188785
Camera Phones	71035	75909	96886	100512
Music Phones	65942	24923	34590	15696
Wireless PDAs	67604	58793	44483	35095
Satellite Radios	15161	27293	34763	43367
Headsets	9549	6264	2600	4048
Other Accessories	47963	108059	100025	62367

● 2: Design and Create a Worksheet and Chart to Analyze a Budget

To estimate the funds needed by your school's Environmental Club to make it through the upcoming year, you decide to create a budget for the club itemizing the expected quarterly expenses. The anticipated expenses are listed in Table 1–11. Use the concepts and techniques presented in this chapter to create the worksheet and an embedded 3-D Column chart using an appropriate chart style that compares the quarterly cost of each expense. Use the AutoCalculate area to determine the average amount spent per quarter on each expense. Manually insert the averages with appropriate titles in an empty area on the worksheet.

Table 1–11 Quarterly Environmental Club Budget				
	Jan – Mar	**April – June**	**July – Sept**	**Oct – Dec**
Meeting Room Rent	300	300	150	450
Copies and Supplies	390	725	325	640
Travel	450	755	275	850
Refreshments	105	85	215	155
Speaker Fees	200	200	0	500
Miscellaneous	125	110	75	215

Continued >

Cases and Places *continued*

•• 3: Create a 3-D Pie Chart to Analyze Quarterly Revenue

In-the-Villa DVD Rental is a DVD movie rental store. The owner of the store is trying to decide if it is feasible to hire more employees during certain times of the year. You have been asked to develop a worksheet totaling all the revenue received last year by quarter. The revenue per quarter is: Quarter 1, $52,699.23; Quarter 2, $111,244.32; Quarter 3, $70,905.03; and Quarter 4, $87,560.10. Create a 3-D Pie chart to illustrate quarterly revenue contribution by quarter. Use the AutoCalculate area to find the average, maximum, and minimum quarterly revenue and manually enter them and their corresponding identifiers in an empty area of the worksheet.

•• 4: Design and Create a Workbook to Analyze Your Field of Interest

Make It Personal

Based on your college major, area of interest, or career, use an Internet search engine or other research material to determine the total number of people employed in your chosen field of interest in the country over the past five years. For each year, break the yearly number down into two or more categories. For example, the number for each year can be broken into management and nonmanagement employees. Create an Excel worksheet that includes this data. Place the data in appropriate rows and columns for each year and category. Create totals for each row, totals for each column, and a grand total. Format the worksheet title, column headings, and data using the concepts presented in this chapter. Create a properly formatted Clustered Cone chart for the data and place it below the data in the worksheet. Make certain that years are on the X axis and number of employees is on the Y axis.

•• 5: Design and Create a Workbook to Analyze Your School

Working Together

Visit the registrar's office at your school and obtain data, such as age, gender, and full-time versus part-time status, for the students majoring in at least six different academic departments this semester. Have each member of your team divide the data into different categories. For example, separate the data by:

1. Age, divided into four different age groups

2. Gender, divided into male and female

3. Status, divided into full-time and part-time

After coordinating the data as a group, have each member independently use the concepts and techniques presented in this chapter to create a worksheet and appropriate chart to show the total students by characteristics by academic department. As a group, critique each worksheet and have each member modify his or her worksheet based on the group recommendations.

2 Formulas, Functions, Formatting, and Web Queries

Objectives

You will have mastered the material in this chapter when you can:

- Enter formulas using the keyboard and Point mode
- Apply the AVERAGE, MAX, and MIN functions
- Verify a formula using Range Finder
- Apply a theme to a workbook
- Add conditional formatting to cells
- Change column width and row height
- Check the spelling of a worksheet

- Set margins, headers and footers in Page Layout View
- Preview and print versions of a worksheet
- Use a Web query to get real-time data from a Web site
- Rename sheets in a workbook
- E-mail the active workbook from within Excel

2 | Formulas, Functions, Formatting, and Web Queries

Introduction

In Chapter 1, you learned how to enter data, sum values, format the worksheet to make it easier to read, and draw a chart. You also learned about using Help and saving, printing, and opening a workbook. This chapter continues to highlight these topics and presents some new ones.

The new topics covered in this chapter include using formulas and functions to create a worksheet. A **function** is a prewritten formula that is built into Excel. Other new topics include smart tags and option buttons, verifying formulas, applying a theme to a worksheet, adding borders, formatting numbers and text, using conditional formatting, changing the widths of columns and heights of rows, spell checking, e-mailing from within an application, renaming worksheets, using alternative types of worksheet displays and printouts, and adding page headers and footers to a worksheet. One alternative worksheet display and printout shows the formulas in the worksheet, instead of the values. When you display the formulas in the worksheet, you see exactly what text, data, formulas, and functions you have entered into it. Finally, this chapter covers Web queries to obtain real-time data from a Web site.

Project — Worksheet with Formulas, Functions, and Web Queries

The project in the chapter follows proper design guidelines and uses Excel to create the two worksheets shown in Figure 2–1. The Silver Dollars Stock Club was started and is owned by a national academic fraternity, which pools contributions from a number of local chapters. Each local chapter contributes $150 per month; the money is then invested in the stock market for the benefit of the organization and as a tool to help members learn about investing. At the end of each month, the club's treasurer summarizes the club's financial status in a portfolio summary. This summary includes information such as the stocks owned by the club, the cost of the stocks to the club, and the gain or loss that the club has seen over time on the stock. As the complexity of the task of creating the summary increases, the treasurer wants to use Excel to create the monthly portfolio summary. The treasurer also sees an opportunity to use Excel's built-in capability to access real-time stock quotes over the Internet.

Recall that the first step in creating an effective worksheet is to make sure you understand what is required. The people who will use the worksheet usually provide requirements. The requirements document for the Silver Dollars Stock Club Portfolio Summary worksheet includes the following: needs, source of data, summary of calculations, Web requirements, and other facts about its development (Figure 2–2 on page EX 84). The real-time stock quotes (shown in Figure 2–1b) will be accessed via a Web query. The stock quotes will be returned to the active workbook on a separate worksheet. Microsoft determines the content and format of the Real-Time Stock Quotes worksheet.

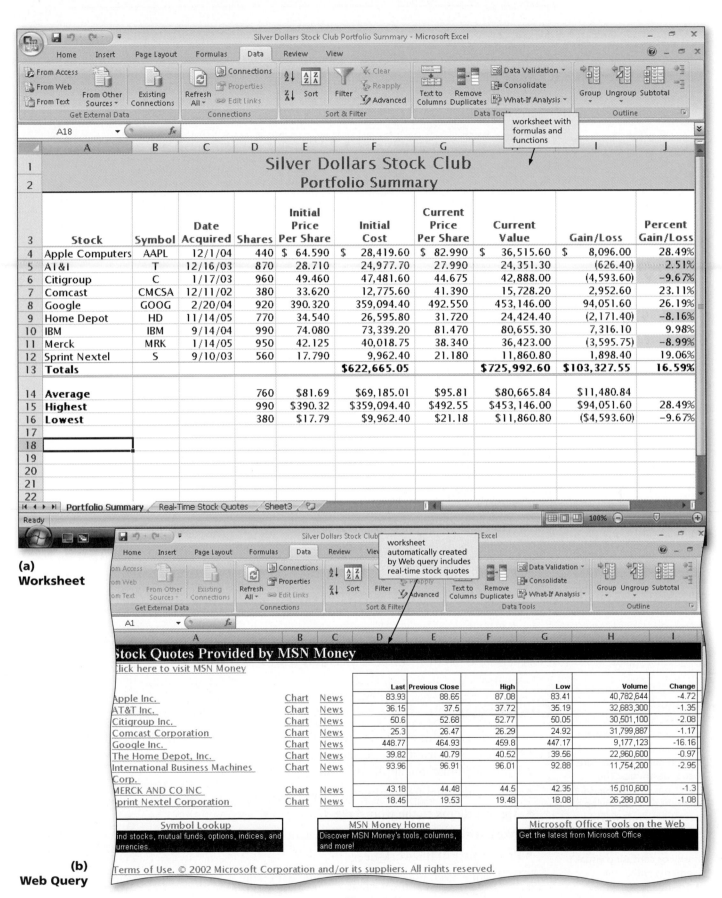

(a) Worksheet

(b) Web Query

Figure 2–1

REQUEST FOR NEW WORKSHEET

Date Submitted:	April 8, 2008
Submitted By:	Juan Castillo
Worksheet Title:	Silver Dollars Stock Club Portfolio Summary
Needs:	An easy-to-read worksheet that summarizes the club's investments (Figure 2-3). For each stock, the worksheet is to include the stock name, stock symbol, date acquired, shares, initial price per share, initial cost, current price per share, current value, gain/loss, and percent gain/loss. Also include totals and the average, highest value, and lowest value for each column of numbers. Use the import data capabilities of Excel to access real-time stock quotes using Web queries.
Source of Data:	The data supplied by Juan includes the stock names, symbols, dates acquired, number of shares, initial price per share, and current price per share. This data is shown in Table 2-1 on page EX 89.
Calculations:	The following calculations must be made for each of the stocks: 1. Initial Cost = Shares × Initial Price Per Share 2. Current Value = Shares × Current Price Per Share 3. Gain/Loss = Current Value − Initial Cost 4. Percent Gain/Loss = Gain/Loss / Initial Cost 5. Compute the totals for initial cost, current value, and gain/loss. 6. Use the AVERAGE function to determine the average for the number of shares, initial price per share, initial cost per share, current price per share, current value, and gain/loss. 7. Use the MAX and MIN functions to determine the highest and lowest values for the number of shares, initial price per share, initial cost per share, current price per share, current value, gain/loss, and percent gain/loss.
Web Requirements:	Use the Web query feature of Excel to get real-time stock quotes for the stocks owned by the Silver Dollars Stock Club.

Approvals

Approval Status:	X	Approved
		Rejected
Approved By:	Members of the Silver Dollars Stock Club	
Date:	April 15, 2008	
Assigned To:	J. Quasney, Spreadsheet Specialist	

Figure 2–2

BTW

Aesthetics versus Function
In designing a worksheet, functional considerations should come first, before visual aesthetics. The function, or purpose, of a worksheet is to provide a user with direct ways to accomplish tasks. Avoid the temptation to use flashy or confusing visual elements within the worksheet, unless they will help the user more easily complete a task.

Overview

As you read this chapter, you will learn how to create the worksheet shown in Figure 2–1 by performing these general tasks:

- Enter formulas and apply functions in the worksheet
- Add conditional formatting to the worksheet
- Apply a theme to the worksheet
- Work with the worksheet in Page Layout View
- Print a part of the worksheet
- Perform a Web query to get real-time data from a Web site and create a new worksheet
- E-mail the worksheet

General Project Decisions

While creating an Excel worksheet, you need to make several decisions that will determine the appearance and characteristics of the finished worksheet. As you create the worksheet required to meet the requirements shown in Figure 2–2, you should follow these general guidelines:

1. **Plan the layout of the worksheet.** As discussed in Chapter 1 and shown in Figure 2–3, rows typically contain items analogous to items in a list. In the case of the stock club's data, the individual stocks serve this purpose and each stock should be placed in a row. As the club adds more stocks, the number of rows in the worksheet will increase. Information about each stock and associated calculations should appear in columns.

2. **Determine the necessary formulas and functions needed.** Values such as initial cost and current value are calculated from known values. The formulas for these calculations should be known in advance of creating the worksheet. Values such as the average, highest, and lowest values can be calculated using Excel functions as opposed to relying on complex formulas.

3. **Identify how to format various elements of the worksheet.** As discussed in Chapter 1 and shown in Figure 2–3, the appearance of the worksheet affects its ability to communicate clearly. Numeric data should be formatted in generally accepted formats, such as using commas as thousands separators and parentheses for negative values.

4. **Establish rules for conditional formatting.** Conditional formatting allows you to format a cell based on the contents of the cell. Decide under which circumstances you would like a cell to stand out from similar cells and determine in what way the cell will stand out. In the case of the Percent Gain/Loss column on the worksheet, placing a different background color in cells that show losses is an appropriate format for the column.

5. **Specify how the printed worksheet should appear.** When it is possible that a person will want to print a worksheet, care should be taken in the development of the worksheet to ensure that the contents can be printed in a readable manner. Excel prints worksheets in landscape or portrait orientation and margins can be adjusted to fit more or less data on each page. Headers and footers add an additional level of customization to the printed page.

(continued)

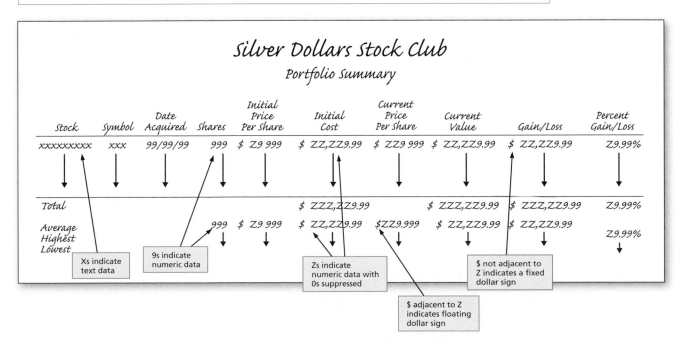

Figure 2–3

(continued)

6. **Gather information regarding the needed Web query.** You must also know what information the Web query requires in order for it to generate results that you can use in Excel.

7. **Choose names for the worksheets.** When a workbook includes multiple worksheets, each worksheet should be named. A good worksheet name is succinct, unique to the workbook, and meaningful to any user of the workbook.

In addition, using a sketch of the worksheet can help you visualize its design. The sketch for Silver Dollars Stock Club Portfolio Summary worksheet (Figure 2–3 on the previous page) includes a title, a subtitle, column and row headings, and the location of data values. It also uses specific characters to define the desired formatting for the worksheet as follows:

1. The row of Xs below the leftmost column defines the cell entries as text, such as stock names and stock symbols.

2. The rows of Zs and 9s with slashes, dollar signs, decimal points, commas, and percent signs in the remaining columns define the cell entries as numbers. The Zs indicate that the selected format should instruct Excel to suppress leading 0s. The 9s indicate that the selected format should instruct Excel to display any digits, including 0s.

3. The decimal point means that a decimal point should appear in the cell entry and indicates the number of decimal places to use.

4. The commas indicate that the selected format should instruct Excel to display a comma separator only if the number has enough digits to the left of the decimal point.

5. The slashes in the third column identify the cell entry as a date.

6. The dollar signs that are not adjacent to the Zs in the first row below the column headings and in the total row signify a fixed dollar sign. The dollar signs that are adjacent to the Zs below the total row signify a floating dollar sign, or one that appears next to the first significant digit.

7. The percent sign (%) in the far right column indicates a percent sign should appear after the number.

When necessary, more specific details concerning the above guidelines are presented at appropriate points in the chapter. The chapter also will identify the actions you perform and decisions made regarding these guidelines during the creation of the worksheet shown in Figure 2–3 on page EX 85.

With a good understanding of the requirements document, an understanding of the necessary decisions, and a sketch of the worksheet, the next step is to use Excel to create the worksheet.

To Start Excel

If you are using a computer to step through the project in this chapter and you want your screen to match the figures in this book, you should change your computer's resolution to 1024 × 768. For information about how to change a computer's resolution, read Appendix E.

The following steps, which assume Windows Vista is running, start Excel based on a typical installation of Microsoft Office on your computer. You may need to ask your instructor how to start Excel for your computer.

Note: If you are using Windows XP, see Appendix F for alternate steps.

1 Click the Start button on the Windows Vista taskbar to display the Start menu.

2 Point to All Programs at the bottom of the left pane on the Start menu to display the All Programs list.

3 Click Microsoft Office in the All Programs list to display the Microsoft Office list.

4 Click Microsoft Office Excel to start Excel and display a blank worksheet in the Excel window.

5 If the Excel window is not maximized, click the Maximize button next to the Close button on its title bar to maximize the window.

6 If the worksheet window in Excel is not maximized, click the Maximize button next to the Close button on its title bar to maximize the worksheet window within Excel.

BTW

Starting Excel
You can use a command-line switch to start Excel and control how it starts. First, click the Start button on the Windows Vista taskbar, and then click the Start Search box. Next, enter the complete path to Excel's application file including the switch (for example, C:\Program Files\Microsoft Office\ Office12\Excel.exe/e). The switch /e starts Excel without opening a new workbook; /i starts Excel with a maximized window; /p "folder" sets the active path to folder and ignores the default folder; /r "filename" opens filename in read-only mode; and /s starts Excel in safe mode.

Entering the Titles and Numbers into the Worksheet

The first step in creating the worksheet is to enter the titles and numbers into the worksheet.

To Enter the Worksheet Title and Subtitle

The following steps enter the worksheet title and subtitle into cells A1 and A2.

1 If necessary, select cell A1. Type `Silver Dollars Stock Club` in the cell and then press the DOWN ARROW key to enter the worksheet title in cell A1.

2 Type `Portfolio Summary` in cell A2 and then press the DOWN ARROW key to enter the worksheet subtitle in cell A2 (Figure 2–4 on page EX 89).

To Enter the Column Titles

The column titles in row 3 begin in cell A3 and extend through cell J3. The column titles in Figure 2–3 include multiple lines of text. To start a new line in a cell, press ALT+ENTER after each line, except for the last line, which is completed by clicking the Enter box, pressing the ENTER key, or pressing one of the arrow keys. When you see ALT+ENTER in a step, press the ENTER key while holding down the ALT key and then release both keys.

The stock names and the row titles Totals, Average, Highest, and Lowest in the leftmost column begin in cell A4 and continue down to cell A16. This data is entered into rows 4 through 12 of the worksheet. The remainder of this section explains the steps required to enter the column titles, stock data, and row titles as shown in Figure 2–4 on page EX 89 and then save the workbook.

1 With cell A3 selected, type `Stock` and then press the RIGHT ARROW key.

2 Type `Symbol` in cell B3 and then press the RIGHT ARROW key.

BTW

Wrapping Text
If you have a long text entry, such as a paragraph, you can instruct Excel to wrap the text in a cell, rather than pressing ALT+ENTER to end a line. To wrap text, right-click in the cell, click Format Cells on the shortcut menu, click the Alignment tab, click Wrap text, and then click OK. Excel will increase the height of the cell automatically so the additional lines will fit. If you want to control where each line ends in the cell, rather than letting Excel wrap based on the cell width, however, then you must end each line with ALT+ENTER.

③ In cell C3, type Date and then press ALT+ENTER. Type Acquired and then press the RIGHT ARROW key.

④ In cell D3, type Shares and then press the RIGHT ARROW key.

⑤ In cell E3, type Initial and then press ALT+ENTER. Type Price and then press ALT+ENTER. Type Per Share and then press the RIGHT ARROW key.

⑥ Type Initial in cell F3 and then press ALT+ENTER. Type Cost and then press the RIGHT ARROW key.

⑦ In cell G3, type Current and then press ALT+ENTER. Type Price and then press ALT+ENTER. Type Per Share and then press the RIGHT ARROW key.

⑧ Type Current in cell H3 and then press ALT+ENTER. Type Value and then press the RIGHT ARROW key.

⑨ In cell I3, type Gain/Loss and then press the RIGHT ARROW key.

⑩ In cell J3, type Percent and then press ALT+ENTER. Type Gain/Loss.

To Enter the Portfolio Summary Data

The portfolio summary data in Table 2–1 includes a purchase date for each stock. Excel considers a date to be a number and, therefore, it displays the date right-aligned in the cell. The following steps enter the portfolio summary data shown in Table 2–1.

BTW

Two-Digit Years
When you enter a two-digit year value, Excel changes a two-digit year less than 30 to 20xx and a two-digit year of 30 and greater to 19xx. Use four-digit years to ensure that Excel interprets year values the way you intend, if necessary.

① Select cell A4, type Apple Computers, and then press the RIGHT ARROW key.

② Type AAPL in cell B4 and then press the RIGHT ARROW key.

③ Type 12/1/04 in cell C4 and then press the RIGHT ARROW key.

④ Type 440 in cell D4 and then press the RIGHT ARROW key.

⑤ Type 64.59 in cell E4 and then click cell G4.

⑥ Type 82.99 in cell G4 and then click cell A5.

⑦ Enter the portfolio summary data in Table 2–1 for the eight remaining stocks in rows 5 through 12 (Figure 2–4).

BTW

Formatting a Worksheet
With early worksheet programs, users often skipped rows to improve the appearance of the worksheet. With Excel it is not necessary to skip rows because you can increase row heights to add white space between information.

To Enter the Row Titles

① Select cell A13. Type Totals and then press the DOWN ARROW key. Type Average in cell A14 and then press the DOWN ARROW key.

② Type Highest in cell A15 and then press the DOWN ARROW key. Type Lowest in cell A16 and then press the ENTER key. Select cell F4 (Figure 2–4).

Table 2–1 Silver Dollars Stock Club Portfolio Summary Data					
Stock	Symbol	Date Acquired	Shares	Initial Price Per Share	Current Price Per Share
Apple Computers	AAPL	12/1/04	440	64.59	82.99
AT&T	T	12/16/03	870	28.71	27.99
Citigroup	C	1/17/03	960	49.46	44.675
Comcast	CMCSA	12/11/02	380	33.62	41.39
Google	GOOG	2/20/04	920	390.32	492.55
Home Depot	HD	11/14/05	770	34.54	31.72
IBM	IBM	9/14/04	990	74.08	81.47
Merck	MRK	1/14/05	950	42.125	38.34
Sprint Nextel	S	9/10/03	560	17.79	21.18

Figure 2–4

BTW

To Change Workbook Properties and Save the Workbook

With the data entered into the worksheet, the following steps save the workbook using the file name, Silver Dollars Stock Club Portfolio Summary. As you are building a workbook, it is a good idea to save it often so that you do not lose your work if the computer is turned off or if you lose electrical power. The first time you save a workbook, you should change the workbook properties.

Entering Numbers in a Range
An efficient way to enter data into a range of cells is to select a range and then enter the first number in the upper-left cell of the range. Excel responds by entering the value and moving the active cell selection down one cell. When you enter the last value in the first column, Excel moves the active cell selection to the top of the next column.

1 Click the Office Button, click Prepare on the Office Button menu, and then click Properties.

2 Update the document properties with your name and any other information required.

3 Click the Close button on the Document Properties pane.

Note: If you are using Windows XP, see Appendix F for alternate steps.

4 With a USB flash drive connected to one of the computer's USB ports, click the Save button on the Quick Access Toolbar.

5 When Excel displays the Save As dialog box, type `Silver Dollars Stock Club Portfolio Summary` in the File name text box.

6 If the Folders list is displayed below the Folders button, click the Folders button to remove the Folders list.

7 If Computer is not displayed in the Favorite Links section, drag the top or bottom edge of the Save As dialog box until Computer is displayed.

8 Click Computer in the Favorite Links section. If necessary, scroll until UDISK 2.0 (E:) appears in the list of available drives. Double-click UDISK 2.0 (E:) (your USB flash drive may have a different name and letter). Click the Save button in the Save As dialog box to save the workbook on the USB flash drive using the file name, Silver Dollars Stock Club Portfolio Summary.

Entering Formulas

One of the reasons Excel is such a valuable tool is that you can assign a **formula** to a cell and Excel will calculate the result. Consider, for example, what would happen if you had to multiply 440×64.59 and then manually enter the product, 28,419.60, in cell F4. Every time the values in cells D4 or E4 changed, you would have to recalculate the product and enter the new value in cell F4. By contrast, if you enter a formula in cell F4 to multiply the values in cells D4 and E4, Excel recalculates the product whenever new values are entered into those cells and displays the result in cell F4.

Plan Ahead

Determine the necessary formulas and functions needed.
The formulas needed in the worksheet are noted in the requirements document as follows:

1. Initial Cost (column F) = Shares $\times$ Initial Price Per Share

2. Current Value (column H) = Shares $\times$ Current Price Per Share

3. Gain/Loss (column I) = Current Value – Initial Cost

4. Percent Gain/Loss (column J) = Gain/Loss / Initial Cost

The necessary functions to determine the average, highest, and lowest numbers are discussed shortly.

To Enter a Formula Using the Keyboard

The initial cost for each stock, which appears in column F, is equal to the number of shares in column D times the initial price per share in column E. Thus, the initial cost for Apple Computers in cell F4 is obtained by multiplying 440 (cell D4) by 64.59 (cell E4) or =D4*E4. The following steps enter the initial cost formula in cell F4 using the keyboard.

1

- With cell F4 selected, type =d4*e4 in the cell to display the formula in the formula bar and in cell F4 and to display colored borders around the cells referenced in the formula (Figure 2–5).

Q&A

What is happening on the worksheet as I enter the formula?

The **equal sign** (=) preceding d4*e4 is an important part of the formula. It alerts Excel that you are entering a formula or function and not text. Because the most common error when entering a formula is to reference the wrong cell in a formula mistakenly, Excel colors the borders of the cells referenced in the formula. The coloring helps in the reviewing process to ensure the cell references are correct. The **asterisk** (*) following d4 is the arithmetic operator that directs Excel to perform the multiplication operation.

Figure 2–5

2

- Press the RIGHT ARROW key twice to complete the arithmetic operation indicated by the formula, display the result, 28419.6, and to select cell H4 (Figure 2–6).

Figure 2–6

Arithmetic Operations

Table 2–2 describes multiplication and other valid Excel arithmetic operators.

Table 2–2 Summary of Arithmetic Operators			
Arithmetic Operator	**Meaning**	**Example of Usage**	**Meaning**
–	Negation	–34	Negative 34
%	Percentage	=72%	Multiplies 72 by 0.01
^	Exponentiation	=4 ^ 6	Raises 4 to the sixth power
*	Multiplication	=22.6 * F4	Multiplies the contents of cell F4 by 22.6
/	Division	=C3 / C6	Divides the contents of cell C3 by the contents of cell C6
+	Addition	=7 + 3	Adds 7 and 3
–	Subtraction	=F12 – 22	Subtracts 22 from the contents of cell F12

BTW

Troubling Formulas
If Excel does not accept a formula, remove the equal sign from the left side and complete the entry as text. Later, after you have entered additional data or determined the error, reinsert the equal sign to change the text back to a formula and edit the formula as needed.

You can enter the cell references in formulas in uppercase or lowercase, and you can add spaces before and after arithmetic operators to make the formulas easier to read. The formula, =d4*e4, is the same as the formulas, =d4 * e4, =D4 * e4, or =D4 * E4.

Order of Operations

When more than one arithmetic operator is involved in a formula, Excel follows the same basic order of operations that you use in algebra. Moving from left to right in a formula, the **order of operations** is as follows: first negation (–), then all percentages (%), then all exponentiations (^), then all multiplications (*) and divisions (/), and finally, all additions (+) and subtractions (–).

You can use parentheses to override the order of operations. For example, if Excel follows the order of operations, 5 * 9 + 8 equals 53. If you use parentheses, however, to change the formula to 5 * (9 + 8), the result is 85, because the parentheses instruct Excel to add 9 and 8 before multiplying by 5. Table 2–3 illustrates several examples of valid Excel formulas and explains the order of operations.

Table 2–3 Examples of Excel Formulas	
Formula	**Meaning**
=K12	Assigns the value in cell K12 to the active cell.
=10 + 4^2	Assigns the sum of 10 + 16 (or 26) to the active cell.
=3 * C20 or =C20 * 3 or =(3 * C20)	Assigns three times the contents of cell C20 to the active cell.
=50% * 12	Assigns the product of 0.50 times 12 (or 6) to the active cell.
– (H3 * Q30)	Assigns the negative value of the product of the values contained in cells H3 and Q30 to the active cell.
=12 * (N8 – O8)	Assigns the product of 12 times the difference between the values contained in cells N8 and O8 to the active cell.
=M9 / Z8 – C3 * Q19 + A3 ^ B3	Completes the following operations, from left to right: exponentiation (A3 ^ B3), then division (M9 / Z8), then multiplication (C3 * Q19), then subtraction (M9 / Z8) – (C3 * Q19), and finally addition (M9 / Z8 – C3 * Q19) + (A3 ^ B3). If cells A3 = 2, B3 = 4, C3 = 6, M9 = 3, Q19 = 4, and Z8 = 3, then Excel assigns the active cell the value 18; that is, 3 / 3 – 6 * 4 + 2 ^ 4 = -7.

To Enter Formulas Using Point Mode

The sketch of the worksheet in Figure 2–3 on page EX 85 calls for the current value, gain/loss, and percent gain/loss of each stock to appear in columns H, I, and J respectively. All three of these values are calculated using formulas in row 4:

Current Value (cell H4) = Shares × Current Price Per Share or =D4*G4

Gain/Loss (cell I4) = Current Value – Initial Cost or H4-F4

Percent Gain/Loss (cell J4) = Gain/Loss / Initial Cost or I4/F4

An alternative to entering the formulas in cells H4, I4, and J4 using the keyboard is to enter the formulas using the mouse and Point mode. **Point mode** allows you to select cells for use in a formula by using the mouse. The following steps enter formulas using Point mode.

- With cell H4 selected, type = (equal sign) to begin the formula and then click cell D4 to add a reference to cell D4 to the formula (Figure 2–7).

Figure 2–7

- Type * (asterisk) and then click cell G4 to add a multiplication operator and reference to cell G4 to the formula (Figure 2–8).

Figure 2–8

- Click the Enter box and then click cell I4 to select cell I4.

- Type = (equal sign) and then click cell H4 to add a reference to cell H4 to the formula.

- Type – (minus sign) and then click cell F4 to add a subtraction operator and reference to cell F4 to the formula (Figure 2–9).

Q&A

When should I use Point mode to enter formulas?

Using Point mode to enter formulas often is faster and more accurate than using the keyboard to type the entire formula when the cell you want to select does not require you to scroll. In many instances, as in these steps, you may want to use both the keyboard and mouse when entering a formula in a cell. You can use the keyboard to begin the formula, for example, and then use the mouse to select a range of cells.

Figure 2–9

❹

- Click the Enter box to enter the formula in cell I4.

- Select cell J4. Type = (equal sign) and then click cell I4 to add a reference to cell I4 to the formula.

- Type / (forward slash) and then click cell F4 to add a reference to cell F4 to the formula.

- Click the Enter box to enter the formula in cell J4 (Figure 2–10).

Q&A

Why do only six decimal places show in cell J4?

The actual value assigned by Excel to cell J4 from the division operation in Step 4 is 0.284873819. While not all the decimal places appear in Figure 2–10, Excel maintains all of them for computational purposes. Thus, if referencing cell J4 in a formula, the value used for computational purposes is 0.284873819, not 0.284874. Excel displays the value in cell J4 as 0.284874 because the cell formatting is set to display only six digits after the decimal point. If you change the cell formatting of column J to display nine digits after the decimal point, then Excel displays the true value 0.284873819.

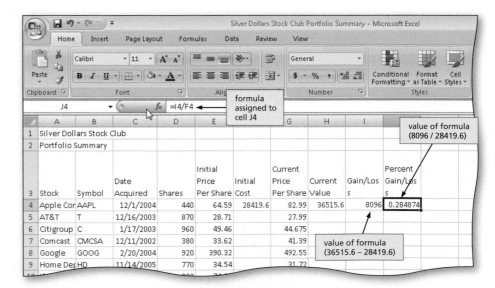

Figure 2–10

To Copy Formulas Using the Fill Handle

The four formulas for Apple Computers in cells F4, H4, I4, and J4 now are complete. You could enter the same four formulas one at a time for the eight remaining stocks. A much easier method of entering the formulas, however, is to select the formulas in row 4 and then use the fill handle to copy them through row 12. Recall from Chapter 1 that the fill handle is a small rectangle in the lower-right corner of the active cell or active range. The following steps copy the formulas using the fill handle.

- Select cell F4 and then point to the fill handle.

- Drag the fill handle down through cell F12 and continue to hold the mouse button to select the destination range (Figure 2–11).

Figure 2–11

- Release the mouse button to copy the formula in cell F4 to the cells in the range F5:F12.

- Select the range H4:J4 and then point to the fill handle (Figure 2–12).

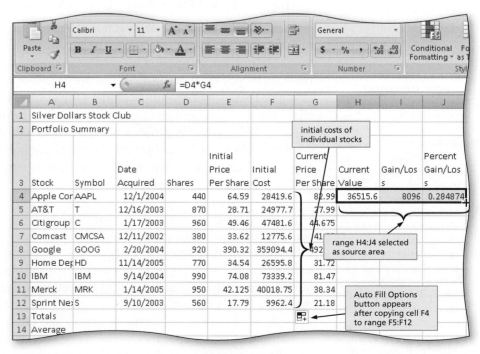

Figure 2–12

3

- Drag the fill handle down through the range H5:J12 to copy the three formulas =D4*G4 in cell H4, =H4-F4 in cell I4, and =I4/F4 in cell J4 to the range H5:J12 (Figure 2–13).

Q&A

How does Excel adjust the cell references in the formulas in the destination area?

Recall that when you copy a formula, Excel adjusts the cell references so the new formulas contain references corresponding to the new location and performs calculations using the appropriate values. Thus, if you copy downward, Excel adjusts the row portion of cell references. If you copy across, then Excel adjusts the column portion of cell references. These cell references are called **relative cell references**.

Figure 2–13

Other Ways

1. Select source area, click Copy button on Ribbon, select destination area, click Paste button on Ribbon

2. Select source area, right-click copy area, click Copy on shortcut menu, select destination area, right-click paste area, click Paste on shortcut menu

BTW

Automatic Recalculation
Every time you enter a value into a cell in the worksheet, Excel automatically recalculates all formulas. You can change to manual recalculation by clicking the Calculation Options button on the Formulas tab on the Ribbon and then clicking Manual. In manual calculation mode, press the F9 key to instruct Excel to recalculate all formulas.

Smart Tags and Option Buttons

Excel can identify certain actions to take on specific data in workbooks using **smart tags**. Data labeled with smart tags includes dates, financial symbols, people's names, and more. To use smart tags, you must turn on smart tags using the AutoCorrect Options in the Excel Options dialog box. To change AutoCorrect options, click the Office Button, click the Excel Options button on the Office Button menu, point to Proofing, and then click AutoCorrect Options. Once smart tags are turned on, Excel places a small purple triangle, called a **smart tag indicator**, in a cell to indicate that a smart tag is available. When you move the insertion point over the smart tag indicator, the Smart Tag Actions button appears. Clicking the Smart Tag Actions button arrow produces a list of actions you can perform on the data in that specific cell.

In addition to smart tags, Excel also displays Options buttons in a workbook while you are working on it to indicate that you can complete an operation using automatic features such as AutoCorrect, Auto Fill, error checking, and others. For example, the Auto Fill Options button shown in Figure 2–13 appears after a fill operation, such as dragging the fill handle. When an error occurs in a formula in a cell, Excel displays the Trace Error button next to the cell and identifies the cell with the error by placing a green triangle in the upper left of the cell.

Table 2–4 summarizes the smart tag and Options buttons available in Excel. When one of these buttons appears on your worksheet, click the button arrow to produce the list of options for modifying the operation or to obtain additional information.

Table 2–4 Smart Tag and Options Buttons in Excel

Button	Name	Menu Function
	Auto Fill Options	Gives options for how to fill cells following a fill operation, such as dragging the fill handle.
	AutoCorrect Options	Undoes an automatic correction, stops future automatic corrections of this type, or causes Excel to display the AutoCorrect Options dialog box.
	Insert Options	Lists formatting options following an insertion of cells, rows, or columns.
	Paste Options	Specifies how moved or pasted items should appear (for example, with original formatting, without formatting, or with different formatting).
	Smart Tag Actions	Lists information options for a cell containing data recognized by Excel, such as a stock symbol.
	Trace Error	Lists error checking options following the assignment of an invalid formula to a cell.

To Determine Totals Using the Sum Button

The next step is to determine the totals in row 13 for the initial cost in column F, current value in column H, and gain/loss in column I. To determine the total initial cost in column F, the values in the range F4 through F12 must be summed. To do so, enter the function =sum(f4:f12) in cell F13 or select cell F13 and then click the Sum button on the Ribbon and then press the ENTER key. Recall that a function is a prewritten formula that is built into Excel. Similar SUM functions or the Sum button can be used in cells H13 and I13 to determine total current value and total gain/loss, respectively.

1 Select cell F13. Click the Sum button on the Ribbon and then click the Enter button.

2 Select the range H13:I13. Click the Sum button on the Ribbon to display the totals in row 13 as shown in Figure 2–14.

BTW

Selecting a Range
You can select a range using the keyboard. Press the F8 key and then use the arrow keys to select the desired range. After you are finished, make sure to press the F8 key to turn off the selection or you will continue to select ranges.

Figure 2–14

To Determine the Total Percent Gain/Loss

With the totals in row 13 determined, the next step is to copy the percent gain/loss formula in cell J12 to cell J13 as performed in the following steps.

1 Select cell J12 and then point to the fill handle.

2 Drag the fill handle down through cell J13 to copy the formula in cell J12 to cell J13 (Figure 2–15).

Q&A

Why was the formula I13/F13 not copied to cell J13 earlier?

The formula, I13/F13, was not copied to cell J13 when cell J4 was copied to the range J5:J12 because both cells involved in the computation (I13 and F13) were blank, or zero, at the time. A **blank cell** in Excel has a numerical value of zero, which would have resulted in an error message in cell J13. Once the totals were determined, both cells I13 and F13 (especially F13, because it is the divisor) had nonzero numerical values.

	Stock	Symbol	Date Acquired	Shares	Initial Price Per Share	Initial Cost	Current Price Per Share	Current Value	Gain/Loss	Percent Gain/Loss
3	Stock	Symbol	Date Acquired	Shares	Initial Price Per Share	Initial Cost	Current Price Per Share	Current Value	Gain/Loss	Percent Gain/Loss
4	Apple Cor	AAPL	12/1/2004	440	64.59	28419.6	82.99	36515.6	8096	0.284874
5	AT&T	T	12/16/2003	870	28.71	24977.7	27.99	24351.3	-626.4	-0.02508
6	Citigroup	C	1/17/2003	960	49.46	47481.6	44.675	42888	-4593.6	-0.09674
7	Comcast	CMCSA	12/11/2002	380	33.62	12775.6	41.39	15728.2	2952.6	0.231112
8	Google	GOOG	2/20/2004	920	390.32	359094.4	492.55	453146	94051.6	0.261913
9	Home Dep	HD	11/14/2005	770	34.54	26595.8	31.72	24424.4	-2171.4	-0.08164
10	IBM	IBM	9/14/2004	990	74.08	73339.2	81.47	80655.3	7316.1	0.099757
11	Merck	MRK	1/14/2005	950	42.125	40018.75	38.34	36423	-3595.75	-0.08985
12	Sprint Nex	S	9/10/2003	560	17.79	9962.4	21.18	11860.8	1898.4	0.190556
13	Totals					622665.1		725992.6	103327.6	0.165944
14	Average									
15	Highest									
16	Lowest									

formula is =I12/F12

formula is =I13/F13

Auto Fill Options button appears after copying cell J12 to cell J13

Figure 2–15

BTW

Entering Functions
You can drag the Function Arguments dialog box (Figure 2–20 on page EX 101) out of the way in order to select a range. You also can click the Collapse Dialog button to the right of the Number 1 box to hide the Function Arguments dialog box. After selecting the range, click the Collapse Dialog button a second time.

BTW

Statistical Functions
Excel usually considers a blank cell to be equal to 0. The statistical functions, however, ignore blank cells. Excel thus calculates the average of 3 cells with values of 7, blank, and 5 to be 6 or (7 + 5) / 2 and not 4 or (7 + 0 + 5) / 3.

Using the AVERAGE, MAX, and MIN Functions

The next step in creating the Silver Dollars Stock Club Portfolio Summary worksheet is to compute the average, highest value, and lowest value for the number of shares listed in the range D4:D12 using the AVERAGE, MAX, and MIN functions in the range D14:D16. Once the values are determined for column D, the entries can be copied across to the other columns.

Excel includes prewritten formulas called functions to help you compute these statistics. A **function** takes a value or values, performs an operation, and returns a result to the cell. The values that you use with a function are called **arguments**. All functions begin with an equal sign and include the arguments in parentheses after the function name. For example, in the function =AVERAGE(D4:D12), the function name is AVERAGE, and the argument is the range D4:D12.

With Excel, you can enter functions using one of five methods: (1) the keyboard or mouse; (2) the Insert Function box in the formula bar; (3) the Sum menu; (4) the AutoSum command on the Formulas tab on the Ribbon; and (5) the Name box area in the formula bar (Figure 2–16). The method you choose will depend on your typing skills and whether you can recall the function name and required arguments.

In the following pages, each of the first three methods will be used. The keyboard and mouse method will be used to determine the average number of shares (cell D14). The Insert Function button in the formula bar method will be used to determine the highest number of shares (cell D15). The Sum menu method will be used to determine the lowest number of shares (cell D16).

To Determine the Average of a Range of Numbers Using the Keyboard and Mouse

The **AVERAGE function** sums the numbers in the specified range and then divides the sum by the number of nonzero cells in the range. The following steps use the AVERAGE function to determine the average of the numbers in the range D4:D12.

1

- Select cell D14.

- Type =av in the cell to display the Formula AutoComplete list.

- Point to the AVERAGE function name (Figure 2–16).

Q&A

What is happening as I type?

As you type the equal sign followed by the characters in the name of a function, Excel displays the Formula AutoComplete list. This list contains those functions that alphabetically match the letters you have typed. Because you typed =av, Excel displays all the functions that begin with the letters av.

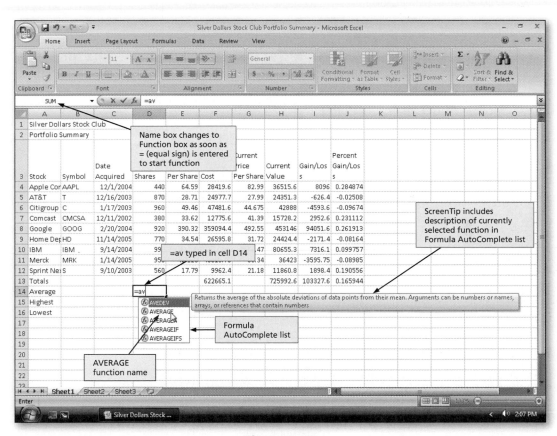

Figure 2–16

2

- Double-click AVERAGE in the Formula AutoComplete list to select the AVERAGE function.

- Select the range D4:D12 to insert the range as the argument to the AVERAGE function (Figure 2–17).

Q&A

As I drag, why does the function in cell D14 change?

When you click cell D4, Excel appends cell D4 to the left parenthesis in the formula bar and surrounds cell D4 with a marquee. When you begin dragging, Excel appends to the argument a colon (:) and the cell reference of the cell where the mouse pointer is located.

3

- Click the Enter box to compute the average of the nine numbers in the range D4:D12 and display the result in cell D14 (Figure 2–18).

Q&A

Can I use the arrow keys to complete the entry instead?

No. When you use Point mode you cannot use the arrow keys to complete the entry. While in Point mode, the arrow keys change the selected cell reference in the range you are selecting.

Q&A

What is the purpose of the parentheses in the function?

The AVERAGE function requires that the argument (in this case, the range D4:D12) be included within parentheses following the function name. Excel automatically appends the right parenthesis to complete the AVERAGE function when you click the Enter box or press the ENTER key.

SUM | =AVERAGE(D4:D12

AVERAGE function with range to average shows in active cell and formula bar

	A	B	C	D	E	F	G	H	I	J
1	Silver Dollars Stock Club									
2	Portfolio Summary									
3	Stock	Symbol	Date Acquired	Shares	Initial Price Per Share	Initial Cost	Current Price Per Share	Current Value	Gain/Loss	Percent Gain/Loss
4	Apple Cor	AAPL	12/1/2004	440	64.59	28419.6	82.99	36515.6	8096	0.28487
5			/16/2003	870	28.71	24977.7	27.99	24351.3	-626.4	-0.0250
6			/17/2003	960	49.46	47481.6	44.675	42888	-4593.6	-0.0967
7	Comcast	CMCSA	12/11/2002	380	33.62	12775.6	41.39	15728.2	2952.6	0.231112
8	Google	GOOG	2/20/2004	920	390.32	359094.4	492.55	453146	94051.6	0.261913
9	Home Dep	HD	11/14/2005	770	34.54	26595.8	31.72	24424.4	-2171.4	-0.08164
10	IBM	IBM	9/14/2004	990	74.08	73339.2	81.47	80655.3	7316.1	0.099757
11	Merck	MRK	1/14/2005	950	42.125	40018.75	38.34	36423	-3595.75	-0.08985
12	Sprint Ne	S	9/10/2003	560	17.79	9962.4	21.18	11860.8	1898.4	0.190556
13	Total					622665.1		725992.6	103327.6	0.165944
14	Aver			=AVERAGE(D4:D12						
15	Highest									
16	Lowest									
17										

Enter box

marquee surrounds selected range D4:D12

AVERAGE function ScreenTip

AVERAGE(**number1**, [number2], ...)

Figure 2–17

Function box changes back to Name box

when cell D14 is active cell, formula bar displays AVERAGE function

right parenthesis automatically appended when Enter box clicked or ENTER key pressed

D14 | =AVERAGE(D4:D12)

	A	B	C	D	E	F	G	H	I	J
1	Silver Dollars Stock Club									
2	Portfolio Summary									
3	Stock	Symbol	Date Acquired	Shares	Initial Price Per Share	Initial Cost	Current Price Per Share	Current Value	Gain/Loss	Percent Gain/Loss
4	Apple Cor	AAPL	12/1/2004	440	64.59	28419.6	82.99	36515.6	8096	0.28487
5	AT&T	T	12/16/2003	870	28.71	24977.7	27.99	24351.3	-626.4	-0.0250
6	Citigroup	C	1/17/2003	960	49.46	47481.6	44.675	42888	-4593.6	-0.0967
7	Comcast	CMCSA	12/11/2002	380	33.62	12775.6	41.39	15728.2	2952.6	0.231112
8	Google	GOOG	2/20/2004	920	390.32	359094.4	492.55	453146	94051.6	0.261913
9	Home Dep	HD	11/14/2005	770	34.54	26595.8	31.72	24424.4	-2171.4	-0.08164
10	IBM	IBM	9/14/2004	990	74.08	73339.2	81.47	80655.3	7316.1	0.099757
11	Merck	MRK	1/14/2005	950	42.125	40018.75	38.34	36423	-3595.75	-0.08985
12	Sprint Ne	S	9/10/2003	560	17.79	9962.4	21.18	11860.8	1898.4	0.190556
13	Totals							725992.6	103327.6	0.165944
14	Average			760						
15	Hi									

average shares per stock

Figure 2–18

Other Ways

1. Click Insert Function box in formula bar, click AVERAGE function

2. Click Sum button arrow on Ribbon, click Average function

3. Click Formulas tab on Ribbon, click AutoSum button arrow, click Average function

To Determine the Highest Number in a Range of Numbers Using the Insert Function Box

The next step is to select cell D15 and determine the highest (maximum) number in the range D4:D12. Excel has a function called the **MAX function** that displays the highest value in a range. Although you could enter the MAX function using the keyboard and Point mode as described in the previous steps, an alternative method to entering the function is to use the Insert Function box in the formula bar, as performed in the following steps.

- Select cell D15.

- Click the Insert Function box in the formula bar to display the Insert Function dialog box.

- When Excel displays the Insert Function dialog box, click MAX in the 'Select a function' list (Figure 2–19).

Figure 2–19

- Click the OK button.

- When Excel displays the Function Arguments dialog box, type d4:d12 in the Number1 box (Figure 2–20).

Q&A

Why did numbers appear in the Function Arguments dialog box?

As shown in Figure 2–20, Excel displays the value the MAX function will return to cell D15 in the Function Arguments dialog box. It also lists the first few numbers in the selected range, next to the Number1 box.

Figure 2–20

- Click the OK button to display the highest value in the range D4:D12 in cell D15 (Figure 2–21).

Q&A

Why should I not just enter the highest value that I see in the range D4:D12 in cell D15?

In this example, rather than entering the MAX function, you easily could scan the range D4:D12, determine that the highest number of shares is 990, and manually enter the number 990 as a constant in cell D15. Excel would display the number the same as in Figure 2–21. Because it contains a constant, however, Excel will continue to display 990 in cell D15, even if the values in the range D4:D12 change. If you use the MAX function, Excel will recalculate the highest value in the range D4:D9 each time a new value is entered into the worksheet.

D15 ▾ (fx =MAX(D4:D12)

MAX function determines highest value in range D4:D12

	A	B	C	D	E	F	G	H	I	J
1	Silver Dollars Stock Club									
2	Portfolio Summary									
3	Stock	Symbol	Date Acquired	Shares	Initial Price Per Share	Initial Cost	Current Price Per Share	Current Value	Gain/Loss	Percent Gain/Loss
4	Apple Cor	AAPL	12/1/2004	440	64.59	28419.6	82.99	36515.6	8096	0.28487
5	AT&T	T	12/16/2003	870	28.71	24977.7	27.99	24351.3	-626.4	-0.02505
6	Citigroup	C	1/17/2003	960	49.46	47481.6	44.675	42888	-4593.6	-0.09674
7	Comcast	CMCSA	12/11/2002	380	33.62	12775.6	41.39	15728.2	2952.6	0.231111
8	Google	GOOG	2/20/2004	920	390.32	359094.4	492.55	453146	94051.6	0.261913
9	Home Dep	HD	11/14/2005	770	34.54	26595.8	31.72	24424.4	-2171.4	-0.08164
10	IBM	IBM	9/14/2004	990	74.08	73339.2	81.47	80655.3	7316.1	0.099757
11	Merck	MRK	1/14/2005	950	42.125	40018.75	38.34	36423	-3595.75	-0.08985
12	Sprint Nex	S	9/10/2003	560	17.79	9962.4	21.18	11860.8	1898.4	0.190556
13	Totals					622665.1		725992.6	103327.6	0.165944
14	Average			760						
15	Highest			990						
16	Lowest									
17										

highest value in range D4:D12

Figure 2–21

Other Ways

1. Click Sum button arrow on Ribbon, click Max function
2. Click Formulas tab on Ribbon, click AutoSum button arrow, click Max function
3. Type =MAX in cell

To Determine the Lowest Number in a Range of Numbers Using the Sum Menu

The next step is to enter the **MIN function** in cell D16 to determine the lowest (minimum) number in the range D4:D12. Although you can enter the MIN function using either of the methods used to enter the AVERAGE and MAX functions, the following steps perform an alternative using the Sum button on the Ribbon.

- Select cell D16.

- Click the Sum button arrow on the Ribbon to display the Sum button menu (Figure 2–22).

Q&A

Why should I use the Sum button menu?

Using the Sum button menu allows you to enter one of five often-used functions easily into a cell, without having to memorize its name or the required arguments.

Figure 2–22

2

• Click Min to display the function =MIN(D14:D15) in the formula bar and in cell D16 (Figure 2–23).

Why does Excel select the range D14:D15?

The range D14:D15 automatically selected by Excel is not correct. Excel attempts to guess which cells you want to include in the function by looking for adjacent ranges to the selected cell that contain numeric data.

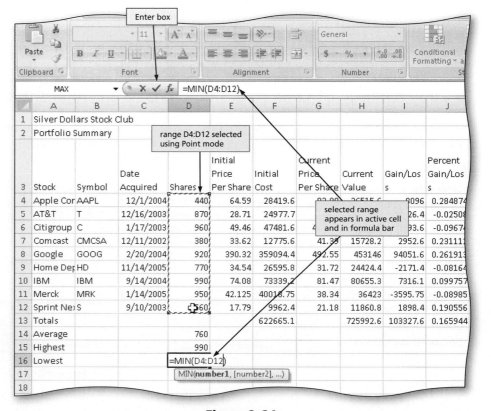

Figure 2–23

3

• Click cell D4 and then drag through cell D12 to display the function in the formula bar and in cell D14 with the new range (Figure 2–24).

Figure 2–24

4

- Click the Enter box to determine the lowest value in D4:D12 and display the result in the formula bar and in cell D14 (Figure 2–25).

Q&A

How can I use other functions?

Excel has more than 400 additional functions that perform just about every type of calculation you can imagine. These functions are categorized in the Insert Function dialog box shown in Figure 2–19 on page EX 101. To view the categories, click the 'Or select a category' box arrow. To obtain a description of a selected function, select its name in the Insert Function dialog box. Excel displays the description of the function below the Select a function list in the dialog box.

Figure 2–25

Other Ways
1. Click Insert Function box in formula bar, click MIN function   2. Click Formulas tab on Ribbon, click AutoSum button arrow, click Min function   3. Type =MIN in cell

To Copy a Range of Cells across Columns to an Adjacent Range Using the Fill Handle

The next step is to copy the AVERAGE, MAX, and MIN functions in the range D14:D16 to the adjacent range E14:J16. The following steps use the fill handle to copy the functions.

1

- Select the range D14:D16.

- Drag the fill handle in the lower-right corner of the selected range through cell J16 and continue to hold down the mouse button (Figure 2–26).

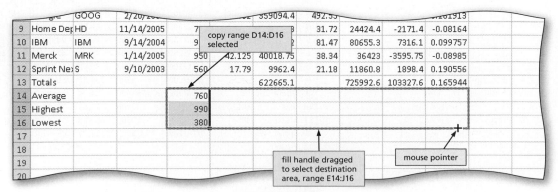

Figure 2–26

2

- Release the mouse button to copy the three functions to the range E14:J16 (Figure 2–27).

 How can I be sure that the function arguments are proper for the cells in range E14:J16?

Remember that Excel adjusts the cell references in the copied functions so each function refers to the range of numbers above it in the same column. Review the numbers in rows 14 through 16 in Figure 2–27. You should see that the functions in each column return the appropriate values, based on the numbers in rows 4 through 12 of that column.

	Stock	Symbol	Date Acquired	Shares	Per Share	Cost	Price Per Share	Current Value	Gain/Los s	s
3	Stock	Symbol	Acquired	Shares	Per Share	Cost	Per Share	Value	s	s
4	Apple Cor	AAPL	12/1/2004	440	64.59	28419.6	82.99	36515.6	8096	0.284874
5	AT&T	T	12/16/2003	870	28.71	24977.7	27.99	24351.3	-626.4	-0.02508
6	Citigroup	C	1/17/2003	960	49.46	47481.6	44.675	42888	-4593.6	-0.09674
7	Comcast	CMCSA	12/11/2002	380	33.62	12775.6	41.39	15728.2	2952.6	0.231112
8	Google	GOOG	2/20/2004	920	390.32	359094.4	492.55	453146	94051.6	0.261913
9	Home Dep	HD	11/14/2005	770	34.54	26595.8	31.72	24424.4	-2171.4	-0.08164
10	IBM	IBM	9/14/2004	990	74.08	73339.2	81.47	80655.3	7316.1	0.099757
11	Merck	MRK	1/14/2005	950	42.125	40018.75	38.34	36423	-3595.75	-0.08985
12	Sprint Nes	S	9/10/2003	560	17.79	9962.4	21.18	11860.8	1898.4	0.190556
13	Totals					622665.1		725992.6	103327.6	0.165944
14	Average			760	81.69278	69185.01	95.81167	80665.84	11480.84	0.086099
15	Highest			990	390.32	359094.4	492.55	453146	94051.6	0.284874
16	Lowest			380	17.79	9962.4	21.18	11860.8	-4593.6	-0.09674
17										

AVERAGE, MAX, and MIN functions in range D14:D16 copied to range E14:J16

Auto Fill Options button

Ready   Count: 21   Max: 453146   Sum: 1088082.908

Silver Dollars Stock ...

Figure 2–27

3

- Select cell J14 and press the DELETE key to delete the average of the percent gain/loss (Figure 2–28).

 Why is the formula in cell J14 deleted?

The average of the percent gain/loss in cell J14 is deleted because an average of percentages of this type is mathematically invalid.

Other Ways

1. Select source area and point to border of range, while holding down CTRL key, drag source area to destination area

2. Select source area, on Ribbon click Copy button, select destination area, on Ribbon click Paste button

3. Right-click source area, click Copy on shortcut menu, right-click destination area, click Paste on shortcut menu

4. Select source area, press CTRL+C, select destination area, press CTRL+V

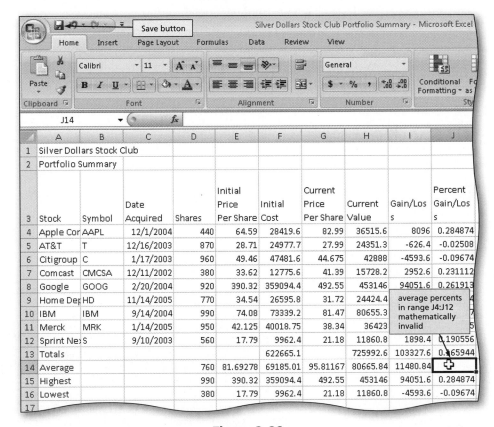

Figure 2–28

To Save a Workbook Using the Same File Name

Earlier in this project, an intermediate version of the workbook was saved using the file name, Silver Dollars Stock Club Portfolio Summary. The following step saves the workbook a second time using the same file name.

1 Click the Save button on the Quick Access Toolbar to save the workbook on the USB flash drive using the file name, Silver Dollars Stock Club Portfolio Summary.

Q&A

Why did Excel not display the Save As dialog box?

When you save a workbook a second time using the same file name, Excel will not display the Save As dialog box as it does the first time you save the workbook. Excel automatically stores the latest version of the workbook using the same file name, Silver Dollars Stock Club Portfolio Summary. You also can click Save on the Office Button menu or press SHIFT+F12 or CTRL+S to save a workbook again.

Verifying Formulas Using Range Finder

One of the more common mistakes made with Excel is to include a wrong cell reference in a formula. An easy way to verify that a formula references the cells you want it to reference is to use Excel's Range Finder. Use the **Range Finder** to check which cells are referenced in the formula assigned to the active cell. Range Finder allows you to make immediate changes to the cells referenced in a formula.

To use Range Finder to verify that a formula contains the intended cell references, double-click the cell with the formula you want to check. Excel responds by highlighting the cells referenced in the formula so you can check that the cell references are correct.

To Verify a Formula Using Range Finder

The following steps use Range Finder to check the formula in cell J4.

1
- Double-click cell J4 to activate Range Finder (Figure 2–29).

2
- Press the ESC key to quit Range Finder and then select cell A18.

Figure 2–29

Formatting the Worksheet

Although the worksheet contains the appropriate data, formulas, and functions, the text and numbers need to be formatted to improve their appearance and readability.

In Chapter 1, cell styles were used to format much of the worksheet. This section describes how to change the unformatted worksheet in Figure 2–30a to the formatted worksheet in Figure 2–30b using a theme and other commands on the Ribbon. A **theme** is a predefined set of colors, fonts, chart styles, cell styles, and fill effects that can be applied to an entire workbook. Every new workbook that you create is assigned a default theme named Office. The colors and fonts that are used in the worksheet shown in Figure 2–30b are those that are associated with the Concourse theme.

(a) Unformatted Worksheet

(b) Formatted Worksheet

Figure 2–30

Plan Ahead

Identify how to format various elements of the worksheet.

The following outlines the formatting suggested in the sketch of the worksheet in Figure 2–3 on page EX 85:

1. Workbook theme - Concourse

2. Worksheet title and subtitle

   a. Alignment — center across columns A through J

   b. Cell style —Title

   c. Font size — title 18; subtitle 16

   d. Background color (range A1:J2) — Turquoise Accent 1, Lighter 60%

   e. Border — thick box border around range A1:J2

3. Column titles

   a. Cell style — Heading 3

   b. Alignment — center

4. Data

   a. Alignment — center data in column B

   b. Dates in column C — mm/dd/yy format

   c. Numbers in top row (range E4:I4) — Accounting style

   d. Numbers below top row (range E5:I12) — Comma style and decimal places

5. Total line

   a. Cell style — Total

   b. Numbers — Accounting style

6. Average, Highest, and Lowest rows

   a. Font style of row titles in range A14:A16 — bold

   b. Numbers — Currency style with floating dollar sign in the range E14:I16

7. Percentages in column J

   a. Numbers — Percentage style with two decimal places; if a cell in range J4:J12 is less than zero, then cell appears with background color of light red

8. Column widths

   a. Column A — 14.11 characters

   b. Columns B and C — best fit

   c. Column D — 6.00 characters

   d. Column E, G, and J — 9.00 characters

   e. Columns F, H, and I — 12.67 characters

9. Row heights

   a. Row 3 — 60.00 points

   b. Row 14 — 26.25 points

   c. Remaining rows — default

BTW

Colors
Knowing how people perceive colors helps you emphasize parts of your worksheet. Warmer colors (red and orange) tend to reach toward the reader. Cooler colors (blue, green, and violet) tend to pull away from the reader. Bright colors jump out of a dark background and are easiest to see. White or yellow text on a dark blue, green, purple, or black background is ideal.

To Change the Workbook Theme

The Concourse theme includes fonts and colors that provide the worksheet a professional and subtly colored appearance. The following steps change the workbook theme to the Concourse theme.

1

- Click the Page Layout tab on the Ribbon.

- Click the Themes button on the Ribbon to display the Theme gallery (Figure 2–31).

 Experiment

- Point to several themes in the Theme gallery to see a live preview of the themes.

Q&A Why should I change the theme of a workbook?

A company or department may standardize on a specific theme so that all of their documents have a similar appearance. Similarly, an individual may want to have a theme that sets their work apart from others. Other Office applications, such as Word and PowerPoint, include the same themes included with Excel, meaning that all of your Microsoft Office documents can share a common theme.

Figure 2–31

2

- Click Concourse in the Theme gallery to change the workbook theme to Concourse (Figure 2–32).

Q&A Why did the cells in the worksheet change?

The cells in the worksheet originally were formatted with the default font for the default Office theme. The default font for the Concourse theme is different than that of the default font for the Office theme and therefore changed on the worksheet when you changed the theme. If you had modified the font for any of the cells, those cells would not receive the default font for the Concourse theme.

Figure 2–32

BTW

Background Colors
The most popular
background color is
blue. Research shows
that the color blue is
used most often because
this color connotes
serenity, reflection, and
proficiency.

To Format the Worksheet Titles

The following steps merge and center the worksheet titles, apply the Title cells style to the worksheet titles, and decrease the font of the worksheet subtitle.

1 Click the Home tab on the Ribbon.

2 Select the range A1:J1 and then click the Merge & Center button on the Ribbon.

3 Select the range A2:J2 and then click the Merge & Center button on the Ribbon.

4 Select the range A1:A2, click the Cell Styles button on the Ribbon, and then click the Title cell style in the Cell Styles gallery.

5 Select cell A2 and then click the Decrease Font Size button on the Ribbon (Figure 2–33).

Q&A

What is the effect of clicking the Decrease Font Size button?

When you click the Decrease Font Size button Excel assigns the next lowest font size in the Font Size gallery to the selected range. The Increase Font Size button works in a similar manner, but causes Excel to assign the next highest font size in the Font Size gallery to the selected range.

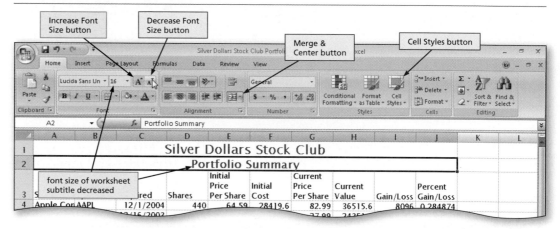

Figure 2–33

To Change the Background Color and Apply a Box Border to the Worksheet Title and Subtitle

The final formats assigned to the worksheet title and subtitle are the turquoise background color and thick box border (Figure 2–30b on page EX 107). The following steps complete the formatting of the worksheet titles.

1

• Select the range A1:A2 and then click the Fill Color button arrow on the Ribbon to display the Fill Color palette (Figure 2–34).

Figure 2–34

2
- Click Turquoise Accent 1, lighter 60% (column 5, row 3) on the Fill Color palette to change the background color of cells A1 and A2 from white to turquoise (Figure 2–35).

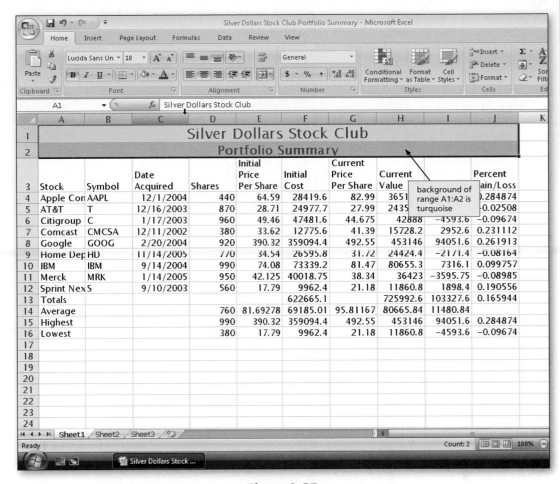

Figure 2–35

3
- Click the Borders button arrow on the Ribbon to display the Borders gallery (Figure 2–36).

Figure 2–36

● Click the Thick Box Border command on the Borders gallery to display a thick box border around the range A1:A2.

● Click cell A18 to deselect the range A1:A2 (Figure 2–37).

Other Ways

1. On Ribbon click Format Cells Dialog Box Launcher, click appropriate tab, click desired format, click OK button

2. Right-click range, click Format Cells on shortcut menu, click appropriate tab, click desired format, click OK button

3. Press CTRL+1, click appropriate tab, click desired format, click OK button

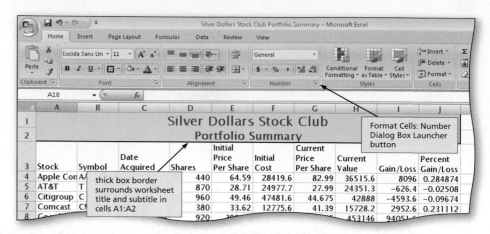

Figure 2–37

To Apply a Cell Style to the Column Headings and Format the Total Rows

As shown in Figure 2–30b on page EX 107, the column titles (row 3) have the Heading 3 cell style and the total row (row 13) has the Total cell style. The summary information headings in the range A14:A16 should be bold. The following steps assign these styles to row 3 and row 13 and the range A14:A16.

1 Select the range A3:J3.

2 Apply the Heading 3 cell style to the range A3:J3.

3 Apply the Total cell style to the range A13:J13.

4 Select the range A14:A16 and then click the Bold button on the Ribbon (Figure 2–38).

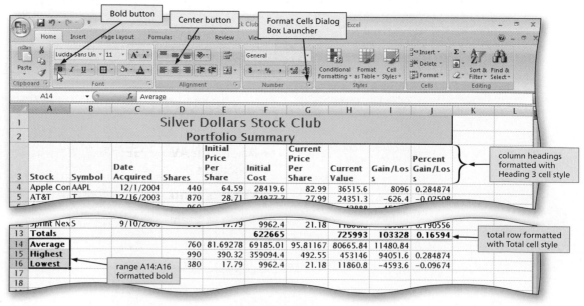

Figure 2–38

To Center Data in Cells and Format Dates

With the column titles and total rows formatted, the next step is to center the stock symbols in column B and format the dates in column C. If a cell entry is short, such as the stock symbols in column B, centering the entries within their respective columns improves the appearance of the worksheet. The following steps center the data in the range B4:B12 and format the dates in the range C4:C12.

- Select the range B4:B12 and then click the Center button on the Ribbon to center the data in the range B4:B12.

2

- Select the range C4:C12.

- Click the Format Cells: Number Dialog Box Launcher on the Ribbon to display the Format Cells dialog box.

- When Excel displays the Format Cells dialog box, if necessary click the Number tab, click Date in the Category list, and then click 3/14/01 in the Type list to choose the format for the range C4:C12 (Figure 2–39).

Figure 2–39

- Click the OK button to format the dates in column C using the date format style, mm/dd/yy.

- Select cell E4 to deselect the range C4:C13 (Figure 2–40).

Q&A

Can I format an entire column at once?

Yes. Rather than selecting the range B4:B12 in Step 1, you could have clicked the column B heading immediately above cell B1, and then clicked the Center button on the Ribbon. In this case, all cells in column B down to the last cell in the worksheet would have been formatted to use center alignment. This same procedure could have been used to format the dates in column C.

	E4		f_x	64.59			
	A	B	C	D	E	F	G	H

Silver Dollars Stock Club
Portfolio Summary

	Stock	Symbol	Date Acquired	Shares	Initial Price Per Share	Initial Cost	Current Price Per Share	Current Value
4	Apple Con	AAPL	12/1/04	440	64.59	28419.6	82.99	3651
5	AT&T	T	12/16/03	870	28.71	24977.7	27.99	2435
6	Citigroup	C	1/17/03	960	49.46	47481.6	44.675	428
7	Comcast	CMCSA	12/11/02	380	33.62	12775.6	41.39	1572
8	Google	GOOG	2/20/04	920	390.32	359094.4	492.55	4531
9	Home Dep	HD	11/14/05	770	34.54	26595.8	31.72	24424
10	IBM	IBM	9/14/04	990	74.08	73339.2	81.47	80655
11	Merck	MRK	1/14/05		43.125	48018.75	38.34	3642
12	Sprint Nex	S	9/10/03			9962.4	21.18	11860
13	**Totals**					22665		7259
14	**Average**					185.01	95.81167	80665
15	**Highest**			990	390.32	359094.4	492.55	4531
16	**Lowest**			380	17.79	9962.4	21.18	1186

Excel displays dates in range C4:C12 using date style format, mm/dd/yy

Figure 2–40

Other Ways

1. Right-click range, click Format Cells on shortcut menu, click appropriate tab, click desired format, click OK button
2. Press CTRL+1, click appropriate tab, click desired format, click OK button

Formatting Numbers Using the Ribbon

As shown in Figure 2–30b on page EX 107, the worksheet is formatted to resemble an accounting report. For example, in columns E through I, the numbers in the first row (row 4), the totals row (row 13), and the rows below the totals (rows 14 through 16) have dollar signs, while the remaining numbers (rows 5 through 12) in columns E through I do not.

To append a dollar sign to a number, you should use the Accounting number format. Excel displays numbers using the **Accounting number format** with a dollar sign to the left of the number, inserts a comma every three positions to the left of the decimal point, and displays numbers to the nearest cent (hundredths place). Clicking the Accounting Number Format button on the Ribbon assigns the desired Accounting number format. When you use the Accounting Number Format button to assign the Accounting number format, Excel displays a **fixed dollar sign** to the far left in the cell, often with spaces between it and the first digit. To assign a **floating dollar sign** that appears immediately to the left of the first digit with no spaces, use the Currency style in the Format Cells dialog box.

The Comma style format is used to instruct Excel to display numbers with commas and no dollar signs. The **Comma style format**, which can be assigned to a range of cells by clicking the Comma Style button on the Ribbon, inserts a comma every three positions to the left of the decimal point and causes numbers to be displayed to the nearest hundredths.

BTW

Rotating and Shrinking Entries in Cells
In addition to aligning entries horizontally and vertically, you also can rotate and shrink entries to fit in a cell. To rotate or shrink entries to fit in a cell, click Format Cells on the shortcut menu, click the Alignment tab in the Format Cells dialog box, and then select the type of control you want.

To Apply an Accounting Style Format and Comma Style Format Using the Ribbon

The following steps show how to assign formats using the Accounting Number Format button and the Comma Style button on the Ribbon.

1

• Select the range E4:I4.

• While holding down the CTRL key, select the ranges F13:I13.

• Click the Accounting Number Format button on the Ribbon (Figure 2–41) to apply the Accounting style format with fixed dollar signs to the nonadjacent ranges E4:I4 and F13:I13 (Figure 2–41).

Q&A

What is the effect of applying the Accounting style format?

The Accounting Number Format button assigns a fixed dollar sign to the numbers in the ranges E4:I4 and F13:I13. In each cell in these ranges, Excel displays the dollar sign to the far left with spaces between it and the first digit in the cell.

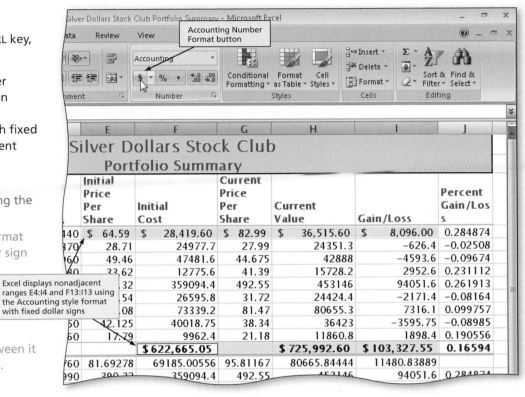

Figure 2–41

2

• Select the range E5:I12.

• Click the Comma Style button on the Ribbon to assign the Comma style format to the range E5:I12 (Figure 2–42).

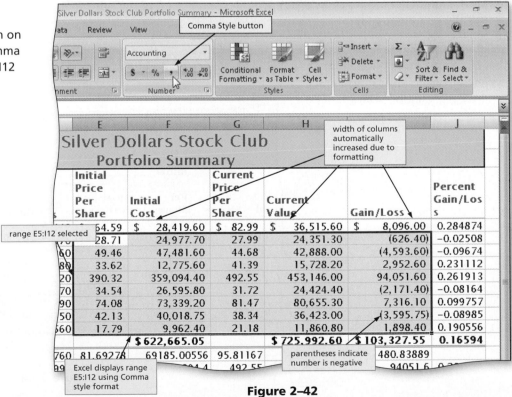

Figure 2–42

3

- Click cell E4.

- While holding down the CTRL key, select cell G4.

- Click the Increase Decimal button on the Ribbon to increase the number of decimal places displayed in cell E4 and G4.

- Select the range E5:E12. While holding down the CTRL key, select the range G5:G12.

- Click the Increase Decimal button on the Ribbon to increase the number of decimal places displayed in selected ranges (Figure 2–43).

Q&A

What is the effect of clicking the Increase Decimal button?

The Increase Decimal button instructs Excel to display additional decimal places in a cell. Each time you click the Increase Decimal button, Excel adds a decimal place to the selected cell.

Figure 2–43

To Apply a Currency Style Format with a Floating Dollar Sign Using the Format Cells Dialog Box

The following steps use the Format Cells dialog box to apply the Currency style format with a floating dollar sign to the numbers in the ranges E14:I16.

1

- Select the range E14:I16 and then point to the Format Cells: Number Dialog Box Launcher on the Ribbon (Figure 2–44).

Figure 2–44

2

- Click the Format Cells: Number Dialog Box Launcher.

- If necessary, click the Number tab in the Format Cells dialog box.

- Click Currency in the Category list and then click the third style ($1,234.10) in the Negative numbers list (Figure 2–45).

Q&A

How do I select the proper format?

You can choose from 12 categories of formats. Once you select a category, you can select the number of decimal places, whether or not a dollar sign should be displayed, and how negative numbers should appear. Selecting the appropriate negative numbers format is important, because doing so adds a space to the right of the number in order to align the numbers in the worksheet on the decimal points. Some of the available negative number formats do not align the numbers in the worksheet on the decimal points.

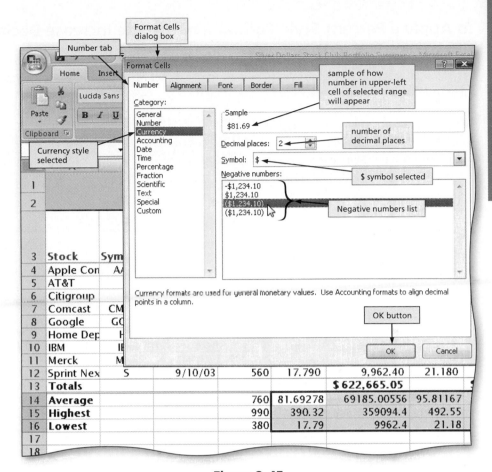

Figure 2–45

3

- Click the OK button to assign the Currency style format with a floating dollar sign to the range E14:I16 (Figure 2–46).

Q&A

Should I click the Accounting Number Style button on the Ribbon or use the Format Cells dialog box?

Recall that a floating dollar sign always appears immediately to the left of the first digit, and the fixed dollar sign always appears on the left side of the cell. Cell E4, for example, has a fixed dollar sign, while cell E14 has a floating dollar sign. The Currency style was assigned to cell E14 using the Format Cells dialog box and the result is a floating dollar sign.

Figure 2–46

Other Ways

1. Press CTRL+1, click Number tab, click Currency in Category list, select format, click OK button

2. Press CTRL+SHIFT+ DOLLAR SIGN ($)

To Apply a Percent Style Format and Use the Increase Decimal Button

The next step is to format the percent gain/loss in column J. Currently, Excel displays the numbers in column J as a decimal fraction (for example, 0.284874 in cell J4). The following steps format the range J4:J16 to the Percent style format with two decimal places.

- Select the range J4:J16.

- Click the Percent Style button on the Ribbon to display the numbers in column J as a rounded whole percent.

Q&A

What is the result of clicking the Percent Style button?

The Percent Style button instructs Excel to display a value as a percentage, determined by multiplying the cell entry by 100, rounding the result to the nearest percent, and adding a percent sign. For example, when cell J4 is formatted using the Percent Style and Increase Decimal buttons, Excel displays the actual value 0.284874 as 28.49%.

- Click the Increase Decimal button on the Ribbon two times to display the numbers in column J with the Percent style format and two decimal places (Figure 2–47).

	Percent Style button	Increase Decimal button			

Silver Dollars Stock Club Portfolio Summary - Microsoft E...

Decrease Decimal button

	E	F	G	H	I	J
Silver Dollars Stock Club						
Portfolio Summary						
	Initial Price Per Share	Initial Cost	Current Price Per Share	Current Value	Gain/Loss	Percent Gain/Los s
440	$ 64.590	$ 28,419.60	$ 82.990	$ 36,515.60	$ 8,096.00	28.49%
870	28.710	24,977.70	27.990	24,351.30	(626.40)	-2.51%
960	49.460	47,481.60	44.675	4_,___.__	(__,593.60)	-9.67%
80	33.620	12,775.60	41.390	1	_52.60	23.11%
20	390.320	359,094.40	492.550	45	_51.60	26.19%
70	34.540	26,595.80	31.720	2	_71.40)	-8.16%
90	74.080	73,339.20	81.470	80,655.30	7,316.10	9.98%
50	42.125	40,018.75	38.340	36,423.00	(3,595.75)	-8.99%
60	17.790	9,962.40	21.180	11,860.80	1,898.40	19.06%
		$ 622,665.05		**$ 725,992.60**	**$ 103,327.55**	**16.59%**
760	$81.69	$69,185.01	$95.81	$80,665.84	$11,480.84	
990	$390.32	$359,094.40	$492.55	$453,146.00	$94,051.60	28.49%
380	$17.79	$9,962.40	$21.18	$11,860.80	($4,593.60)	-9.67%

Excel displays range J4:J16 using Percent style format with two decimal places

Figure 2–47

Other Ways

1. Right-click range, click Format Cells on shortcut menu, click Number tab, click Percentage in Category list, select format, click OK button

2. Press CTRL+1, click Number tab, click Percentage in Category list, select format, click OK button

3. Press CTRL+SHIFT+ PERCENT SIGN (%)

Conditional Formatting

The next step is to emphasize the negative percentages in column J by formatting them to appear with a tinted background. The Conditional Formatting button on the Ribbon will be used to complete this task.

Excel lets you apply formatting that appears only when the value in a cell meets conditions that you specify. This type of formatting is called **conditional formatting**. You can apply conditional formatting to a cell, a range of cells, the entire worksheet, or the entire workbook. Usually, you apply conditional formatting to a range of cells that contains values you want to highlight, if conditions warrant. For example, you can instruct Excel to change the color of the background of a cell if the value in the cell meets a condition, such as being less than 0 as shown in Figure 2–48.

A **condition**, which is made up of two values and a relational operator, is true or false for each cell in the range. If the condition is true, then Excel applies the formatting. If the condition is false, then Excel suppresses the formatting. What makes conditional formatting so powerful is that the cell's appearance can change as you enter new values in the worksheet.

To Apply Conditional Formatting

The following steps assign conditional formatting to the range J4:J12, so that any cell value less than zero will cause Excel to display the number in the cell with a light red background.

1
- Select the range J4:J12.

- Click the Conditional Formatting button on the Ribbon to display the Conditional Formatting gallery (Figure 2–48).

Figure 2–48

2
- Click New Rule in the Conditional Formatting gallery to display the New Formatting Rule dialog box.

- Click 'Format only cells that contain' in the Select a Rule Type area.

- In the Edit the Rule Description area, click the box arrow in the relational operator box (second text box) and then select less than.

- Type 0 (zero) in the rightmost box in the Edit the Rule Description area (Figure 2–49).

Figure 2–49

- Click the Format button.

- When Excel displays the Format Cells dialog box, click the Fill tab and then click the light red color in column 6, row 2 (Figure 2–50).

Figure 2–50

- Click the OK button to close the Format Cells dialog box and display the New Formatting Rule dialog box with the desired color displayed in the Preview box (Figure 2–51).

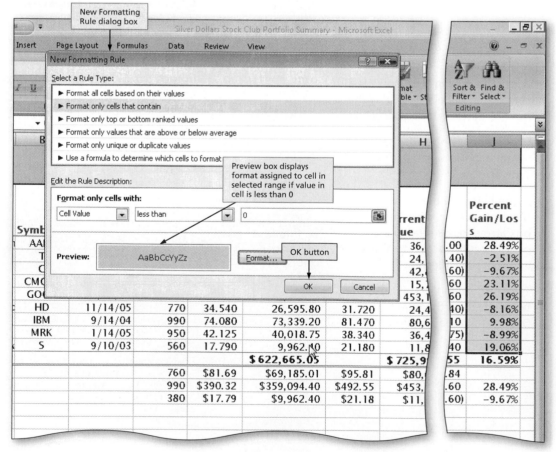

Figure 2–51

5

- Click the OK button to assign the conditional format to the range J4:J12.

- Click cell A18 to deselect the range J4:J12 (Figure 2–52).

Figure 2–52

Conditional Formatting Operators

As shown in Figure 2–49 on page EX 119, the second text box in the New Formatting Rule dialog box allows you to select a relational operator, such as less than, to use in the condition. The eight different relational operators from which you can choose for conditional formatting in the New Formatting Rule dialog box are summarized in Table 2–5.

BTW

Conditional Formatting
You can assign any format to a cell, a range of cells, a worksheet, or an entire workbook conditionally. If the value of the cell changes and no longer meets the specified condition, Excel suppresses the conditional formatting.

Table 2–5 Summary of Conditional Formatting Relational Operators	
Relational Operator	**Description**
Between	Cell value is between two numbers
Not between	Cell value is not between two numbers
Equal to	Cell value is equal to a number
Not equal to	Cell value is not equal to a number
Greater than	Cell value is greater than a number
Less than	Cell value is less than a number
Greater than or equal to	Cell value is greater than or equal to a number
Less than or equal to	Cell value is less than or equal to a number

BTW

Hidden Columns
Trying to unhide a range of columns using the mouse can be frustrating. An alternative is to use the keyboard: select the columns to the right and left of the hidden columns and then press CTRL+SHIFT+) (RIGHT PARENTHESIS). To use the keyboard to hide a range of columns, press CTRL+0 (ZERO).

Changing the Widths of Columns and Heights of Rows

When Excel starts and displays a blank worksheet on the screen, all of the columns have a default width of 8.43 characters, or 64 pixels. A character is defined as a letter, number, symbol, or punctuation mark in 11-point Calibri font, the default font used by Excel. An average of 8.43 characters in 11-point Calibri font will fit in a cell.

Another measure of the height and width of cells is pixels, which is short for picture element. A **pixel** is a dot on the screen that contains a color. The size of the dot is based on your screen's resolution. At a common resolution of 1024 × 768, 1024 pixels appear across the screen and 768 pixels appear down the screen for a total of 786,432 pixels. It is these 786,432 pixels that form the font and other items you see on the screen.

The default row height in a blank worksheet is 15 points (or 20 pixels). Recall from Chapter 1 that a point is equal to 1/72 of an inch. Thus, 15 points is equal to about 1/5 of an inch. You can change the width of the columns or height of the rows at any time to make the worksheet easier to read or to ensure that Excel displays an entry properly in a cell.

To Change the Widths of Columns

When changing the column width, you can set the width manually or you can instruct Excel to size the column to best fit. **Best fit** means that the width of the column will be increased or decreased so the widest entry will fit in the column. Sometimes, you may prefer more or less white space in a column than best fit provides. Excel thus allows you to change column widths manually.

When the format you assign to a cell causes the entry to exceed the width of a column, Excel automatically changes the column width to best fit. If you do not assign a format to a cell or cells in a column, the column width will remain 8.43 characters. To set a column width to best fit, double-click the right boundary of the column heading above row 1.

The following steps change the column widths: column A to 14.11 characters; columns B and C to best fit; column D to 6.00 characters; columns E, G, and J to 9.00 characters; and columns F, H, and I to 12.67 characters.

1

- Point to the boundary on the right side of the column A heading above row 1.

- When the mouse pointer changes to a split double arrow, drag until the ScreenTip indicates Width: 14.11 (134 pixels). Do not release the mouse button (Figure 2–53).

Q&A

What happens if I change the column width to zero (0)?

If you decrease the column width to 0, the column is hidden. **Hiding cells** is a technique you can use to hide data that might not be relevant to a particular report or sensitive data that you do not want others to see. To instruct Excel to display a hidden column, position the mouse pointer to the right of the column heading boundary where the hidden column is located and then drag to the right.

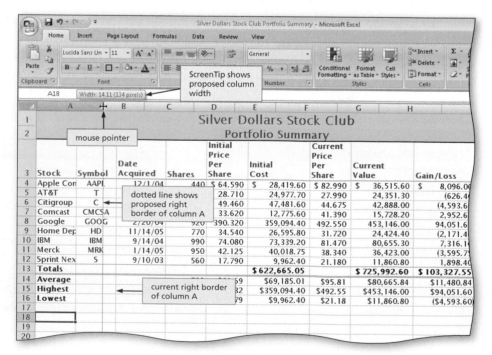

Figure 2–53

2

- Release the mouse button.

- Drag through column headings B and C above row 1.

- Point to the boundary on the right side of column heading C to cause the mouse pointer to become a split double arrow (Figure 2–54).

Q&A

What if I want to make a large change to the column width?

If you want to increase or decrease column width significantly, you can right-click a column heading and then use the Column Width command on the shortcut menu to change the column's width. To use this command, however, you must select one or more entire columns.

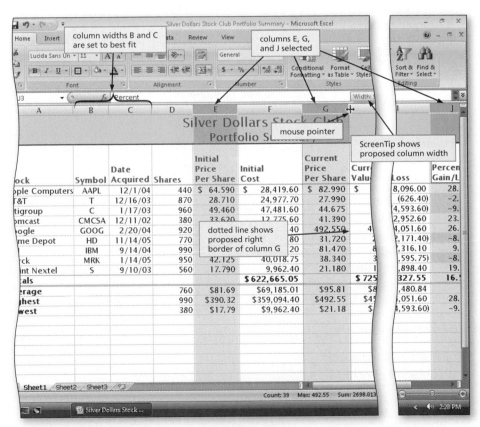

Figure 2–54

3

- Double-click the right boundary of column heading C to change the width of columns B and C to best fit.

- Click the column E heading above row 1.

- While holding down the CTRL key, click the column G heading and then the column J heading above row 1 so that columns E, G, and J are selected.

- If necessary, scroll the worksheet to the right so that the right border of column J is visible. Point to the boundary on the right side of the column J heading above row 1.

- Drag until the ScreenTip indicates Width: 9.00 (88 pixels). Do not release the mouse button (Figure 2–55).

Figure 2–55

4

- Release the mouse button.

- Click the column F heading above row 1 to select column F.

- While holding down the CTRL key, click the column H heading and then the column I heading above row 1, to select columns F, H, and I.

- Point to the boundary on the right side of the column I heading above row 1.

- Drag to the left until the ScreenTip indicates Width: 12.67 (121 pixels). Do not release the mouse button (Figure 2–56).

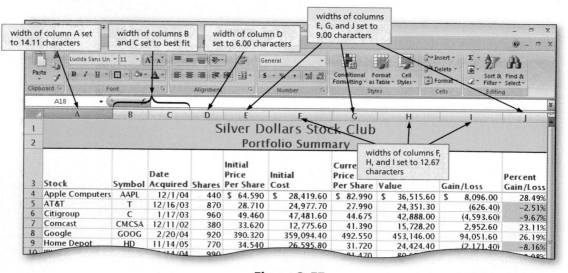

Figure 2–56

5

- Release the mouse button.

- Point to the boundary on the right side of the column D heading above row 1.

- Drag to the left until the ScreenTip indicates Width: 6.00 (61 pixels) and then release the mouse button to display the worksheet with the new column widths.

- Click cell A18 to deselect columns F, H, and I (Figure 2–57).

Figure 2–57

Other Ways

1. Right-click column heading or drag through multiple column headings and right-click, click Column Width on shortcut menu, enter desired

   column width, click OK button

2. Right-click column heading or drag through multiple column headings and right-

   click, click Format button on Ribbon, click Column Width in Format gallery, enter desired column width, click OK button

To Change the Heights of Rows

When you increase the font size of a cell entry, such as the title in cell A1, Excel automatically increases the row height to best fit so it can display the characters properly. Recall that Excel did this earlier when multiple lines were entered in a cell in row 3, and when the cell style of the worksheet title and subtitle was changed.

You also can increase or decrease the height of a row manually to improve the appearance of the worksheet. The following steps show how to improve the appearance of the worksheet by increasing the height of row 3 to 60.00 points, and increasing the height of row 14 to 26.25 points.

1

- Point to the boundary below row heading 3.

- Drag down until the ScreenTip indicates Height: 60.00 (80 pixels). Do not release the mouse button (Figure 2–58).

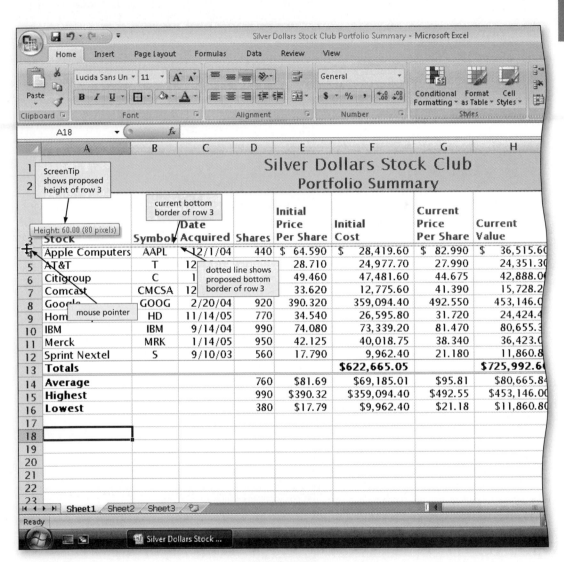

Figure 2–58

2

- Release the mouse button.

- Point to the boundary below row heading 14.

- Drag down until the ScreenTip indicates Height: 26.25 (35 pixels). Do not release the mouse button (Figure 2–59).

Figure 2–59

3

- Release the mouse button to change the row height of row 14 to 26.25.

- Select cells A3:J3 and then click the Center button on the Ribbon to center the column headings.

- Select cell A18 (Figure 2–60).

Q&A

Can I hide a row?

Yes. As with column widths, when you decrease the row height to 0, the row is hidden. To instruct Excel to display a hidden row, position the mouse pointer just below the row heading boundary where the row is hidden and then drag down. To set a row height to best fit, double-click the bottom boundary of the row heading.

Figure 2–60

Other Ways

1. Right-click row heading or drag through multiple row headings and right-click, click Row Height on shortcut menu, enter desired row height, click OK button

Checking Spelling

Excel has a **spell checker** you can use to check the worksheet for spelling errors. The spell checker looks for spelling errors by comparing words on the worksheet against words contained in its standard dictionary. If you often use specialized terms that are not in the standard dictionary, you may want to add them to a custom dictionary using the Spelling dialog box.

When the spell checker finds a word that is not in either dictionary, it displays the word in the Spelling dialog box. You then can correct it if it is misspelled.

BTW

Hidden Rows
You can use the keyboard to unhide a range of rows by selecting the rows immediately above and below the hidden rows and then pressing CTRL+SHIFT+((LEFT PARENTHESIS). To use the keyboard to hide a range of rows, press CTRL+9.

To Check Spelling on the Worksheet

To illustrate how Excel responds to a misspelled word, the word, Stock, in cell A3 is misspelled purposely as the word, Stcok, as shown in Figure 2–61.

1

- Click cell A3 and then type Stcok to misspell the word Stock.

- Click cell A1.

- Click the Review tab on the Ribbon.

- Click the Spelling button on the Ribbon to run the spell checker and display the misspelled word, Stcok, in the Spelling dialog box (Figure 2–61).

Q&A

What happens when the spell checker finds a misspelled word?

When the spell checker identifies that a cell contains a word not in its standard or custom dictionary, it selects that cell as the active cell and displays the Spelling dialog box. The Spelling dialog box (Figure 2–61) lists the word not found in the dictionary and a list of suggested corrections.

Figure 2–61

- With the word Stock highlighted in the Suggestions list, click the Change button to change the misspelled word, Stcok, to the correct word, Stock (Figure 2–62).

- If the Microsoft Office Excel dialog box is displayed, click the OK button.

3

- Select cell A18.

- Click the Home tab on the Ribbon.

- Click the Save button on the Quick Access Toolbar to save the workbook.

Q&A

What other actions can I take in the Spelling dialog box?

If one of the words in the Suggestions list is correct, click it and then click the Change button. If none of the suggestions is correct, type the correct word in the Not in Dictionary text box and then click the Change button. To change the word throughout the worksheet, click the Change All button instead of the Change button. To skip correcting the word, click the Ignore Once button. To have Excel ignore the word for the remainder of the worksheet, click the Ignore All button.

Figure 2–62

Other Ways
1. Press F7

Additional Spell Checker Considerations

Consider these additional guidelines when using the spell checker:

- To check the spelling of the text in a single cell, double-click the cell to make the formula bar active and then click the Spelling button on the Review tab on the Ribbon.

- If you select a single cell so that the formula bar is not active and then start the spell checker, Excel checks the remainder of the worksheet, including notes and embedded charts.

- If you select a cell other than cell A1 before you start the spell checker, Excel will display a dialog box when the spell checker reaches the end of the worksheet, asking if you want to continue checking at the beginning.

- If you select a range of cells before starting the spell checker, Excel checks the spelling of the words only in the selected range.

- To check the spelling of all the sheets in a workbook, click Select All Sheets on the sheet tab shortcut menu and then start the spell checker. To instruct Excel to display the sheet tab shortcut menu, right-click any sheet tab.

- To add words to the dictionary such as your last name, click the Add to Dictionary button in the Spelling dialog box (Figure 2–61 on page EX 127) when Excel identifies the word as not in the dictionary.

- Click the AutoCorrect button (Figure 2–61) to add the misspelled word and the correct version of the word to the AutoCorrect list. For example, suppose you misspell the word, do, as the word, dox. When the spell checker displays the Spelling dialog box with the correct word, do, in the Change to box, click the AutoCorrect button. Then, anytime in the future that you type the word, dox, Excel automatically will change it to the word, do.

Preparing to Print the Worksheet

Excel allows for a great deal of customization in how a worksheet appears when printed. For example, the margins on the page can be adjusted. A header or footer can be added to each printed page as well. Excel also has the capability to work on the worksheet in Page Layout View. **Page Layout View** allows you to create or modify a worksheet while viewing how it will look in printed format. The default view that you have worked in up until this point in the book is called **Normal View**.

Specify how the printed worksheet should appear.

Before printing a worksheet, you should consider how the worksheet will appear when printed. In order to fit as much information on the printed page as possible, the margins of the worksheet should be set to a reasonably small width and height. The current Portfolio Summary worksheet will print on one page. If, however, the club added more data to the worksheet, then it may extend to multiple pages. It is, therefore, a good idea to add a page header to the worksheet that prints in the top margin of each page.

In Chapter 1, the worksheet was printed in **portrait orientation**, which means the printout is printed across the width of the page. **Landscape orientation** means the printout is printed across the length of the page. Landscape orientation is a good choice for the Silver Dollars Stock Club Portfolio Summary because the printed worksheet's width is greater than its length.

BTW

Spell Checking
While Excel's spell checker is a valuable tool, it is not infallible. You should proofread your workbook carefully by pointing to each word and saying it aloud as you point to it. Be mindful of misused words such as its and it's, through and though, and to and too. Nothing undermines a good impression more than a professional looking report with misspelled words.

BTW

Error Checking
Always take the time to check the formulas of a worksheet before submitting it to your supervisor. You can check formulas by clicking the Error Checking button on the Formulas tab on the Ribbon. You also should test the formulas by employing data that tests the limits of formulas. Experienced spreadsheet specialists spend as much time testing a workbook as they do creating it, before placing it into production.

Plan Ahead

BTW

Certification
The Microsoft Certified Application Specialist (MCAS) program provides an opportunity for you to obtain a valuable industry credential – proof that you have the Excel 2007 skills required by employers. For more information, see Appendix G or visit the Excel 2007 Certification Web page (scsite.com/ex2007/cert).

To Change the Worksheet's Margins, Header, and Orientation in Page Layout View

The following steps change to Page Layout View, narrow the margins of the worksheet, change the header of the worksheet, and set the orientation of the worksheet to landscape.

1

- Click the Page Layout View button on the status bar to view the worksheet in Page Layout View (Figure 2–63).

 Q&A

What are some key features of Page Layout View?

Page Layout View shows the worksheet divided into pages. A blue background separates each page. The white areas surrounding each page indicate the print margins. The top of each page includes a Header area, and the bottom of each page includes a Footer area. Page Layout View also includes a ruler at the top of the page that assists you in placing objects on the page, such as charts and pictures.

Figure 2–63

2

- Click the Page Layout tab on the Ribbon.

- Click the Margins button on the Ribbon to display the Margins gallery (Figure 2–64).

Figure 2–64

❸

- Click Narrow in the Margins gallery to change the worksheet margins to the Narrow margin style.

- Drag the scroll bar on the right side of the worksheet to the top so that row 1 of the worksheet is displayed.

- Click above the worksheet title in cell A1 in the Header area.

- Type `Treasurer: Juan Castillo` and then press the ENTER key. Type `castillo_juan37@hotmail.com` to complete the worksheet header (Figure 2–65).

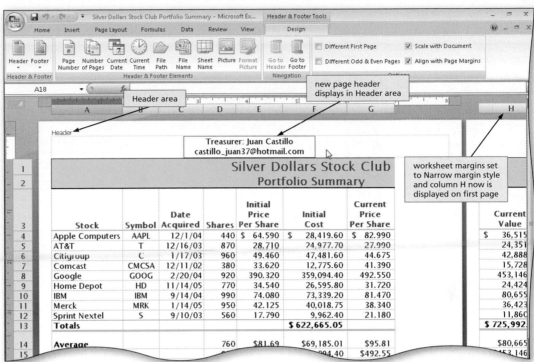

Figure 2–65

❹

- Select cell B16 to deselect the header. Click the Orientation button on the Ribbon to display the Orientation gallery.

- Point to Landscape but do not click the mouse button (Figure 2–66).

Figure 2–66

- Click Landscape in the Orientation gallery to change the worksheet's orientation to landscape (Figure 2–67).

Q&A

Do I need to change the orientation every time I want to print the worksheet?

No. Once you change the orientation and save the workbook, Excel will save the orientation setting for that workbook until you change it. When you open a new workbook, Excel sets the orientation to portrait.

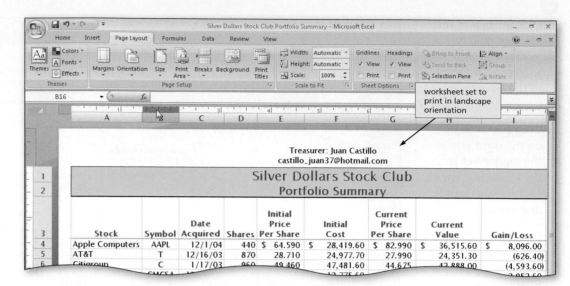

Figure 2–67

Other Ways

1. Click Page Layout tab on Ribbon, click Page Setup Dialog Box Launcher, click Page tab, click Portrait or Landscape, click OK button

Previewing and Printing the Worksheet

In Chapter 1, the worksheet was printed without first previewing it on the screen. By **previewing the worksheet**, however, you see exactly how it will look without generating a printout. Previewing a worksheet using the Print Preview command can save time, paper, and the frustration of waiting for a printout only to discover it is not what you want.

To Preview and Print a Worksheet

The following steps preview and then print the worksheet.

- Click the Office Button and then point to Print on the Office Button menu to display the Print submenu (Figure 2–68).

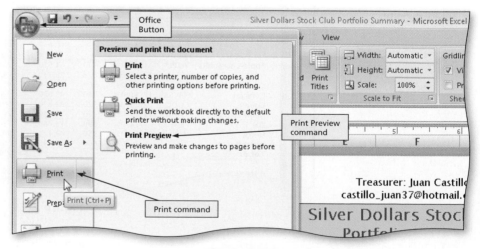

Figure 2–68

2

- Click Print Preview on the Print submenu to display a preview of the worksheet in landscape orientation (Figure 2–69).

Q&A

What is the purpose of the buttons in the Print Preview area?

The Print button displays the Print dialog box and allows you to print the worksheet. The Page Setup button displays the Page Setup dialog box. The Zoom button allows you to zoom in and out of the page displayed in the Preview window. You also can click the previewed page in the Preview window when the mouse pointer shape is a magnifying glass to carry out the function of the Zoom button.

Figure 2–69

3

- Click the Print button to display the Print dialog box (Figure 2–70).

Q&A

How can I use the Print dialog box?

When you click the Print command on the Print submenu of the Office Button menu or a Print button in a dialog box or Preview window, Excel displays the Print dialog box shown in Figure 2–70. Excel does not display the Print dialog box when you use the Print button on the Quick Access Toolbar, as was the case in Chapter 1. The Print dialog box allows you to select a printer, instruct Excel what to print, and indicate how many copies of the printout you want.

Figure 2–70

- Click the OK button to print the worksheet (Figure 2–71).

worksheet printed in landscape orientation

Treasurer: Juan Castillo
castillo_juan37@hotmail.com

Silver Dollars Stock Club
Portfolio Summary

Stock	Symbol	Date Aquired	Shares	Initial Price Per Share	Initial Cost	Current Price Per Share	Current Value	Gain/Loss
Apple Computers	AAPL	12/1/04	440	$ 64.590	$ 28,419.60	$ 82.990	$ 36,515.60	$ 8,096.00
AT&T	T	12/16/03	870	28.710	24,977.70	27.990	24,351.30	(626.40)
Citigroup	C	1/17/04	960	49.460	47,481.60	44.675	42,888.00	(4,593.60)
Comcast	CMCSA	2/11/02	380	33.620	12,775.60	41.390	15,728.20	2,952.60
Google	GOOG	2/20/04	920	390.320	359,094.40	492.550	453,146.00	94,051.60
Home Depot	HD	11/14/05	770	34.540	26,595.80	31.720	24,424.40	(2,171.40)
IBM	IBM	9/14/04	990	74.080	73,339.20	81.470	80,655.30	7,316.10
Merck	MRK	1/14/05	950	42.125	40,018.75	38.340	36,423.00	(3,595.75)
Sprint Nextel	S	9/10/03	560	17.790	9,962.40	21.180	11,860.80	1,898.40
Totals					$ 622,665.05		$ 725,992.60	$ 103,327.55
Average			760	$81.69	$69,185.01	$95.81	$80,665.84	$11,480.84
Highest			990	$390.32	$359,094.40	$492.55	$453,146.00	$94,051.60
Lowest			380	$17.79	$9,962.40	$21.18	$11,860.80	($4,593.60)

Figure 2–71

Other Ways

1. Click Page Layout tab on Ribbon, click Page Setup Dialog Box Launcher, click appropriate tab, change desired options, click Print, click OK button

To Print a Section of the Worksheet

You might not always want to print the entire worksheet. You can print portions of the worksheet by selecting the range of cells to print and then clicking the Selection option button in the Print what area in the Print dialog box. The following steps print the range A3:F16.

- Select the range A3:F16.

- Click the Office Button and then click Print on the Office Button menu to display the Print dialog box.

- Click Selection in the Print what area to instruct Excel to print only the selected range (Figure 2–72).

Figure 2–72

2

- Click the OK button to print the selected range of the worksheet on the printer (Figure 2–73).

- Click the Normal View button on the status bar.

- Click cell A18 to deselect the range A3:F13.

Q&A

What are the options in the Print what area?

The Print what area of the Print dialog box includes four option buttons (Figure 2–72). As shown in the previous steps, the Selection option button instructs Excel to print the selected range. The Active sheet(s) option button instructs Excel to print the active worksheet (the worksheet currently on the screen) or the selected worksheets. Finally, the Entire workbook option button instructs Excel to print all of the worksheets in the workbook.

header prints → Treasurer: Juan Castillo
castillo_juan37@hotmail.com ← selected range prints

Stock	Symbol	Date Acquired	Shares	Initial Price Per Share	Initial Cost
Apple Computers	AAPL	12/1/04	440	$ 64.590	$ 28,419.60
AT&T	T	12/16/03	870	28.710	24,977.70
Citigroup	C	1/17/04	960	49.460	47,481.60
Comcast	CMCSA	2/11/02	380	33.620	12,775.60
Google	GOOG	2/20/04	920	390.320	359,094.40
Home Depot	HD	11/14/05	770	34.540	26,595.80
IBM	IBM	9/14/04	990	74.080	73,339.20
Merck	MRK	1/14/05	950	42.125	40,018.75
Sprint Nextel	S	9/10/03	560	17.790	9,962.40
Totals					$ 622,665.05
Average			760	$81.69	$69,185.01
Highest			990	$390.32	$359,094.40
Lowest			380	$17.79	$9,962.40

Figure 2–73

Other Ways

1. Select range, click Page Layout tab on Ribbon, click Print Area button, click Set Print Area, click Quick Print button on Quick Access Toolbar, click Print Area button, click Clear Print Area button

Displaying and Printing the Formulas Version of the Worksheet

Thus far, you have been working with the **values version** of the worksheet, which shows the results of the formulas you have entered, rather than the actual formulas. Excel also can display and print the **formulas version** of the worksheet, which shows the actual formulas you have entered, rather than the resulting values. You can toggle between the values version and formulas version by holding down the CTRL key while pressing the ACCENT MARK (`) key, which is located to the left of the number 1 key on the keyboard.

The formulas version is useful for debugging a worksheet. **Debugging** is the process of finding and correcting errors in the worksheet. Viewing and printing the formulas version instead of the values version makes it easier to see any mistakes in the formulas.

When you change from the values version to the formulas version, Excel increases the width of the columns so the formulas and text do not overflow into adjacent cells on the right. The formulas version of the worksheet thus usually is significantly wider than the values version. To fit the wide printout on one page, you can use landscape orientation, which has already been selected for the workbook, and the Fit to option in the Page sheet in the Page Setup dialog box.

BTW

Values versus Formulas
When completing class assignments, do not enter numbers in cells that require formulas. Most instructors require their students to hand in both the values version and formulas version of the worksheet. The formulas version verifies that you entered formulas, rather than numbers, in formula-based cells.

To Display the Formulas in the Worksheet and Fit the Printout on One Page

The following steps change the view of the worksheet from the values version to the formulas version of the worksheet and then print the formulas version on one page.

- Press CTRL+ACCENT MARK (`).

- When Excel displays the formulas version of the worksheet, click the right horizontal scroll arrow until column J appears to display the worksheet with formulas (Figure 2–74).

Figure 2–74

- If necessary, click the Page Layout tab on the Ribbon and then click the Page Setup Dialog Box Launcher to display the Page Setup dialog box.

- If necessary, click Landscape to select it and then click Fit to in the Scaling area.

3

- Click the Print button in the Page Setup dialog box to print the formulas in the worksheet on one page in landscape orientation (Figure 2–75).

- When Excel displays the Print dialog box, click the OK button.

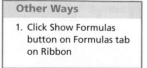

Figure 2–75

4

- After viewing and printing the formulas version, press CTRL+ACCENT MARK (`) to instruct Excel to display the values version.

- Click the left horizontal scroll arrow until column A appears.

Other Ways

1. Click Show Formulas button on Formulas tab on Ribbon

To Change the Print Scaling Option Back to 100%

Depending on your printer, you may have to change the Print Scaling option back to 100% after using the Fit to option. The following steps reset the Print Scaling option so future worksheets print at 100%, instead of being resized to print on one page.

1 If necessary, click the Page Layout tab on the Ribbon and then click the Page Setup Dialog Box Launcher to display the Page Setup dialog box.

2 Click Adjust to in the Scaling area.

3 If necessary, type 100 in the Adjust to box.

4 Click the OK button to set the print scaling to normal.

5 Click the Home tab on the Ribbon.

Q&A What is the purpose of the Adjust to box in the Page Setup dialog box?

The Adjust to box allows you to specify the percentage of reduction or enlargement in the printout of a worksheet. The default percentage is 100%. When you click the Fit to option, this percentage automatically changes to the percentage required to fit the printout on one page.

Importing External Data from a Web Source Using a Web Query

One of the major features of Excel is its capability of importing external data from Web sites. To import external data from a Web site, you must have access to the Internet. You then can import data stored on a Web site using a **Web query**. When you run a Web query, Excel imports the external data in the form of a worksheet. As described in Table 2–6, three Web queries are available when you first install Excel. All three Web queries relate to investment and stock market activities.

BTW

Web Queries
Most Excel specialists that build Web queries use the worksheet returned from the Web query as an engine to supply data to another worksheet in the workbook. With 3-D cell references, you can create a worksheet similar to the Silver Dollars Stock Club worksheet to feed the Web query stock symbols and get refreshed stock prices in return.

Table 2–6 Excel Web Queries	
Query	**External Data Returned**
MSN MoneyCentral Investor Currency Rates	Currency rates
MSN MoneyCentral Investor Major Indices	Major indices
MSN MoneyCentral Investor Stock Quotes	Up to 20 stocks of your choice

Gather information regarding the needed Web query.
As shown in Table 2–6, the MSN Money Central Investor Stock Quotes feature that is included with Excel allows you to retrieve information on up to 20 stocks of your choice. The Web query requires that you supply the stock symbols. The stock symbols are located in column B of the Portfolio Summary worksheet.

Plan Ahead

To Import Data from a Web Source Using a Web Query

Although you can have a Web query return data to a blank workbook, the following steps have the data for the nine stock symbols in column B of the Portfolio Summary worksheet returned to a blank worksheet in the Silver Dollars Stock Club Portfolio Summary workbook. The data returned by the stock-related Web queries is real time in the sense that it is no more than 20 minutes old during the business day.

- With the Silver Dollars Stock Club Portfolio Summary workbook open, click the Sheet2 tab at the bottom of the window.

- With cell A1 active, click the Data tab on the Ribbon, and then click the Existing Connections button to display the Existing Connections dialog box (Figure 2–76).

Figure 2–76

2

- Double-click MSN MoneyCentral Investor Stock Quotes to display the Import Data dialog box (Figure 2–77).

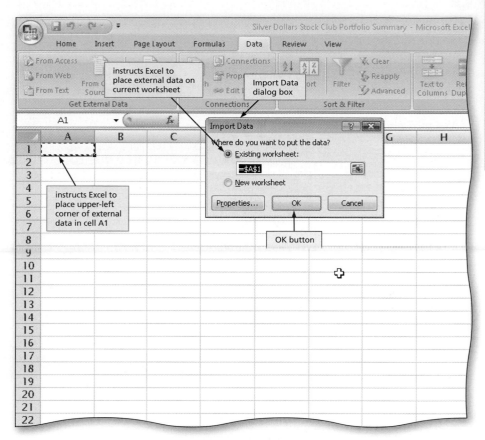

Figure 2–77

3

- Click the OK button.

- When Excel displays the Enter Parameter Value dialog box, type the nine stock symbols aapl t c cmcsa goog hd ibm mrk s in the text box.

- Click the 'Use this value/reference for future refreshes' check box to select it (Figure 2–78).

Q&A

What is the purpose of clicking the check box?

Once Excel displays the worksheet, you can refresh the data as often as you want. To refresh the data for all the stocks, click the Refresh All button on the Data tab on the Ribbon. Because the 'Use this value/reference for future refreshes' check box was selected, Excel will continue to use the same stock symbols each time it refreshes.

Figure 2–78

4

- Click the OK button to retrieve the stock quotes and display a new worksheet with the desired data (Figure 2–79).

Q&A

What composes the new worksheet?

As shown in Figure 2–79, Excel displays the data returned from the Web query in an organized, formatted worksheet, which has a worksheet title, column titles, and a row of data for each stock symbol entered. Other than the first column, which contains the stock name and stock symbol, you have no control over the remaining columns of data returned. The latest price of each stock appears in column D.

Figure 2–79

Other Ways

1. Press ALT+A, X, select data source

Changing the Worksheet Names

The sheet tabs at the bottom of the window allow you to view any worksheet in the workbook. You click the sheet tab of the worksheet you want to view in the Excel window. By default, Excel presets the names of the worksheets to Sheet1, Sheet2, and so on. The worksheet names become increasingly important as you move towards more sophisticated workbooks, especially workbooks in which you reference cells between worksheets.

Plan Ahead

Choose names for the worksheets.
Use simple, meaningful names for each worksheet. Name the first worksheet that includes the portfolio summary Portfolio Summary. The second worksheet that includes the stock quotes should be named Real-Time Stock Quotes to reflect its contents.

To Change the Worksheet Names

The following steps show how to rename worksheets by double-clicking the sheet tabs.

1

- Double-click the sheet tab labeled Sheet2 in the lower-left corner of the window.

- Type `Real-Time Stock Quotes` as the worksheet name and then press the ENTER key to display the new worksheet name on the sheet tab (Figure 2–80).

Q&A

What is the maximum length for a worksheet tab?

Worksheet names can be up to 31 characters (including spaces) in length. Longer worksheet names, however, mean that fewer sheet tabs will show. To view more sheet tabs, you can drag the tab split box (Figure 2–81) to the right. This will reduce the size of the scroll bar at the bottom of the screen. Double-click the tab split box to reset it to its normal position.

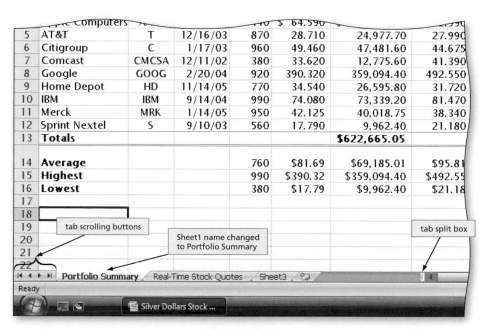

Figure 2–80

2

- Double-click the sheet tab labeled Sheet1 in the lower-left corner of the window.

- Type `Portfolio Summary` as the worksheet name and then press the ENTER key to change the name of the worksheet from Sheet 1 to Portfolio Summary (Figure 2–81).

Q&A

How can I quickly move between worksheet tabs?

You can use the tab scrolling buttons to the left of the sheet tabs (Figure 2–81) to move between worksheets. The leftmost and rightmost scroll buttons move to the first or last worksheet in the workbook. The two middle scroll buttons move one worksheet to the left or right.

Figure 2–81

3

- Click the Home tab on the Ribbon.

BTW

Obtaining an E-Mail Account
Several Web sites that allow you to sign up for free e-mail are available. Some choices are MSN Hotmail, Yahoo! Mail, and Google Gmail.

E-Mailing a Workbook from within Excel

The most popular service on the Internet is electronic mail, or **e-mail**, which is the electronic transmission of messages and files to and from other computers using the Internet. Using e-mail, you can converse with friends across the room or on another continent. One of the features of e-mail is the capability to attach Office files, such as Word documents or Excel workbooks, to an e-mail message and send it to a coworker. In the past, if you wanted to e-mail a workbook, you saved the workbook, closed the file, started your e-mail program, and then attached the workbook to the e-mail message before sending it. With Excel, you have the capability of e-mailing a worksheet or workbook directly from within Excel. For these steps to work properly, you must have an e-mail address and one of the following as your e-mail program: Microsoft Outlook, Microsoft Outlook Express, Microsoft Exchange Client, or another 32-bit e-mail program compatible with Messaging Application Programming Interface.

To E-Mail a Workbook from within Excel

The following steps show how to e-mail the Silver Dollars Stock Club Portfolio Summary workbook from within Excel to Juan Castillo at the e-mail address castillo_juan37@hotmail.com.

- With the Silver Dollars Stock Club Portfolio Summary workbook open, click the Office Button and then click Send to display the Send submenu (Figure 2–82).

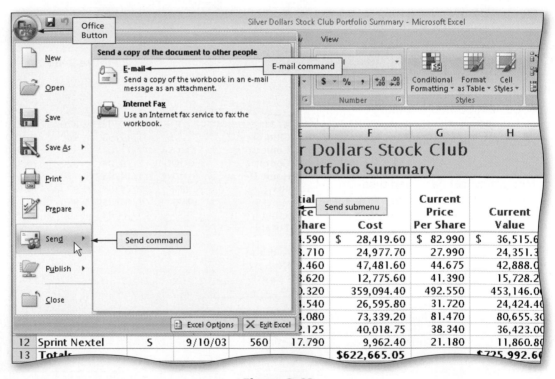

Figure 2–82

2

- Click E-mail on the Send submenu.

- When the e-mail Message window appears, type castillo_ juan37@hotmail. com in the To text box.

- Type the message shown in the message area in Figure 2–83.

3

- Click the Send button to send the e-mail with the attached workbook to castillo_juan37@ hotmail.com.

Q&A

How can the recipient use the attached workbook?

Because the workbook was sent as an attachment, Juan Castillo can double-click the attachment in the e-mail to open it in Excel, or he can save it on disk and then open it later.

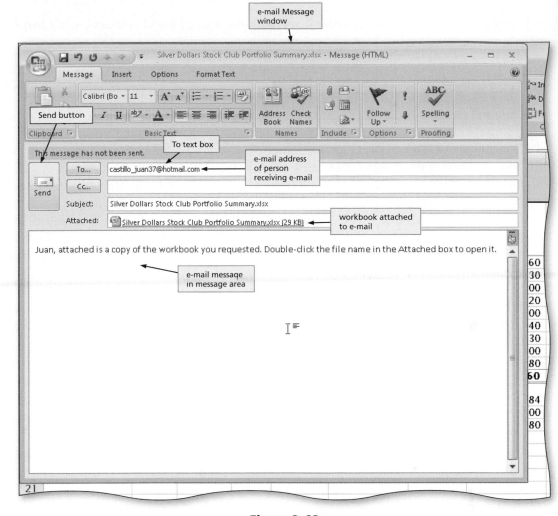

Figure 2–83

To Save the Workbook and Quit Excel

With the workbook complete and e-mailed, the following steps save the workbook and quit Excel.

1 Click the Save button on the Quick Access Toolbar.

2 Click the Close button on the upper-right corner of the title bar.

BTW

Quick Reference
For a table that lists how to complete the tasks covered in this book using the mouse, Ribbon, shortcut menu, and keyboard, see the Quick Reference Summary at the back of this book, or visit the Excel 2007 Quick Reference Web page (scsite.com/ex2007/qr).

Chapter Summary

In creating the Silver Dollars Stock Club Portfolio Summary workbook, you learned how to enter formulas, calculate an average, find the highest and lowest numbers in a range, verify formulas using Range Finder, draw borders, align text, format numbers, change column widths and row heights, and add conditional formatting to a range of numbers. In addition, you learned to spell check a worksheet, preview a worksheet, print a section of a worksheet, display and print the formulas version of the worksheet using the Fit to option, complete a Web query, rename sheet tabs, and send an e-mail directly from within Excel with the opened workbook as an attachment. The items listed below include all the new Excel skills you have learned in this chapter.

1. Enter a Formula Using the Keyboard (EX 91)
2. Enter Formulas Using Point Mode (EX 93)
3. Copy Formulas Using the Fill Handle (EX 95)
4. Determine the Average of a Range of Numbers Using the Keyboard and Mouse (EX 99)
5. Determine the Highest Number in a Range of Numbers Using the Insert Function Box (EX 101)
6. Determine the Lowest Number in a Range of Numbers Using the Sum Menu (EX 102)
7. Copy a Range of Cells across Columns to an Adjacent Range Using the Fill Handle (EX 104)
8. Verify a Formula Using Range Finder (EX 106)
9. Change the Workbook Theme (EX 109)
10. Change the Background Color and Apply a Box Border to the Worksheet Title and Subtitle (EX 110)
11. Center Data in Cells and Format Dates (EX 113)
12. Apply an Accounting Number Format and Comma Style Format Using the Ribbon (EX 115)
13. Apply a Currency Style Format with a Floating Dollar Sign Using the Format Cells Dialog Box (EX 116)
14. Apply a Percent Style Format and Use the Increase Decimal Button (EX 118)
15. Apply Conditional Formatting (EX 119)
16. Change the Widths of Columns (EX 122)
17. Change the Heights of Rows (EX 125)
18. Check Spelling on the Worksheet (EX 127)
19. Change the Worksheet's Margins, Header, and Orientation in Page Layout View (EX 130)
20. Preview and Print a Worksheet (EX 132)
21. Print a Section of the Worksheet (EX 134)
22. Display the Formulas in the Worksheet and Fit the Printout on One Page (EX 136)
23. Import Data from a Web Source Using a Web Query (EX 138)
24. Change the Worksheet Names (EX 141)
25. E-Mail a Workbook from within Excel (EX 142)

If you have a SAM user profile, you may have access to hands-on instruction, practice, and assessment. Log in to your SAM account (http://sam2007.course.com) to launch any assigned training activities or exams that relate to the skills covered in this chapter.

Learn It Online

Learn It Online is a series of online student exercises that test your knowledge of chapter content and key terms.

Instructions: To complete the Learn It Online exercises, start your browser, click the Address bar, and then enter the Web address `scsite.com/ex2007/learn`. When the Excel 2007 Learn It Online page is displayed, click the link for the exercise you want to complete and then read the instructions.

Chapter Reinforcement TF, MC, and SA
A series of true/false, multiple choice, and short answer questions that test your knowledge of the chapter content.

Flash Cards
An interactive learning environment where you identify chapter key terms associated with displayed definitions.

Practice Test
A series of multiple choice questions that test your knowledge of chapter content and key terms.

Who Wants To Be a Computer Genius?
An interactive game that challenges your knowledge of chapter content in the style of a television quiz show.

Wheel of Terms
An interactive game that challenges your knowledge of chapter key terms in the style of the television show *Wheel of Fortune*.

Crossword Puzzle Challenge
A crossword puzzle that challenges your knowledge of key terms presented in the chapter.

Apply Your Knowledge

Reinforce the skills and apply the concepts you learned in this chapter.

Profit Analysis Worksheet

Instructions Part 1:   Start Excel. Open the workbook Apply 2-1 Car-B-Clean Profit Analysis. See the inside back cover of this book for instructions for downloading the Data Files for Students or see your instructor for information on accessing the files required in this book. The purpose of this exercise is to open a partially completed workbook, enter formulas and functions, copy the formulas and functions, and then format the worksheet titles and numbers. As shown in Figure 2–84, the completed worksheet analyzes profits by product.

	Item	Unit Cost	Unit Profit	Units Sold	Total Sales	Total Profit	% Total Profit
					Car-B-Clean Accessories		
					Profit Analysis		
4	Brush	$ 5.84	$ 3.15	36,751	$ 330,391.49	$ 115,765.65	35.039%
5	Bucket	7.14	2.75	57,758	571,226.62	158,834.50	27.806%
6	Drying Cloth	3.52	1.17	42,555	199,582.95	49,789.35	24.947%
7	Duster	2.55	1.04	78,816	282,949.44	81,968.64	28.969%
8	Polish	7.19	7.80	57,758	865,792.42	450,512.40	52.035%
9	Soap	8.52	4.09	50,646	638,646.06	207,142.14	32.435%
10	Sponge	2.05	1.84	23,154	90,069.06	42,603.36	47.301%
11	Wax	10.15	7.44	53,099	934,011.41	395,056.56	42.297%
12	Vacuum	43.91	33.09	17,780	1,369,060.00	588,340.20	42.974%
13	**Totals**			**418,317**	**$5,281,729.45**	**$2,090,012.80**	**39.571%**
14	Lowest	$2.05	$1.04	17,780	$90,069.06	$42,603.36	24.947%
15	Highest	$43.91	$33.09	78,816	$1,369,060.00	$588,340.20	52.035%
16	Average	$10.10	$6.93	46,480	$586,858.83	$232,223.64	

Figure 2–84

Perform the following tasks.

1. Use the following formulas in cells E4, F4, and G4:

   Total Sales (cell E4) = Units Sold * (Unit Cost + Unit Profit) or =D4 * (B4 + C4)

   Total Profit (cell F4) = Units Sold * Unit Profit or = D4 * C4

   % Total Profit (cell G4) = Total Profit / Total Sales or = F4 / E4

   Use the fill handle to copy the three formulas in the range E4:G4 to the range E5:G12.

2. Determine totals for the units sold, total sales, and total profit in row 13. Copy cell G12 to G13 to assign the formula in cell G12 to G13 in the total line.

Continued >

Apply Your Knowledge *continued*

3. In the range B14:B16, determine the lowest value, highest value, and average value, respectively, for the values in the range B4:B12. Use the fill handle to copy the three functions to the range C14:G16. Delete the average from cell G16, because an average of percentages of this type is mathematically invalid.

4. Format the worksheet as follows:

   a. change the workbook theme to Concourse by using the Themes button on the Page Layout tab on the Ribbon

   b. cell A1 — change to font size 24 with a green (column 6 of standard colors) background and white font color by using the buttons in the Font group on the Home tab on the Ribbon

   c. cell A2 — change to a green (column 6 of standard colors) background and white font color

   d. cells B4:C4, E4:F4, and E13:F13 — Accounting style format with two decimal places and fixed dollar signs (use the Accounting Style button on the Home tab on the Ribbon)

   e. cells B5:C12 and E5:F12 — Comma style format with two decimal places (use the Comma Style button on the Home tab on the Ribbon)

   f. cells D4:D16 — Comma style format with no decimal places

   g. cells G4:G15 — Percent style format with three decimal places

   h. cells B14:C16 and E14:F16 — Currency style format with floating dollar signs (use the Format Cells: Number Dialog Box Launcher on the Home tab on the Ribbon)

5. Switch to Page Layout View and enter your name, course, laboratory assignment number (Apply 2-1), date, and any other information requested by your instructor in the Header area. Preview and print the worksheet in landscape orientation. Change the document properties, as specified by your instructor. Save the workbook using the file name, Apply 2-1 Car-B-Clean Profit Analysis Complete in the format specified by your instructor.

6. Use Range Finder to verify the formula in cell F4.

7. Print the range A3:E16. Press CTRL+ACCENT MARK (`) to change the display from the values version of the worksheet to the formulas version. Print the formulas version in landscape orientation on one page (Figure 2–85) by using the Fit to option in the Page sheet in the Page Setup dialog box. Press CTRL+ACCENT MARK (`) to change the display of the worksheet back to the values version. Do not save the workbook. If requested, submit the three printouts to your instructor.

Instructions Part 2:

1. Do not save the workbook in this part. In column C, use the keyboard to add manually $1.00 to the profit of each product with a unit profit less than $7.00 and $3.00 to the profits of all other products. You should end up with $2,765,603.80 in cell F13.

2. Print the worksheet. Do not save the workbook. If requested, submit the revised workbook in the format specified by your instructor.

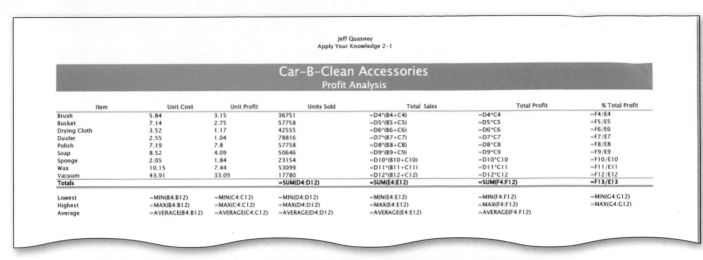

Jeff Quasney
Apply Your Knowledge 2-1

	Car-B-Clean Accessories					
	Profit Analysis					
Item	Unit Cost	Unit Profit	Units Sold	Total Sales	Total Profit	% Total Profit
Brush	5.84	3.15	36751	=D4*(B4+C4)	=D4*C4	=F4/E4
Bucket	7.14	2.75	57758	=D5*(B5+C5)	=D5*C5	=F5/E5
Drying Cloth	3.52	1.17	42555	=D6*(B6+C6)	=D6*C6	=F6/E6
Duster	2.55	1.04	78816	=D7*(B7+C7)	=D7*C7	=F7/E7
Polish	7.19	7.8	57758	=D8*(B8+C8)	=D8*C8	=F8/E8
Soap	8.52	4.09	50646	=D9*(B9+C9)	=D9*C9	=F9/E9
Sponge	2.05	1.84	23154	=D10*(B10+C10)	=D10*C10	=F10/E10
Wax	10.15	7.44	53099	=D11*(B11+C11)	=D11*C11	=F11/E11
Vacuum	43.91	33.09	17780	=D12*(B12+C12)	=D12*C12	=F12/E12
Totals			=SUM(D4:D12)	=SUM(E4:E12)	=SUM(F4:F12)	=F13/E13
Lowest	=MIN(B4:B12)	=MIN(C4:C12)	=MIN(D4:D12)	=MIN(E4:E12)	=MIN(F4:F12)	=MIN(G4:G12)
Highest	=MAX(B4:B12)	=MAX(C4:C12)	=MAX(D4:D12)	=MAX(E4:E12)	=MAX(F4:F12)	=MAX(G4:G12)
Average	=AVERAGE(B4:B12)	=AVERAGE(C4:C12)	=AVERAGE(D4:D12)	=AVERAGE(E4:E12)	=AVERAGE(F4:F12)	

Figure 2–85

Extend Your Knowledge

Extend the skills you learned in this chapter and experiment with new skills. You may need to use Help to complete the assignment.

Applying Conditional Formatting to Cells

Instructions: Start Excel. Open the workbook Extend 2-1 Biology 201 Midterm Scores. See the inside back cover of this book for instructions for downloading the Data Files for Students, or see your instructor for information on accessing the files required in this book. Perform the following tasks to apply new conditional formatting to the worksheet.

1. Select the range C4:C18. Click the Conditional Formatting button on the Home tab on the Ribbon and then select New Rule in the Conditional Formatting gallery. Select 'Format only top or bottom ranked values' in the Select a Rule Type area (Figure 2–86). Enter a value between 20 and 35 of your choosing in the text box in the Edit the Rule Description area and click the '% of the selected range' check box to select it. Click the Format button and choose a format to assign to this conditional format. Click the OK button in each dialog box to close the dialog boxes and view the worksheet.

2. With range C4:C18 selected, apply a conditional format to the range that highlights scores that are below average.

3. With range D4:D18 selected, apply a conditional format to the range that highlights any grade that is a D or an F.

4. With range B4:B18 selected, apply a conditional format to the range that uses a red color to highlight any duplicate student names.

5. Change the document properties, as specified by your instructor. Change the worksheet header with your name, course number, and other information requested by your instructor. Save the workbook using the file name, Extend 2-1 Biology 201 Midterm Scores Complete, and submit the revised workbook as specified by your instructor.

Figure 2–86

STUDENT ASSIGNMENTS

Make It Right

Analyze a workbook and correct all errors and/or improve the design.

Correcting Functions and Formulas in a Worksheet

Instructions: Start Excel. Open the workbook Make It Right 2-1 El Centro Diner Payroll Report. See the inside back cover of this book for instructions for downloading the Data Files for Students, or see your instructor for information on accessing the files required for this book. Correct the following formatting, function, and formula problems (Figure 2–87) in the worksheet.

	A	B	C	D	E	F	G	H	I	J	K
					El Centro Diner						
					Payrol Report						
3	**Employee**	Dependents	Rate per Hou	Hours Worked	Gross Pay	Federal Tax	State Tax	Net Pay	% Taxes		
4	Vincent Flores	1	$9.90	20.00	$198.00	$34.97	$7.92	$162.03	21.660%		
5	Wonda Jefferson	2	11.20	40.00	448.00	80.33	17.92	365.67	21.931%		
6	Anthony Sanchez	2	15.90	21.25	337.88	58.31	13.52	277.57	21.257%		
7	Alexa Martin	3	11.30	23.50	265.55	39.21	10.62	223.34	18.765%		
8	Maria Reyes	1	10.30	21.25	218.88	39.14	8.76	178.73	21.883%		
9	Lori Romanoff	2	10.75	40.00	430.00	76.73	17.20	351.27	21.845%		
10	Carmen Alvarez	1	12.60	21.50	270.90	49.55	10.84	220.35	22.289%		
11	Peter Lane	4	14.50	37.50	543.75	90.21	21.75	449.54	20.591%		
12	Claudi Moreno	1	16.00	33.00	528.00	100.97	21.12	426.03	23.122%		
13	Wayne Vargas	3	8.00	29.25	234.00	32.90	9.36	198.10	18.059%		
14	**Totals**			287.25	$3,474.95	$ 602.31	$ 139.00	$2,852.64	21.333%		
15	Average	1.8888889	$12.49	28.67	$360.11	$60.23	$13.90	$294.95	21.140%		
16	Highest	4	$16.00	40.00	$543.75	$100.97	$21.75	$449.54	23.122%		
17	Lowest	1	$8.00	20.00	$198.00	$32.90	$7.92	$162.03	18.059%		

Figure 2–87

1. Adjust the width of column B to 11.25 pixels so that the word in the column header does not wrap.

2. Spell check the worksheet and correct any spelling mistakes that are found, but ignore any spelling mistakes found with the worksheet title and the employee names.

3. The averages in several columns do not include the employee in row 13. Adjust the functions in these cells so that all employees are included in the calculation.

4. The net pay calculation should be:

    Net Pay = Gross Pay − (Federal Taxes + State Taxes)

    Adjust the formulas in the range H4:H13 so that the correct formula is used.

5. The value for the highest value in column C was entered as a number rather than as a function. Replace the value with the appropriate function.

6. The currency values in row 4 should be formatted with the Accounting Number Format button on the Home tab on the Ribbon. They are currently formatted with the Currency format.

7. Delete the function in the cell containing the average of % Taxes because it is mathematically invalid.

8. Change the document properties, as specified by your instructor. Change the worksheet header with your name, course number, and other information requested by your instructor. Save the workbook using the file name, Make It Right 2-1 El Centro Diner Payroll Report Corrected. Submit the revised workbook as specified by your instructor.

In the Lab

Create a workbook using the guidelines, concepts, and skills presented in this chapter. Labs are listed in order of increasing difficulty.

Lab 1: Sales Analysis Worksheet

Problem: You have been asked to build a sales analysis worksheet for Facade Importers that determines the sales quota and percentage of quota met for the sales representatives in Table 2–8. The desired worksheet is shown in Figure 2–88.

Table 2–8 Facade Importers Sales Data			
Sales Representative	**Sales Amount**	**Sales Return**	**Sales Quota**
Polizzi, Bernard	591518	12638	765130
Li, Grace	895050	12015	776381
Volpe, Pamela	716502	18141	733309
Khan, Anwer	709672	22326	566940
Hudson, Emma	802525	11138	712222
Huerta, Teresa	885156	18721	778060

A	B	C	D	E	F
		Facade Importers			
		Sales Analysis			
Sales Representative	*Sales Amount*	*Sales Return*	*Net Sales*	*Sales Quota*	*Above Quota*
Polizzi, Bernard	$591,518.00	$12,638.00	$578,880.00	$765,130.00	($186,250.00)
Li, Grace	895,050.00	12,015.00	883,035.00	776,381.00	106,654.00
Volpe, Pamela	716,502.00	18,141.00	698,361.00	733,309.00	(34,948.00)
Khan, Anwer	709,672.00	22,326.00	687,346.00	566,940.00	120,406.00
Hudson, Emma	802,525.00	11,138.00	791,387.00	712,222.00	79,165.00
Huerta, Terese	885,156.00	18,721.00	866,435.00	778,060.00	88,375.00
Total	$4,600,423.00	$94,979.00	$4,505,444.00	$4,332,042.00	$173,402.00
Average	$766,737.17	$15,829.83	$750,907.33	$722,007.00	$28,900.33
Highest	$895,050.00	$22,326.00	$883,035.00	$778,060.00	$120,406.00
Lowest	$591,518.00	$11,138.00	$578,880.00	$566,940.00	($186,250.00)
% of Quota Sold ====>	104.00%				

Figure 2–88

Continued >

In the Lab *continued*

Instructions Part 1: Perform the following tasks to build the worksheet shown in Figure 2–88.

1. Apply the Aspect theme to the worksheet by using the Themes button on the Page Layout tab on the Ribbon.

2. Increase the width of column A to 19.00 points and the width of columns B through F to 13.50 points.

3. Enter the worksheet title Facade Importers in cell A1 and the worksheet subtitle Sales Analysis in cell A2. Enter the column titles in row 3 as shown in Figure 2–88. In row 3, use ALT+ENTER to start a new line in a cell.

4. Enter the sales data described in Table 2–8 in columns A, B, C, and E in rows 4 through 9. Enter the row titles in the range A10:A14 as shown in Figure 2–88 on the previous page.

5. Obtain the net sales in column D by subtracting the sales returns in column C from the sales amount in column B. Enter the formula in cell D4 and copy it to the range D5:D9.

6. Obtain the above quota amounts in column F by subtracting the sales quota in column E from the net sales in column D. Enter the formula in cell F4 and copy it to the range F5:F9.

7. Obtain the totals in row 10 by adding the column values for each salesperson. In the range B11:B13, use the AVERAGE, MAX, and MIN functions to determine the average, highest value, and lowest value in the range B4:B9. Copy the range B11:B13 to the range C11:F13.

8. Determine the percent of quota sold in cell B14 by dividing the total net sales amount in cell D10 by the total sales quota amount in cell E10. Center this value in the cell.

9. If necessary, click the Home tab on the Ribbon. One at a time, merge and center the worksheet title and subtitle across columns A through F. Select cells A1 and A2 and change the background color to red (column 2 in the Standard Colors area on the Fill Color palette). Apply the Title cell style to cells A1 and B1 by clicking the Cell Styles button on the Home tab on the Ribbon and clicking the Title cell style in the Titles and Headings area in the Cell Styles gallery. Change the worksheet title in cell A1 to 28-point white (column 1, row 1 on the Font Color gallery). Change the worksheet subtitle to the same color. Assign a thick box border from the Borders gallery to the range A1:A2.

10. Center the titles in row 3, columns A through F. Apply the Heading 3 cell style to the range A3:F3. Use the Italic button on the Home tab on the Ribbon to italicize the column titles in row 3 and the row titles in the range A10:A14.

11. Apply the Total cell style to the range A10:F10. Assign a thick box to cell B14. Change the background and font colors for cell B14 to the same colors applied to the worksheet title in Step 9.

12. Change the row heights of row 3 to 33.00 points and rows 11 and 14 to 30.00 points.

13. Select cell B14 and then click the Percent Style button on the Home tab on the Ribbon. Click the Increase Decimal button on the Ribbon twice to display the percent in cell B14 to hundredths.

14. Use the CTRL key to select the ranges B4:F4 and B10:F13. That is, select the range B4:F4 and then while holding down the CTRL key, select the range B10:F13. Use the Format Cells: Number Dialog Box Launcher button on the Home tab on the Ribbon to display the Format Cells dialog box to assign the selected ranges a Floating Dollar Sign style format with two decimal places and parentheses to represent negative numbers. Select the range B5:F9 and click the Comma Style button on the Home tab on the Ribbon.

15. Rename the sheet tab as Sales Analysis. Change the document properties, as specified by your instructor. Change the worksheet header with your name, course number, and other information requested by your instructor.

16. Save the workbook using the file name Lab 2-1 Part 1 Facade Importers Sales Analysis. Print the entire worksheet in landscape orientation. Print only the range A3:B10.

17. Display the formulas version by pressing CTRL+ACCENT MARK (`). Print the formulas version using the Fit to option button in the Scaling area on the Page tab in the Page Setup dialog box. After printing the worksheet, reset the Scaling option by selecting the Adjust to option button on the Page tab in the Page Setup dialog box and changing the percent value to 100%. Change the display from the formulas version to the values version by pressing CTRL+ACCENT MARK (`). Do not save the workbook.

18. Submit the assignment as specified by your instructor.

Instructions Part 2: Open the workbook created in Part 1 and save the workbook as Lab 2-1 Part 2 Facade Importers Sales Analysis. Manually decrement each of the six values in the net sales column by $10,000.00 until the percent of quota sold in cell B14 is below, yet as close as possible to, 100%. All six values in column E must be incremented the same number of times. The percent of quota sold in B14 should equal 99.85%. Update the worksheet header and save the workbook. Print the worksheet. Submit the assignment as specified by your instructor.

Instructions Part 3: Open the workbook created in Part 2 and then save the workbook as Lab 2-1 Part 3 Facade Importers Sales Analysis. With the percent of quota sold in cell B14 equal to 99.85% from Part 2, manually decrement each of the six values in the sales return column by $1,000.00 until the percent of quota sold in cell B14 is above, yet as close as possible to, 100%. Decrement all six values in column C the same number of times. Your worksheet is correct when the percent of quota sold in cell B14 is equal to 100.12%. Update the worksheet header and save the workbook. Print the worksheet. Submit the assignment as specified by your instructor.

In the Lab

Lab 2: Balance Due Worksheet

Problem: You are a spreadsheet intern for Jackson's Bright Ideas, a popular Denver-based light fixture store with outlets in major cities across the western United States. You have been asked to use Excel to generate a report (Figure 2–89) that summarizes the monthly balance due. A graphic breakdown of the data also is desired. The customer data in Table 2–9 is available for test purposes.

Table 2–9 Jackson's Bright Ideas Monthly Balance Due Data				
Customer	**Beginning Balance**	**Credits**	**Payments**	**Purchases**
Costa, Dan	160.68	18.70	99.33	68.28
Hernandez, Abraham	138.11	48.47	75.81	46.72
Mc Cartan, John	820.15	32.11	31.23	29.19
Paoli, Pam	167.35	59.32	52.91	33.90
Ramirez, Alberto	568.34	55.17	18.53	36.34
Vaughn, Noah	449.92	25.90	82.05	99.77
Xiong, James	390.73	48.12	19.35	92.13

Continued >

In the Lab *continued*

Instructions Part 1: Create a worksheet similar to the one shown in Figure 2–89. Include the five columns of customer data in Table 2–9 in the report, plus two additional columns to compute a service charge and a new balance for each customer. Assume no negative unpaid monthly balances.

G16			f_x					
	A	B	C	D	E	F	G	H

1								
			Jackson's Bright Ideas				
2			**Monthly Balance Due Report**				
3	Customer	Beginning Balance	Credits	Payments	Purchases	Service Charge	New Balance
4	Costa, Dan	$160.68	$18.70	$99.33	$68.28	$1.17	$112.10
5	Hernandez, Abraham	138.11	48.47	75.81	46.72	0.38	60.93
6	Mc Cartan, John	820.15	32.11	31.23	29.19	20.81	806.81
7	Paoli, Pam	167.35	59.32	52.91	33.90	1.52	90.54
8	Ramirez, Alberto	568.34	55.17	18.53	36.34	13.60	544.58
9	Vaughn, Noah	449.92	25.90	82.05	99.77	9.40	451.14
10	Xiong, James	390.73	48.12	19.35	92.13	8.89	424.28
11	**Totals**	**$2,695.28**	**$287.79**	**$379.21**	**$406.33**	**$55.78**	**$2,490.39**
12	**Highest**	$820.15	$59.32	$99.33	$99.77	$20.81	$806.81
13	**Lowest**	$138.11	$18.70	$18.53	$29.19	$0.38	$60.93
14	**Average**	$385.04	$41.11	$54.17	$58.05	$7.97	$355.77
15							
16							

Figure 2–89

Perform the following tasks:

1. Enter and format the worksheet title `Jackson's Bright Ideas` and worksheet subtitle `Monthly Balance Due Report` in cells A1 and A2. Change the theme of the worksheet to the Technic theme. Apply the Title cell style to cells A1 and A2. Change the font size in cell A1 to 28 points. One at a time, merge and center the worksheet title and subtitle across columns A through G. Change the background color of cells A1 and A2 to yellow (column 4 in the Standard Colors area in the Font Color palette). Draw a thick box border around the range A1:A2.

2. Change the width of column A to 20.00 characters. Change the widths of columns B through G to 12.00. Change the heights of row 3 to 36.00 and row 12 to 30.00 points.

3. Enter the column titles in row 3 and row titles in the range A11:A14 as shown in Figure 2–89. Center the column titles in the range A3:G3. Apply the Heading 3 cell style to the range A3:G3. Bold the titles in the range A11:A14. Apply the Total cell style to the range A11:G11. Change the font size of the cells in the range A3:G14 to 12 points.

4. Enter the data in Table 2–9 in the range A4:E10.

5. Use the following formulas to determine the service charge in column F and the new balance in column G for the first customer. Copy the two formulas down through the remaining customers.

   a. Service Charge (cell F4) = 2.75% * (Beginning Balance – Payments – Credits)
      or = 0.0275 * (B4 – D4 – C4)

   b. New Balance (G4) = Beginning Balance + Purchases – Credits – Payments + Service Charge
      or =B4 + E4 – C4 – D4 + F4

6. Determine the totals in row 11.

STUDENT ASSIGNMENTS

7. Determine the maximum, minimum, and average values in cells B12:B14 for the range B4:B10 and then copy the range B12:B14 to C12:G14.

8. Use the Format Cells command on the shortcut menu to format the numbers as follows: (a) assign the Currency style with a floating dollar sign to the cells containing numeric data in the ranges B4:G4 and B11:G14; and (b) assign the Comma style (currency with no dollar sign) to the range B5:G10.

9. Use conditional formatting to change the formatting to white font on a red background in any cell in the range C4:C10 that contains a value greater than 50.

10. Change the worksheet name from Sheet1 to Balance Due. Change the document properties, as specified by your instructor. Change the worksheet header with your name, course number, and other information requested by your instructor.

11. Spell check the worksheet. Preview and then print the worksheet in landscape orientation. Save the workbook using the file name, Lab 2-2 Part 1 Jackson's Bright Ideas Monthly Balance Due Report.

12. Print the range A3:D14. Print the formulas version on one page. Close the workbook without saving the changes. Submit the assignment as specified by your instructor.

Instructions Part 2:   This part requires that a 3-D Bar chart with a cylindrical shape be inserted on a new worksheet in the workbook. If necessary, use Excel Help to obtain information on inserting a chart on a separate sheet in the workbook.

1. With the Lab 2-2 Part 1 Jackson's Bright Ideas Monthly Balance Due Report workbook open, save the workbook using the file name, Lab 2-2 Part 2 Jackson's Bright Ideas Monthly Balance Due Report. Draw the 3-D Bar chart with cylindrical shape showing each customer's total new balance as shown in Figure 2–90.

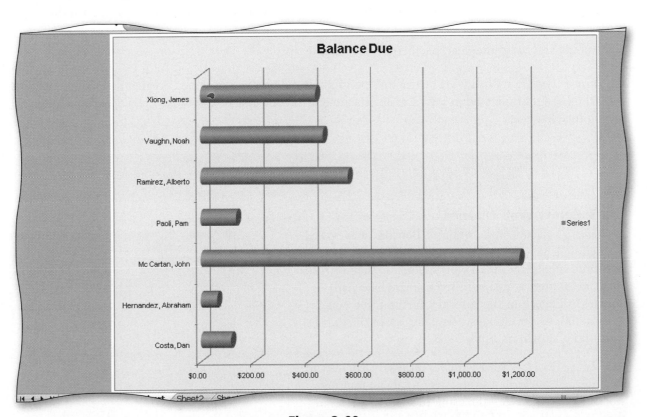

Figure 2–90

2. Use the CTRL key and mouse to select the nonadjacent chart ranges A4:A10 and G4:G10. That is, select the range A4:A10 and then while holding down the CTRL key, select the range G4:G10. The customer names in the range A4:A10 will identify the cylindrical bars, while the data series in the range G4:G10 will determine the length of the bars.

Continued >

In the Lab *continued*

3. Click the Insert tab on the Ribbon. Click the Bar button in the Charts group on the Ribbon and then select Clustered Horizontal Cylinder in the Cylinder area. When the chart is displayed on the worksheet, click the Move Chart button on the Ribbon. When the Move Chart dialog box appears, click New sheet and then type Bar Chart for the sheet name. Click the OK button.

4. When the chart is displayed on the new worksheet, click the chart area, which is a blank area near the edge of the chart, and then click the Format contextual tab. Click the Shape Fill button on the Ribbon and then select Gold, Accent 2, Lighter 80% in the gallery (column 6, row 2). Click the Layout contextual tab. Click the Chart Title button on the Ribbon and then select Above Chart in the Chart Title gallery. If necessary, use the scroll bar on the right side of the worksheet to scroll to the top of the chart. Click the edge of the chart title to select it and then type Balance Due as the chart title.

5. Drag the Balance Due tab at the bottom of the worksheet to the left of the Bar Chart tab to reorder the sheets in the workbook. Preview and print the chart.

6. Click the Balance Due sheet tab. Change the following purchases: customer John Mc Cartan to $406.58, and customer Pam Paoli to $74.99. The company also decided to change the service charge from 2.75% to 3.25% for all customers. After copying the adjusted formula in cell F4 to the range F5:F10, click the Auto Fill Options button and then click Fill without Formatting to maintain the original formatting in the range F5:F10. The total new balance in cell G11 should equal $2,919.01.

7. Select both sheets by holding down the SHIFT key and then clicking the Bar Chart tab. Preview and print the selected sheets. Submit the assignment as requested by your instructor. Save the workbook.

8. Submit the assignment as specified by your instructor.

Instructions Part 3: With your instructor's permission, e-mail the workbook created in this exercise with the changes indicated in Part 2 as an attachment to your instructor. Close the workbook without saving the changes.

In the Lab

Lab 3: Equity Web Queries

Problem: A friend of your family, Benson Yackley, has learned that Excel can connect to the Web, download real-time stock data into a worksheet, and then refresh the data as often as needed. Because you have had courses in Excel and the Internet, he has hired you as a consultant to develop a stock analysis workbook. His portfolio is shown in Table 2–10.

Table 2–10 Benson Yackley's Stock Portfolio	
Company	**Stock Symbol**
Exxon Mobil	XOM
Dell	DELL
Hewlett-Packard	HPQ
Intel	INTC
MetLife	MET
PepsiCo	PEP

Instructions Part 1: Start Excel. If necessary, connect to the Internet. Perform a Web query to obtain multiple stock quotes (Figure 2–91), using the stock symbols in the second column of Table 2–10. Place the results of the Web query in a new worksheet. Rename the worksheet Real-Time Stock Quotes. Change the document properties, as specified by your instructor. Add a header with your name, course number, and other information requested by your instructor. Save the workbook using the file name, Lab 2-3 Part 1 Benson Yackley Equities Online. Preview and then print the worksheet in landscape orientation using the Fit to option.

Click the following links and print the Web page that appears in the browser window: Click here to visit MSN Money; Dell Inc.; Chart (to the right of MetLife, Inc.); and News (to the right of PepsiCo, Inc.). Submit the assignment as specified by your instructor.

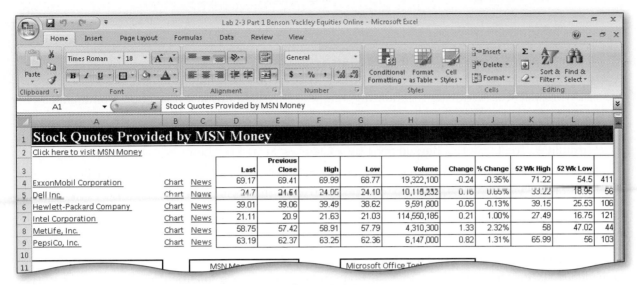

Figure 2–91

Instructions Part 2:   While connected to the Internet and with the Lab 2-3 Benson Yackley Equities Online workbook open, create a worksheet listing the major indices and their current values on Sheet2 of the workbook (Figure 2–92). After clicking the Sheet2 tab, create the worksheet by double-clicking MSN MoneyCentral Investor Major Indices in the Existing Connections dialog box. The dialog box is displayed when you click the Existing Connections button on the Data tab on the Ribbon. Rename the worksheet Major Indices. Preview and then print the Major Indices worksheet in landscape orientation using the Fit to option. Save the workbook using the same file name as in Part 1. Submit the assignment as specified by your instructor.

A1   Stock Quotes Provided by MSN Money

			Last	Previous Close	High	Low	Volume	Change	% Change	52 Wk High	52 Wk Low
1	**Stock Quotes Provided by MSN Money**										
2	Click here to visit MSN Money										
3											
	DOW JONES INDUSTRIAL AVERAGE	Chart News	11992.68	11950.02	12049.03	11947.62	276,354,912	42.66	0.36%	11997.25	10193.45
4	INDEX										
5	DOW JONES COMPOSITE INDEX	Chart News	4030.49	4028.71	4068.22	4013.22	344,654,987	1.78	0.04%	4053.4	3346.66
	DOW JONES TRANSPORTATION	Chart News	4605.27	4648.65	4718.13	4574.62	44,944,975	-43.38	-0.93%	5013.67	3550.55
6	AVERAGE INDEX										
7	DOW JONES UTILITIES INDEX	Chart News	442.81	439.33	443.03	439.35	23,355,100	3.48	0.79%	443.49	378.95
8	$DAX (Invalid symbol)	??? ???	???	???	???	???	???	???	???	???	???
9	$FTSE (Invalid symbol)	??? ???	???	???	???	???	???	???	???	???	???
10	Hang Seng	Chart News	18048.09	18014.84	18048.09	17881.78	0	33.25	0.18%	0	0
	AMEX INTERACTIVE WEEK	Chart News	186.5	187.51	188.97	186.09	0	-1.01	-0.54%	192.64	156.16
11	INTERNET INDEX										
12	NASDAQ COMPOSITE INDEX	Chart News	2337.15	2344.95	2362.09	2330.49	2,091,566,611	-7.8	-0.33%	2375.54	2012.78
13	$NI225 (Invalid symbol)	??? ???	???	???	???	???	???	???	???	???	???
14	$CAC (Invalid symbol)	??? ???	???	???	???	???	???	???	???	???	???
	PHLX SEMICONDUCTOR SECTOR	Chart News	450.79	463.74	462.46	449.51	0	-12.95	-2.79%	559.6	384.28
15	INDEX										

Figure 2–92

Cases and Places

Apply your creative thinking and problem solving skills to design and implement a solution.

● EASIER   ●● MORE DIFFICULT

● 1: Design and Create a Weight-Loss Plan Worksheet

As a summer intern working for Choose to Lose, a local weight-loss clinic, you have been asked to create a worksheet that estimates the monthly weight lost for an individual based on recommended average daily activities. You have been given the numbers of calories burned per hour and the average number of hours for each activity (Table 2–11). Use the following formulas:

Formula A: Total Calories Burned per Day = Calories burned per Hour × Average Hours Daily

Formula B: Total Pounds Lost per Month (30 days) = 30 × Total Calories Burned per Day / 3500

Formula C: Average function

Formula D: Max function

Formula E: Min function

Use the concepts and techniques presented in this project to create and format the worksheet. Include an embedded 3-D Pie chart that shows the contribution of each activity to the total calories burned per day. Use Microsoft Excel Help to create a professional looking 3-D Pie chart with title and data labels.

Table 2–11 Activities with Corresponding Calories Burned per Hour and Worksheet Layout				
Activity	**Calories Burned per Hour**	**Average Hours Daily**	**Total Calories Burned per Day**	**Total Pounds Lost per Month (30 Days)**
Aerobics class	450	0.50	Formula A	Formula B
Brisk walking	350	0.50		
House work	150	1.00		
Office work/sitting	120	6.00		
Sleeping	70	9.00		
Standing	105	2.00		
Swimming	290	0.50		
Tennis	315	0.25		
Walking	240	4.25		
Totals	—		—	—
Average	Formula C			
Highest	Formula D			
Lowest	Formula E			

• 2: Create a Profit Potential Worksheet

You work part-time for Doze-Now, a retailer of sleep-related products. Your manager wants to know the profit potential of their inventory based on the categories of inventory in Table 2–12. Table 2–12 contains the format of the desired report. The required formulas are shown in Table 2–13. Use the concepts and techniques developed in this project to create and format the worksheet. Submit a printout of the values version and formulas version of the worksheet. The company just received a shipment of 175 additional comforters and 273 items of sleepwear. Update the appropriate cells in the Units on Hand column.

Table 2–12 Doze-Now Profit Potential Data and Worksheet Layout

Item	Units on Hand	Average Unit Cost	Total Cost	Average Unit Price	Total Value	Potential Profit
Comforters	216	46.52	Formula A	Formula B	Formula C	Formula D
Night lights	4,283	6.89				
Pillows	691	47.64				
Sleep sound machines	103	45.06				
Sleepwear	489	16.77				
Total	—		—	—	—	—
Average	Formula E					
Lowest	Formula F					
Highest	Formula G					

Table 2–13 Doze-Now Profit Potential Formulas

Formula A = Units on Hand * Average Unit Cost

Formula B = Average Unit Cost * (1 / (1 − .58))

Formula C = Units on Hand * Average Unit Price

Formula D = Total Value − Total Cost

Formula E = AVERAGE function

Formula F = MIN function

Formula G = MAX function

Continued >

Cases and Places *continued*

•• 3: Create a Fund-Raising Analysis Worksheet

You are the chairperson of the fund-raising committee for a local charity. You want to compare various fund-raising ideas to determine which will give you the best profit. The data obtained from six businesses about their products and the format of the desired report are shown in Table 2–14. The required formulas are shown in Table 2–15. Use the concepts and techniques presented in this project to create and format the worksheet.

Table 2–14 Fund-Raising Data and Worksheet Layout

Product	Company	Cost per Unit	Margin	Selling Price	Profit per 2000 Sales	Profit per 5000 Sales
Candles	Woodland Farms	$4.75	40%	Formula A	Formula B	Formula C
Candy	Polkandy	3.00	70%			
Coffee	Garcia Coffee	6.50	45%			
Cookie dough	Oh, Dough!	2.90	65%			
Flower bulbs	Early Bloom	2.40	50%			
T-shirts	Zed's Sports	5.75	42%			
Minimum		Formula D				
Maximum		Formula E				

Table 2–15 Band Fund-Raising Formulas

Formula A = Cost per Unit / (1 – Margin)

Formula B = 2000 * (Selling Price – Cost per Unit)

Formula C = 5000 *110% * (Selling Price – Cost per Unit)

Formula D = MIN function

Formula E = MAX function

•• 4: Design and Create a Projected Budget

Make It Personal

For the next six-month period, forecast your income for each month, your base expenditures for each month, and your special expenditures for each month. Base expenditures include expenses that occur each month, such as food and loan payments. Special expenditures include expenses that are out of the ordinary, such as the purchase of gifts, automobile insurance, and medical expenses. With this data, develop a worksheet calculating the amount of remaining money at the end of each month. You can determine this amount by subtracting both expenses from the anticipated income.

Include a total, average value, highest value, and lowest value for income, base expenditures, special expenditures, and remaining money. Use the concepts and techniques presented in this project to create and format the worksheet.

Create a 3-D Pie chart on a separate sheet illustrating the portion each month's special expenditures deducts from the total remaining money after all six months have passed. Use Microsoft Excel Help to create a professional looking 3-D Pie chart with title and data labels.

•• 5: Design and Create a Stock Analysis Worksheet

Working Together

Have each member of your team select six stocks — two bank stocks, two communications stocks, and two Internet stocks. Each member should submit the stock names, stock symbols, and an approximate six-month-old price. Create a worksheet that lists the stock names, symbols, price, and number of shares for each stock (use 350 shares as the number of shares for all stocks). Format the worksheet so that it has a professional appearance and is as informative as possible.

Have the group do research on the use of 3-D references, which is a reference to a range that spans two or more worksheets in a workbook (use Microsoft Excel Help). Use what the group learns to create a Web query on the Sheet2 worksheet by referencing the stock symbols on the Sheet1 worksheet. On the Sheet1 worksheet, change the cells that list current price per share numbers on the Sheet1 worksheet so that they use 3-D cell references that refer to the worksheet created by the Web query on the Sheet2 worksheet. Present your workbook and findings to the class.

3 | What-If Analysis, Charting, and Working with Large Worksheets

Objectives

You will have mastered the material in this chapter when you can:

- Rotate text in a cell
- Create a series of month names
- Copy, paste, insert, and delete cells
- Format numbers using format symbols
- Freeze and unfreeze titles
- Show and format the system date
- Use absolute cell references in a formula
- Use the IF function to perform a logical test

- Use the Format Painter button to format cells
- Create a 3-D Pie chart on a separate chart sheet
- Color and rearrange worksheet tabs
- Change the worksheet view
- Answer what-if questions
- Goal seek to answer what-if questions

3 | What-If Analysis, Charting, and Working with Large Worksheets

Introduction

Worksheets normally are much larger than those created in the previous chapters, often extending beyond the size of the window. Because you cannot see the entire worksheet on the screen at one time, working with a large worksheet sometimes can be frustrating. This chapter introduces several Excel commands that allow you to control what displays on the screen so you can view critical parts of a large worksheet at one time. One command lets you freeze the row and column titles so Excel always displays them on the screen. Another command splits the worksheet into separate window panes so you can view different parts of a worksheet on the screen at one time. Hiding the Ribbon will allow a larger portion of the worksheet to be visible.

When you set up a worksheet, you should use cell references in formulas whenever possible, rather than constant values. The use of a cell reference allows you to change a value in multiple formulas by changing the value in a single cell. The cell references in a formula are called assumptions. Assumptions are values in cells that you can change to determine new values for formulas. This chapter emphasizes the use of assumptions and shows how to use Excel to answer what-if questions such as, what happens to the semi-annual operating income if you decrease the marketing expenses assumption by 2%? Being able to analyze quickly the effect of changing values in a worksheet is an important skill in making business decisions.

This chapter also introduces you to techniques that will enhance your ability to create worksheets and draw charts. From your work in Chapter 1, you are aware of how easily you can create charts. This chapter covers additional charting techniques that allow you to convey your message in a dramatic pictorial fashion such as an exploded 3-D Pie chart. This chapter also covers other methods for entering values in cells, such as allowing Excel to enter values for you based on a pattern of values that you create, and formatting these values. In addition, you will learn how to use absolute cell references and how to use the IF function to assign a value to a cell based on a logical test.

Project — Financial Projection Worksheet with What-If Analysis and Chart

The project in the chapter follows proper design guidelines and uses Excel to create the worksheet and pie chart shown in Figure 3–1. Campus Clothiers manufactures and sells customized clothing to college students on campuses around the country. Each June and December, the director of finance and accounting submits a plan to the management team to show projected monthly revenues, costs of goods, gross margin, expenses, and operating income for the next six months. The director requires an easy-to-read worksheet that shows financial projections for the next six months. The worksheet should allow for quick analysis if projections for certain numbers change, such as the percentage of expenses allocated to marketing. In addition, a 3-D Pie chart is required that shows the projected operating income contribution for each of the six months.

Walk and Rock Music 1st Quarter Sales - (Autosaved) - M

Home   Insert   Page Layout   Formulas   Data   Review   View

	A	B	C	D	E	F	G	H
1	**Campus Clothiers**							
2	Semiannual Projected Gross Margin, Expenses, and Operating Income							11/5/2008
3		January	February	March	April	May	June	Total
4	Sales	$3,383,909.82	$6,880,576.15	$9,742,702.37	$4,818,493.53	$4,566,722.63	$8,527,504.39	$37,919,908.89
5	Cost of Goods Sold	1,319,724.83	2,683,424.70	3,799,653.92	1,879,212.48	1,781,021.83	3,325,726.71	14,788,764.47
6	Gross Margin	$2,064,184.99	$4,197,151.45	$5,943,048.45	$2,939,281.05	$2,785,700.80	$5,201,777.68	$23,131,144.42
7								
8	Expenses							
9	Bonus	$0.00	$100,000.00	$100,000.00	$100,000.00	$0.00	$100,000.00	$400,000.00
10	Commission	109,977.07	223,618.72	316,637.83	156,601.04	148,418.49	277,143.89	1,232,397.04
11	Marketing	304,551.88	619,251.85	876,843.21	433,664.42	411,005.04	767,475.40	3,412,791.80
12	Research and Development	194,574.81	395,633.13	560,205.39	277,063.38	262,586.55	490,331.50	2,180,394.76
13	Support, General, and Administrative	575,264.67	1,169,697.95	1,656,259.40	819,143.90	776,342.85	1,449,675.75	6,446,384.51
14	Total Expenses	$1,184,368.44	$2,508,201.65	$3,509,945.83	$1,786,472.74	$1,598,352.92	$3,084,626.54	$13,671,968.11
15								
16	Operating Income	$879,816.55	$1,688,949.80	$2,433,102.62	$1,152,808.32	$1,187,347.88	$2,117,151.14	$9,459,176.31
17								
18	*What-if Assumptions*							
19	Bonus	100,000.00						
20	Commission	3.25%						
21	Margin	61.00%						
22	Marketing	9.00%						
23	Research and Development	5.75%						
24	Revenue for Bonus	4,750,000.00						
25	Support, General, and Administrative	17.00%						
26								

(a) Worksheet

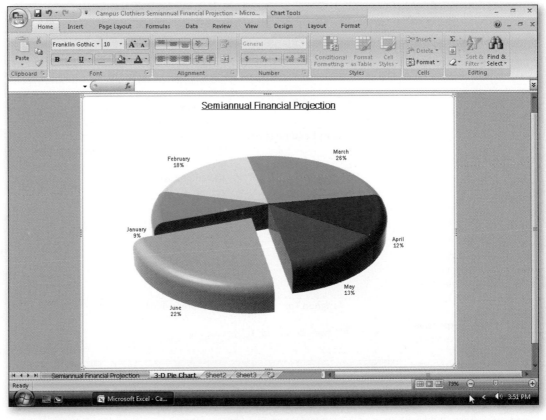

(b) 3-D Pie Chart

Figure 3–1

BTW

Correctness
Studies have shown that more than 25 percent of all business worksheets have errors. If you are not careful entering data and formulas, then your worksheet is prone to errors. You can ensure correctness in your formulas by carefully checking them using Range Finder. The Formula Auditing group on the Formulas tab on the Ribbon also can be helpful when verifying formulas.

The requirements document for the Campus Clothiers Semiannual Financial Projection worksheet is shown in Figure 3–2. It includes the needs, source of data, summary of calculations, chart requirements, and other facts about its development.

REQUEST FOR NEW WORKBOOK

Date Submitted:	October 27, 2008
Submitted By:	Norm Armand
Worksheet Title:	Campus Clothiers Semiannual Projected Gross Margin, Expenses, and Operating Income
Needs:	The needs are: (1) a worksheet (Figure 3-3a) that shows Campus Clothiers's projected monthly sales, cost of goods, gross margin, expenses, and operating income for a six-month period; and (2) a 3-D Pie chart (Figure 3-3b) that shows the projected contribution of each month's operating income to the six-month period operating income.
Source of Data:	The data supplied by the Finance department includes projections of the monthly sales and expenses (Table 3-1) that are based on prior years. All the remaining numbers in the worksheet are determined from these 13 numbers using formulas.
Calculations:	The following calculations must be made for each month: 1. Cost of Goods = Sales – Sales * Margin 2. Gross Margin = Sales – Cost of Goods 3. Bonus Expense = $100,000.00 if the Sales exceeds the Revenue for Bonus; otherwise Bonus Expense = 0 4. Commission Expense = Commission Assumption * Sales 5. Marketing Expense = Marketing Assumption * Sales 6. Research and Development = Research and Development Assumption * Sales 7. Support, General, and Administrative Expense = Support, General, and Administrative Assumption * Sales 8. Total Expenses = Sum of Expenses 9. Operating Income = Gross Margin – Total Expenses
Chart Requirements:	A 3-D Pie chart is required on a separate sheet (Figure 3-3b) to show the contribution of each month's operating income to the six-month period operating income. The chart should also emphasize the month with the greatest operating income.

Approvals

Approval Status:	X	Approved
		Rejected
Approved By:		Shauna Hendricks, CFO
Date:		November 1, 2008
Assigned To:		J. Quasney, Spreadsheet Specialist

Figure 3–2

BTW

Excel's Usefulness
Just a few short years ago, a what-if question of any complexity only could be answered using a large, expensive computer programmed by highly paid computer professionals. Generating a result could take days. Excel gives the noncomputer professional the ability to get complex business-related questions answered instantaneously and economically.

Overview

As you read this chapter, you will learn how to create the worksheet shown in Figure 3–1 by performing these general tasks:

- Create a series of month names
- Use absolute cell references in a formula
- Use the IF function to perform a logical test
- Use the Format Painter button to format cells
- Create a 3-D Pie chart on a separate chart sheet
- Answer what-if questions
- Manipulate large worksheets

Plan Ahead

General Project Decisions

While creating an Excel worksheet, you need to make several decisions that will determine the appearance and characteristics of the finished worksheet. As you create the worksheet required to meet the requirements shown in Figure 3–2, you should follow these general guidelines:

1. Plan the layout of the worksheet. The requirements state that six months are necessary in the worksheet. It is therefore sensible to place the months across columns so that the financial headings can be placed in rows. The what-if assumptions should not clutter the worksheet, but they should be placed in an easily located portion of the worksheet.

2. Determine the necessary formulas and functions needed. Except for the monthly sales numbers, the remaining numbers in the main portion of the worksheet are calculated based on the numbers in the what-if portion of the worksheet. The formulas are stated in the requirements document (Figure 3–2). The Bonus expense is included only if a certain condition is met. A function can check for the condition and include the bonus when necessary.

3. Identify how to format various elements of the worksheet. Sales and Expenses are two distinct categories of financial data and should be separated visually. Gross Margin and Total Expenses should stand out because they are subtotals. The Operating Income is the key piece of information being calculated in the worksheet and, therefore, should be formatted in such a manner as to draw the reader's attention. The what-if assumptions should be formatted in a manner which indicates that they are separate from the main area of the worksheet.

4. Specify how the chart should convey necessary information. The requirements document indicates that the chart should be a 3-D Pie chart and emphasize the month with the greatest operating income. A 3-D Pie chart is a good way to compare visually a small set of numbers. The month, which is emphasized, also should appear closer to the reader in order to draw the reader's attention.

5. Perform what-if analysis and goal seeking using the best techniques. What-if analysis allows you quickly to answer questions regarding various predictions. In Campus Clothiers Semiannual Financial Projection worksheet, the only cells that you should change when performing what-if analysis are those in the what-if portion of the worksheet. All other values in the worksheet, except for the projected sales, are calculated. Goal seeking allows you automatically to modify values in the what-if area of the worksheet based on a goal that you have for another cell in the worksheet.

(continued)

Plan Ahead

(continued)

In addition, using a sketch of the worksheet can help you visualize its design. The sketch of the worksheet (Figure 3-3a) consists of titles, column and row headings, location of data values, calculations, and a rough idea of the desired formatting. The sketch of the 3-D Pie chart (Figure 3–3b) shows the expected contribution of each month's operating income to the semiannual operating income. The projected monthly sales will be entered in row 4 of the worksheet. The assumptions will be entered below the operating income (Figure 3–3a). The projected monthly sales and the assumptions will be used to calculate the remaining numbers in the worksheet.

When necessary, more specific details concerning the above guidelines are presented at appropriate points in the chapter. The chapter also will identify the actions you perform and decisions made regarding these guidelines during the creation of the worksheet shown in Figure 3–1 on page EX 163.

(a) Worksheet

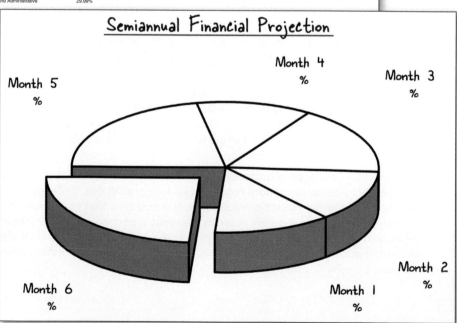

(b) 3-D Pie Chart

Figure 3–3

With a good understanding of the requirements document, an understanding of the necessary decisions, and a sketch of the worksheet, the next step is to use Excel to create the worksheet.

Table 3–1 Campus Clothiers Semiannual Financial Projections Data and What-If Assumptions	
Projected Monthly Total Net Revenues	
January	$3,383,909.82
February	6,880,576.15
March	9,742,702.37
April	4,818,493.53
May	4,566,722.63
June	8,527,504.39
What-If Assumptions	
Bonus	$100,000.00
Commission	3.25%
Margin	61.00%
Marketing	9.00%
Research and Development	5.75%
Revenue for Bonus	$4,750,000.00
Support, General, and Administrative	17.00%

To Start Excel

If you are using a computer to step through the project in this chapter and you want your screen to match the figures in this book, you should change your computer's resolution to 1024 × 768. For information about how to change a computer's resolution, see page APP 36 in Appendix E.

The following steps, which assume Windows Vista is running, start Excel based on a typical installation of Microsoft Office on your computer. You may need to ask your instructor how to start Excel for your computer.

Note: If you are using Windows XP, see Appendix F for alternate steps.

1 Click the Start button on the Windows Vista taskbar to display the Start menu.

2 Click All Programs at the bottom of the left pane on the Start menu to display the All Programs list.

3 Click Microsoft Office in the All Programs list to display the Microsoft Office list.

4 Click Microsoft Office Excel 2007 to start Excel and display a blank worksheet in the Excel window.

5 If the Excel window is not maximized, click the Maximize button next to the Close button on its title bar to maximize the window.

6 If the worksheet window in Excel is not maximized, click the Maximize button next to the Close button on its title bar to maximize the worksheet window within Excel.

To Enter the Worksheet Titles, Change Workbook Properties, Apply a Theme, and Save the Workbook

The worksheet contains two titles, one in cell A1 and another in cell A2. In the previous chapters, titles were centered across the worksheet. With large worksheets that extend beyond the size of a window, it is best to enter titles in the upper-left corner as shown in the sketch of the worksheet in Figure 3–3a. The following steps enter the worksheet titles and save the workbook.

1 Click cell A1 and then enter `Campus Clothiers` as the worksheet title.

2 Click cell A2 and then enter `Semiannual Projected Gross Margin, Expenses, and Operating Income` as the worksheet subtitle and then press the ENTER key.

3 Click the Office Button, click Prepare on the Office Button menu, and then click Properties.

4 Update the document properties with your name and any other relevant information.

5 Click the Close button in the Document Properties pane.

6 Apply the Trek theme to the worksheet by clicking the Themes button on the Page Layout tab on the Ribbon and then return to the Home tab on the Ribbon.

7 With a USB flash drive connected to one of the computer's USB ports, click the Save button on the Quick Access Toolbar.

8 When Excel displays the Save As dialog box, type `Campus Clothiers Semiannual Financial Projection` in the File name text box.

9 If the Folders list is displayed below the Folders button, click the Folders button to remove the Folders list.

10 If Computer is not displayed in the Favorite Links section, drag the top or bottom edge of the Save As dialog box until Computer is displayed.

11 Click Computer in the Favorite Links section. If necessary, scroll until UDISK 2.0 (E:) appears in the list of available drives. Double-click UDISK 2.0 (E:) (your USB flash drive may have a different name and letter). Click the Save button in the Save As dialog box to save the workbook.

Note: If you are using Windows XP, see Appendix F for alternate steps.

BTW

Rotating Text in a Cell
In Excel, you use the Alignment sheet of the Format Cells dialog box, as shown in Figure 3–5, to position data in a cell by centering, left-aligning, or right-aligning; indenting; aligning at the top, bottom, or center; and rotating. If you enter 90 in the Degrees box in the Orientation area, the text will appear vertically and read from bottom to top in the cell.

Rotating Text and Using the Fill Handle to Create a Series

The data on the worksheet, including month names and the What-If Assumptions section, now can be added to the worksheet.

Plan Ahead

> **Plan the layout of the worksheet.**
> The design of the worksheet calls specifically for only six months of data. Because there always will be only six months of data in the worksheet, the months should be placed across the top of the worksheet as column headings rather than as row headings. There are more data items regarding each month than there are months, and it is possible that more expense categories could be added in the future. A proper layout, therefore, includes placing the data items for each month as row headings. The What-If Assumptions section should be placed in an area of the worksheet that is easily accessible, yet does not impair the view of the main section of the worksheet. As shown in Figure 3–3a, the What-If Assumptions should be placed below the calculations in the worksheet.

When you first enter text, its angle is zero degrees (0°), and it reads from left to right in a cell. Text in a cell can be rotated counterclockwise by entering a number between 1° and 90° in the Alignment sheet in the Format Cells dialog box.

To Rotate Text and Use the Fill Handle to Create a Series of Month Names

Chapters 1 and 2 used the fill handle to copy a cell or a range of cells to adjacent cells. The fill handle also can be used to create a series of numbers, dates, or month names automatically. The following steps enter the month name, January, in cell B3; format cell B3 (including rotating the text); and then use the fill handle to enter the remaining month names in the range C3:G3.

- Select cell B3.

- Type `January` as the cell entry and then click the Enter box.

- Click the Format Cells: Alignment Dialog Box Launcher on the Ribbon to display the Format Cells dialog box (Figure 3– 4).

Figure 3–4

- Click the 45° point in the Orientation area to move the Text hand in the Orientation area to the 45° point and to display 45 in the Degrees box (Figure 3–5).

Figure 3–5

- Click the OK button to rotate the text in cell B3 at a 45° angle and automatically increase the height of row 3 to best fit the rotated text (Figure 3–6).

- Point to the fill handle on the lower-right corner of cell B3.

Figure 3–6

4

- Drag the fill handle to the right to select the range C3:G3. Do not release the mouse button (Figure 3–7).

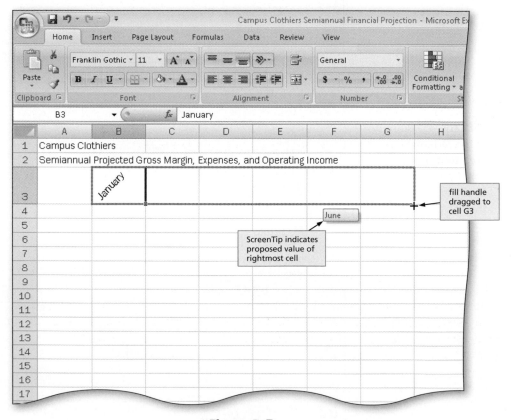

Figure 3–7

5

- Release the mouse button to create a month name series January through June in the range B3:G3 and copy the format in cell B3 to the range C3:G3.

- Click the Auto Fill Options button below the lower-right corner of the fill area to display the Auto Fill Options menu (Figure 3–8).

What if I do not want to copy the format of cell B3 during the auto fill operation?

In addition to creating a series of values, dragging the fill handle instructs Excel to copy the format of cell B3 to the range C3:G3. With some fill operations, you may not want to copy the formats of the source cell or range to the destination cell or range. If this is the case, click the Auto Fill Options button after the range fills (Figure 3–8) and then select the option you desire on the Auto Fill Options menu.

Figure 3–8

6

- Click the Auto Fill Options button to hide the Auto Fill Options menu.

- Click cell H3, type `Total`, and then press the RIGHT ARROW key.

Q&A Why is the word Total automatically formatted with the Heading 3 cell style and 45° rotation?

Excel tries to save you time by automatically recognizing the adjacent cell format in cell G3 and applying it to cell H3. The Heading 3 cell style in cell G3 causes this action to occur.

Using the Auto Fill Options Menu

As shown in Figure 3–8, Fill Series is the default option that Excel uses to fill the area, which means it fills the destination area with a series, using the same formatting as the source area. If you choose another option on the Auto Fill Options menu, then Excel immediately changes the contents of the destination range. Following the use of the fill handle, the Auto Fill Options button remains active until you begin the next Excel operation. Table 3–2 summarizes the options on the Auto Fill Options menu.

Other Ways

1. Enter start month in cell, apply formatting, right-drag fill handle in direction to fill, click Fill Months on shortcut menu

2. Enter start month in cell, apply formatting, select range, click Fill button on Home tab on Ribbon, click Series, click AutoFill

BTW

The Mighty Fill Handle
If you drag the fill handle to the left or up, Excel will decrement the series rather than increment the series. To copy a word, such as January or Monday, which Excel might interpret as the start of a series, hold down the CTRL key while you drag the fill handle to a destination area. If you drag the fill handle back into the middle of a cell, Excel erases the contents.

Table 3–2 Options Available on the Auto Fill Options Menu

Auto Fill Option	Description
Copy Cells	Fill destination area with contents using format of source area. Do not create a series.
Fill Series	Fill destination area with series using format of source area. This option is the default.
Fill Formatting Only	Fill destination area using format of source area. No content is copied unless fill is series.
Fill Without Formatting	Fill destination area with contents, without the formatting of source area.
Fill Months	Fill destination area with series of months using format of source area. Same as Fill Series and shows as an option only if source area contains a month.

You can use the fill handle to create a series longer than the one shown in Figure 3–8. If you drag the fill handle past cell G3 in Step 4, Excel continues to increment the months and logically will repeat January, February, and so on, if you extend the range far enough to the right.

You can create several different types of series using the fill handle. Table 3–3 illustrates several examples. Notice in examples 4 through 7, 9, and 11 that, if you use the fill handle to create a series of numbers or nonsequential months, you must enter the first item in the series in one cell and the second item in the series in an adjacent cell. Next, select both cells and drag the fill handle through the destination area.

Table 3–3 Examples of Series Using the Fill Handle

Example	Contents of Cell(s) Copied Using the Fill Handle	Next Three Values of Extended Series
1	2:00	3:00, 4:00, 5:00
2	Qtr3	Qtr4, Qtr1, Qtr2
3	Quarter 1	Quarter 2, Quarter 3, Quarter 4
4	5-Jan, 5-Mar	5-May, 5-Jul, 5-Sep
5	2007, 2008	2009, 2010, 2011
6	1, 2	3, 4, 5
7	430, 410	390, 370, 350
8	Sun	Mon, Tue, Wed
9	Sunday, Tuesday	Thursday, Saturday, Monday
10	4th Section	5th Section, 6th Section, 7th Section
11	−205, −208	−211, −214, −217

To Increase Column Widths and Enter Row Titles

In Chapter 2, the column widths were increased after the values were entered into the worksheet. Sometimes, you may want to increase the column widths before you enter the values and, if necessary, adjust them later. The following steps increase the column widths and then enter the row titles in column A down to What-If Assumptions in cell A18.

- Move the mouse pointer to the boundary between column heading A and column heading B so that the mouse pointer changes to a split double arrow.

- Drag the mouse pointer to the right until the ScreenTip displays, Width: 35.00 (322 pixels). Do not release the mouse button (Figure 3–9).

Figure 3–9

- Release the mouse button to change the width of column A.

- Click column heading B and then drag through column heading G to select columns B through G.

- Move the mouse pointer to the boundary between column headings B and C and then drag the mouse to the right until the ScreenTip displays, Width: 14.00 (133 pixels). Do not release the mouse button (Figure 3–10).

Figure 3–10

3

- Release the mouse button to change the width of columns B through G.

- Use the technique described in Step 1 to increase the width of column H to 15.00.

- Enter the row titles in the range A4:A18 as shown in Figure 3–11, but without the indents.

- Click cell A5 and then click the Increase Indent button on the Ribbon.

- Select the range A9:A13 and then click the Increase Indent button on the Ribbon.

- Click cell A19 to finish entering the row titles (Figure 3–11).

Q&A

What happens when I click the Increase Indent button?

The Increase Indent button indents the contents of a cell to the right by three spaces each time you click it. The Decrease Indent button decreases the indent by three spaces each time you click it.

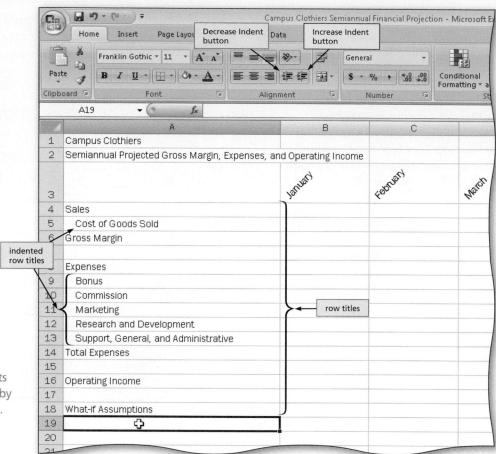

Figure 3–11

Other Ways

1. To indent, right-click range, click Format Cells on shortcut menu, click Alignment tab, click Left (Indent) in Horizontal list, type number of spaces to indent in Indent text box, click OK button

BTW

Fitting Entries in a Cell
An alternative to increasing the column widths or row heights is to shrink the characters in the cell to fit the current width of the column. To shrink to fit, click Format Cells: Alignment Dialog Box Launcher on the Ribbon, and click Shrink to fit in the Text control area. After shrinking entries to fit in a cell, consider using the Zoom slider on the status bar to make the entries more readable.

Copying a Range of Cells to a Nonadjacent Destination Area

As shown in the sketch of the worksheet (Figure 3–3a on page EX 166), the row titles in the Expenses area are the same as the row titles in the What-If Assumptions table, with the exception of the two additional entries in cells A21 (Margin) and A24 (Revenue for Bonus). Hence, the What-If Assumptions table row titles can be created by copying the range A9:A13 to the range A19:A23 and then inserting two rows for the additional entries in cells A21 and A24. The source area (range A9:A13) is not adjacent to the destination area (range A19:A23). The first two chapters used the fill handle to copy a source area to an adjacent destination area. To copy a source area to a nonadjacent destination area, however, you cannot use the fill handle.

A more versatile method of copying a source area is to use the Copy button and Paste button on the Home tab on the Ribbon. You can use these two buttons to copy a source area to an adjacent or nonadjacent destination area.

The Copy button copies the contents and format of the source area to the **Office Clipboard**, a reserved place in the computer's memory that allows you to collect text and graphic items from an Office document and then paste them into any Office document. The Copy command on the Edit menu or shortcut menu works the same as the Copy button. The Paste button copies the item from the Office Clipboard to the destination area.

To Copy a Range of Cells to a Nonadjacent Destination Area

The following steps use the Copy and Paste buttons to copy the range A9:A13 to the nonadjacent range A19:A23.

1

- Select the range A9:A13 and then click the Copy button on the Home tab on the Ribbon to copy the values and formats of the range A9:A13 to the Office Clipboard.

- Click cell A19, the top cell in the destination area (Figure 3–12).

Q&A

Why do I not need to select the entire destination area?

You are not required to select the entire destination area (range A19:A23) before clicking the Paste button. Excel needs to know only the upper-left cell of the destination area. In the case of a single column range, such as A19:A23, the top cell of the destination area (cell A19) also is the upper-left cell of the destination area.

Figure 3–12

2

- Click the Paste button on the Ribbon to copy the values and formats of the last item placed on the Office Clipboard (range A9:A13) to the destination area A19:A23.

- Scroll down so row 5 appears at the top of the window (Figure 3–13).

Q&A

What if data already existed in the destination area?

When you complete a copy, the values and formats in the destination area are replaced with the values and formats of the source area. Any data contained in the destination area prior to the copy and paste is lost. If you accidentally delete valuable data, immediately click the Undo button on the Quick Access Toolbar.

3

- Press the ESC key to remove the marquee from the source area and disable the Paste button on the Ribbon.

Figure 3–13

Other Ways

1. Right-click source area, click Copy on shortcut menu, right-click destination area, click Paste on shortcut menu

2. Select source area and point on border of range; while holding down CTRL key, drag source area to destination area

3. Select source area, press CTRL+C, select destination area, press CTRL+V

Using the Paste Options Menu

After the Paste button is clicked, Excel immediately displays the Paste Options button, as shown in Figure 3–13. If you click the Paste Options button arrow and select an option on the Paste Options menu, Excel modifies the most recent paste operation based on your selection. Table 3–4 summarizes the options available on the Paste Options menu.

Table 3–4 Options Available on the Paste Options Menu

Paste Option	Description
Keep Source Formatting	Copy contents and format of source area. This option is the default.
Match Destination Formatting	Copy contents of source area, but not the format.
Values and Number Formatting	Copy contents and format of source area for numbers or formulas, but use format of destination area for text.
Keep Source Column Widths	Copy contents and format of source area. Change destination column widths to source column widths.
Formatting Only	Copy format of source area, but not the contents.
Link Cells	Copy contents and format and link cells so that a change to the cells in source area updates the corresponding cells in destination area.

The Paste button on the Ribbon (Figure 3–13) includes an arrow, which displays a list of advanced paste options (Paste, Paste Special, and Paste as Hyperlink). These options will be discussed when they are used.

An alternative to clicking the Paste button is to press the ENTER key. The ENTER key completes the paste operation, removes the marquee from the source area, and disables the Paste button so that you cannot paste the copied source area to other destination areas. The ENTER key was not used in the previous set of steps so that the capabilities of the Paste Options button could be discussed. The Paste Options button does not appear on the screen when you use the ENTER key to complete the paste operation.

Using Drag and Drop to Move or Copy Cells

You also can use the mouse to move or copy cells. First, you select the source area and point to the border of the cell or range. You know you are pointing to the border of the cell or range when the mouse pointer changes to a block arrow. To move the selected cell or cells, drag the selection to the destination area. To copy a selection, hold down the CTRL key while dragging the selection to the destination area. You know Excel is in copy mode when a small plus sign appears next to the block arrow mouse pointer. Be sure to release the mouse button before you release the CTRL key. Using the mouse to move or copy cells is called **drag and drop**.

Using Cut and Paste to Move Cells

Another way to move cells is to select them, click the Cut button on the Ribbon (Figure 3–12 on page EX 175) to remove them from the worksheet and copy them to the Office Clipboard, select the destination area, and then click the Paste button on the Ribbon or press the ENTER key. You also can use the Cut command on the shortcut menu, instead of the Cut button.

Inserting and Deleting Cells in a Worksheet

At any time while the worksheet is on the screen, you can insert cells to enter new data or delete cells to remove unwanted data. You can insert or delete individual cells; a range of cells, rows, columns; or entire worksheets.

To Insert a Row

The Insert command on the shortcut menu allows you to insert rows between rows that already contain data. According to the sketch of the worksheet in Figure 3–3a on page EX 166, two rows must be inserted in the What-If Assumptions table, one between Commission and Marketing for the Margin assumption and another between Research and Development and Support, General, and Administrative for the Revenue for Bonus assumption. The following steps accomplish the task of inserting the new rows into the worksheet.

BTW

Move It or Copy It
You may hear someone say, "Move it or copy it, it's all the same." No, it is not the same! When you move a cell, the data in the original location is cleared and the format is reset to the default. When you copy a cell, the data and format of the copy area remain intact. In short, you should copy cells to duplicate entries and move cells to rearrange entries.

BTW

Cutting
When you cut a cell or range of cells using the Cut command or Cut button, Excel copies the cells to the Office Clipboard, but does not remove the cells from the source area until you paste the cells in the destination area by clicking the Paste button or pressing the ENTER key. When you complete the paste, Excel clears the cell entry and its formats from the source area.

BTW

Inserting Multiple Rows
If you want to insert multiple rows, you have two choices. First, you can insert a single row by using the Insert command on the shortcut menu and then repeatedly press F4 to keep inserting rows. Alternatively, you can select any number of existing rows before inserting new rows. For instance, if you want to insert five rows, select five existing rows in the worksheet, right-click the rows, and then click Insert on the shortcut menu.

1

- Right-click row heading 21, the row below where you want to insert a row, to display the shortcut menu and the Mini toolbar (Figure 3–14).

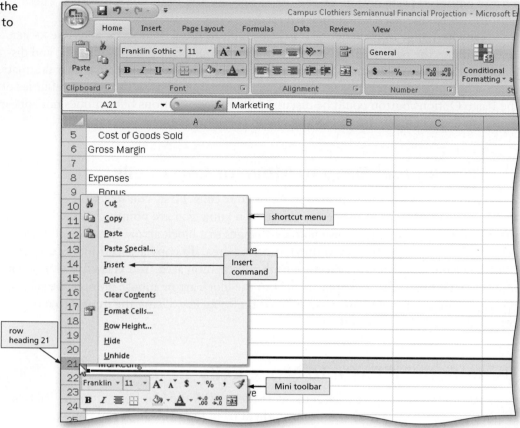

Figure 3–14

2

- Click Insert on the shortcut menu to insert a new row in the worksheet by shifting the selected row 21 and all rows below it down one row.

- Click cell A21 in the new row and then enter Margin as the row title (Figure 3–15).

Q&A

What is the resulting format of the new row?

The cells in the new row inherit the formats of the cells in the row above them. You can change this by clicking the Insert Options button that appears immediately above the inserted row. Following the insertion of a row, the Insert Options button lets you select from the following options: (1) Format Same As Above; (2) Format Same As Below; and (3) Clear Formatting. The Format Same as Above option is the default. The Insert Options button remains active until you begin the next Excel operation.

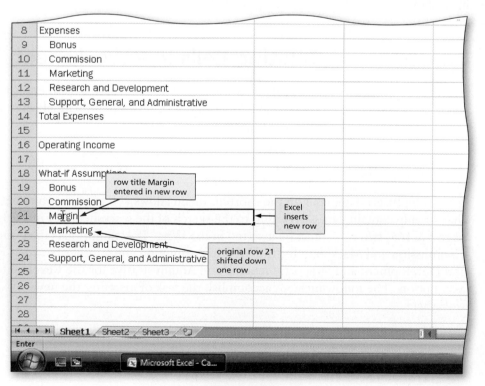

Figure 3–15

3

- Right-click row heading 24 and then click Insert on the shortcut menu to insert a new row in the worksheet.

- Click cell A24 in the new row and then enter `Revenue for Bonus` as the row title (Figure 3–16).

Q&A

What would happen if cells in the shifted rows are included in formulas?

If the rows that are shifted down include cell references in formulas located in the worksheet, Excel automatically adjusts the cell references in the formulas to their new locations. Thus, in Step 2, if a formula in the worksheet references a cell in row 21 before the insert, then the cell reference in the formula is adjusted to row 22 after the insert.

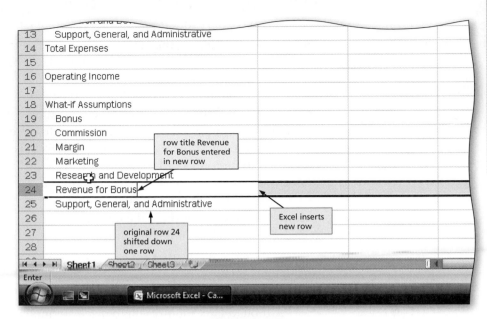

Figure 3–16

Other Ways
1. On Home tab on Ribbon, click Insert, click Insert Sheet Rows	2. Press CTRL+SHIFT+PLUS SIGN, click Entire Row, click OK button

Inserting Columns

You insert columns into a worksheet in the same way you insert rows. To insert columns, select one or more columns immediately to the right of where you want Excel to insert the new column or columns. Select the number of columns you want to insert. Next, click the Insert tab on the Ribbon and then click Insert Sheet Rows in the Insert gallery or click Insert on the shortcut menu. The Insert command on the shortcut menu requires that you select an entire column (or columns) to insert a column (or columns). Following the insertion of a column, Excel displays the Insert Options button, which allows you to modify the insertion in a fashion similar to that discussed earlier when inserting rows.

Inserting Single Cells or a Range of Cells

The Insert command on the shortcut menu or the Cells command on the Insert gallery of the Insert button on the Ribbon allows you to insert a single cell or a range of cells. You should be aware that if you shift a single cell or a range of cells, however, it no longer may be lined up with its associated cells. To ensure that the values in the worksheet do not get out of order, it is recommended that you insert only entire rows or entire columns. When you insert a single cell or a range of cells, Excel displays the Insert Options button so that you can change the format of the inserted cell, using options similar to those for inserting rows and columns.

BTW

Dragging Ranges
You can move and insert a selected cell or range between existing cells by holding down the SHIFT key while you drag the selection to the gridline where you want to insert. You also can copy and insert by holding down the CTRL+SHIFT keys while you drag the selection to the desired gridline.

BTW

The Insert Options Button
When you insert columns or rows, Excel only displays the Insert Options button if formats are assigned to the leftmost column or top row of the selection.

BTW

Ranges and Undo
Copying, deleting, inserting, and moving ranges of cells have the potential to render a worksheet useless. Carefully review these actions before continuing on to the next task. If you are not sure the action is correct, click the Undo button on the Quick Access Toolbar.

Deleting Columns and Rows

The Delete button on the Ribbon or the Delete command on the shortcut menu removes cells (including the data and format) from the worksheet. Deleting cells is not the same as clearing cells. The Clear command, which was described earlier in Chapter 1 on page EX 66, clears the data from the cells, but the cells remain in the worksheet. The Delete command removes the cells from the worksheet and shifts the remaining rows up (when you delete rows) or shifts the remaining columns to the left (when you delete columns). If formulas located in other cells reference cells in the deleted row or column, Excel does not adjust these cell references. Excel displays the error message **#REF!** in those cells to indicate a cell reference error. For example, if cell A7 contains the formula =A4+A5 and you delete row 5, Excel assigns the formula =A4+#REF! to cell A6 (originally cell A7) and displays the error message #REF! in cell A6. It also displays an Error Options button when you select the cell containing the error message #REF!, which allows you to select options to determine the nature of the problem.

Deleting Individual Cells or a Range of Cells

Although Excel allows you to delete an individual cell or range of cells, you should be aware that if you shift a cell or range of cells on the worksheet, it no longer may be lined up with its associated cells. For this reason, it is recommended that you delete only entire rows or entire columns.

Entering Numbers with Format Symbols

The next step in creating the Semiannual Financial Projection worksheet is to enter the what-if assumptions values in the range B19:B25. The numbers in the table can be entered and then formatted as in Chapters 1 and 2, or each one can be entered with format symbols. When a number is entered with a **format symbol**, Excel immediately displays it with the assigned format. Valid format symbols include the dollar sign ($), comma (,), and percent sign (%).

If you enter a whole number, it appears without any decimal places. If you enter a number with one or more decimal places and a format symbol, Excel displays the number with two decimal places. Table 3–5 illustrates several examples of numbers entered with format symbols. The number in parentheses in column 4 indicates the number of decimal places.

Table 3–5 Numbers Entered with Format Symbols			
Format Symbol	**Typed in Formula Bar**	**Displays in Cell**	**Comparable Format**
,	83,341	83,341	Comma (0)
	1,675.8	1,675.80	Comma (2)
$	$278	$278	Currency (0)
	$3818.54	$3,818.54	Currency (2)
	$45,612.3	$45,612.30	Currency (2)
%	23%	23%	Percent (0)
	97.50%	97.50%	Percent (2)
	39.833%	39.83%	Percent (2)

To Enter Numbers with Format Symbols

The following step enters the numbers in the What-If Assumptions table with format symbols.

1

- Enter 100,000.00 in cell B19, 3.25% in cell B20, 61.00% in cell B21, 9.00% in cell B22, 5.75% in cell B23, 4,750,000.00 in cell B24, and 17.00% in cell B25 to display the entries using a format based on the format symbols entered with the numbers (Figure 3–17).

Figure 3–17

Other Ways
1. Right-click range, click Format Cells on shortcut menu, click Number tab, click category in Category list, [select desired format], click OK button
2. Press CTRL+1, click Number tab, click category in Category list, [select desired format], click OK button

Freezing Worksheet Titles

Freezing worksheet titles is a useful technique for viewing large worksheets that extend beyond the window. Normally, when you scroll down or to the right, the column titles in row 3 and the row titles in column A that define the numbers no longer appear on the screen. This makes it difficult to remember what the numbers in these rows and columns represent. To alleviate this problem, Excel allows you to **freeze the titles**, so that Excel displays the titles on the screen, no matter how far down or to the right you scroll.

BTW

Freezing Titles
If you want to freeze only column headings, select the appropriate cell in column A before you click the Freeze Panes button on the View tab on the Ribbon. If you only want to freeze row titles, then select the appropriate cell in row 1. To freeze both column headings and row titles, select the cell that is the intersection of the column and row titles before you click the Freeze Panes button on the View tab on the Ribbon.

To Freeze Column and Row Titles

The following steps use the Freeze Panes button on the View tab on the Ribbon to freeze the worksheet title and column titles in rows 1, 2, and 3, and the row titles in column A.

1

- Press CTRL+HOME to select cell A1 and ensure that Excel displays row 1 and column A on the screen.

- Select cell B4.

- Click the View tab on the Ribbon and then click the Freeze Panes button on the Ribbon to display the Freeze Panes gallery (Figure 3–18).

Figure 3–18

Q&A

Why is cell A1 selected first?

Before freezing the titles, it is important that Excel displays cell A1 in the upper-left corner of the screen. For example, if cell B4 was selected without first selecting cell A1 to ensure Excel displays the upper-left corner of the screen, then Excel would freeze the titles and also hide rows 1 and 2. Excel thus would not be able to display rows 1 and 2 until they are unfrozen.

2

- Click Freeze Panes in the Freeze Panes gallery to freeze column A and rows 1 through 3 (Figure 3–19).

Q&A

What happens after I click the Freeze Panes command?

Excel displays a thin black line on the right side of column A, indicating the split between the frozen row titles in column A and the rest of the worksheet. It also displays a thin black line below row 3, indicating the split between the frozen column titles in rows 1 through 3 and the rest of the worksheet (Figure 3–19).

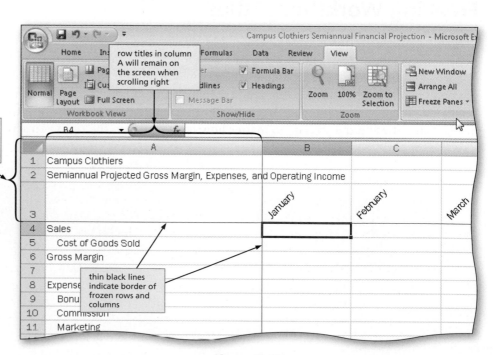

Figure 3–19

Other Ways
1. Press ALT+W, F

To Enter the Projected Monthly Sales

The following steps enter the projected monthly sales, listed earlier in Table 3–1 on page EX 167, in row 4 and compute the projected semiannual sales in cell H4.

1 If necessary, click the Home tab on the Ribbon.

2 Enter 3383909.82 in cell B4, 6880576.15 in cell C4, 9742702.37 in cell D4, 4818493.53 in cell E4, 4566722.63 in cell F4, and 8527504.39 in cell G4.

3 Click cell H4 and then click the Sum button on the Ribbon twice to total the semiannual sales in cell H4 (Figure 3–20).

BTW

Your Age in Days
How many days have you been alive? Enter today's date (e.g., 12/5/2008) in cell A1. Next, enter your birth date (e.g., 6/22/1986) in cell A2. Select cell A3 and enter the formula =A1 - A2. Format cell A3 to the General style using the Number Dialog Box Launcher. Cell A3 will display your age in days.

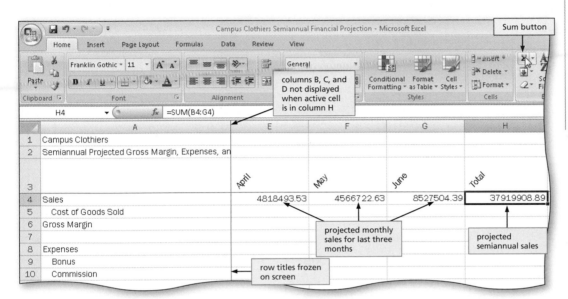

Figure 3–20

Displaying a System Date

The sketch of the worksheet in Figure 3–3a on page EX 166 includes a date stamp on the right side of the heading section. A **date stamp** shows the date a workbook, report, or other document was created or the period it represents. In business, a report often is meaningless without a date stamp. For example, if a printout of the worksheet in this chapter were distributed to the company's analysts, the date stamp would show when the six-month projections were made, as well as what period the report represents.

A simple way to create a date stamp is to use the NOW function to enter the system date tracked by your computer in a cell in the worksheet. The **NOW function** is one of 14 date and time functions available in Excel. When assigned to a cell, the NOW function returns a number that corresponds to the system date and time beginning with December 31, 1899. For example, January 1, 1900 equals 1, January 2, 1900 equals 2, and so on. Noon equals .5. Thus, noon on January 1, 1900 equals 1.5 and 6 P.M. on January 1, 1900 equals 1.75. If the computer's system date is set to the current date, which normally it is, then the date stamp is equivalent to the current date.

Excel automatically formats this number as a date, using the date and time format, mm/dd/yyyy hh:mm, where the first mm is the month, dd is the day of the month, yyyy is the year, hh is the hour of the day, and mm is the minutes past the hour.

BTW

Updating the System Date and Time
If the system date and time appear in an active worksheet, Excel will not update the date and time in the cell until you enter data in another cell or complete some other activity, such as undoing a previous activity or pressing function key F9.

To Enter and Format the System Date

The following steps enter the NOW function and change the format from mm/dd/yyyy hh:mm to mm/dd/yyyy.

- Click cell H2 and then click the Insert Function box in the formula bar.

- When Excel displays the Insert Function dialog box, click the 'Or select a category' box arrow, and then select Date & Time in the list.

- Scroll down in the Select a function list and then click NOW (Figure 3–21).

Figure 3–21

- Click the OK button.

- When Excel displays the Function Arguments dialog box, click the OK button to display the system date and time in cell H2, using the default date and time format mm/dd/yyyy hh:mm.

- Right-click cell H2 to display the shortcut menu (Figure 3–22).

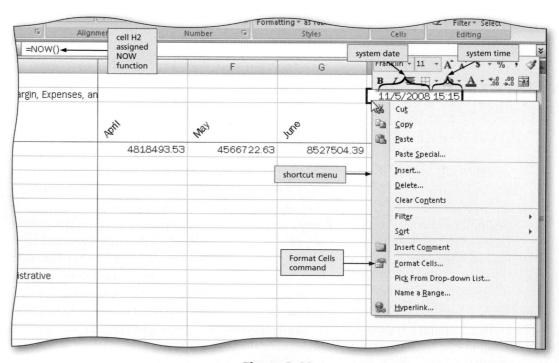

Figure 3–22

3

- Click Format Cells on the shortcut menu.

- When Excel displays the Format Cells dialog box, if necessary, click the Number tab.

- Click Date in the Category list. Scroll down in the Type list and then click 3/14/2001 to display a sample of the data in the active cell (H2) using the selected format in the Sample area (Figure 3–23).

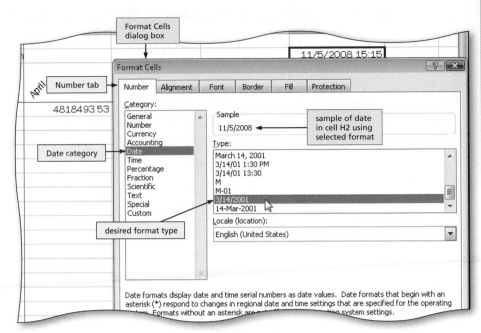

Figure 3–23

4

- Click the OK button in the Format Cells dialog box to display the system date in the form mm/dd/yyyy (Figure 3–24).

Q&A

How does Excel format a date?

In Figure 3–24, the date is displayed right-aligned in the cell because Excel treats a date as a number formatted to display as a date. If you assign the General format (Excel's default format for numbers) to a date in a cell, the date is displayed as a number with two decimal places. For example, if the system time and date is 6:00 PM on December 28, 2007 and the cell containing the NOW function is assigned the General format, then Excel displays the following number in the cell:

Figure 3–24

Number of days since December 31, 1899

time of day is 6:00 PM (portion of day complete)

The whole number portion of the number (39444) represents the number of days since December 31, 1899. The decimal portion of the number (.75) represents 6:00 PM as the time of day, at which point 3/4 of the day is complete. To assign the General format to a cell, click General in the Category list in the Format Cells dialog box (Figure 3–23).

Other Ways

1. On Formulas tab on Ribbon, click Date & Time, click NOW

2. Press CTRL+SEMICOLON (not a volatile date)

3. Press CTRL+SHIFT+# to format date to day-month-year

Absolute versus Relative Addressing

The next sections describe the formulas and functions needed to complete the calculations in the worksheet.

Plan Ahead

> **Determine necessary formulas and functions needed.**
> The next step is to enter the formulas that calculate the following values for January: cost of goods sold (cell B5), gross margin (cell B6), expenses (range B9:B13), total expenses (cell B14), and the operating income (cell B16). The formulas are based on the projected monthly sales in cell B4 and the assumptions in the range B19:B25.
>
> The formulas for each column (month) are the same, except for the reference to the projected monthly sales in row 4, which varies according to the month (B4 for January, C4 for February, and so on). Thus, the formulas for January can be entered in column B and then copied to columns C through G. Table 3–6 shows the formulas for determining the January costs of goods, gross margin, expenses, total expenses, and operating income in column B.
>
> If the formulas are entered as shown in Table 3–6 in column B for January and then copied to columns C through G (February through June) in the worksheet, Excel will adjust the cell references for each column automatically. Thus, after the copy, the February Commission expense in cell C10 would be =C4 * C20. While the cell reference C4 (February Sales) is correct, the cell reference C20 references an empty cell. The formula for cell C7 should read =C4 * B20, rather than =C4 * C20, because B20 references the Commission % value in the What-If Assumptions table. In this instance, a way is needed to keep a cell reference in a formula the same, or constant, when it is copied.

Table 3–6 Formulas for Determining Cost of Goods, Margin, Expenses, Total Expenses, and Operating Income for January

Cell	Row Title	Formula	Comment
B5	Cost of Goods Sold	=B4 * (1 − B21)	Sales times (1 minus Margin %)
B6	Gross Margin	= B4 − B5	Sales minus Cost of Goods
B9	Bonus	=IF(B4 >= B24, B19, 0)	Bonus equals value in B19 or 0
B10	Commission	=B4 * B20	Sales times Commission %
B11	Marketing	=B4 * B22	Sales times Marketing %
B12	Research and Development	=B4 * B23	Sales times Research and Development %
B13	Support, General, and Administrative	=B4 * B25	Sales times Support, General, and Administrative %
B14	Total Expenses	=SUM(B9:B13)	Sum of January Expenses
B16	Operating Income	=B6 − B14	Gross Margin minus Total Expense

BTW

Absolute Referencing
Absolute referencing is one of the more difficult worksheet concepts to understand. One point to keep in mind is that the paste operation is the only operation affected by an absolute cell reference. An absolute cell reference instructs the paste operation to keep the same cell reference as it copies a formula from one cell to another.

To keep a cell reference constant when copying a formula or function, Excel uses a technique called absolute cell referencing. To specify an absolute cell reference in a formula, enter a dollar sign ($) before any column letters or row numbers you want to keep constant in formulas you plan to copy. For example, $B$20 is an absolute cell reference, while B20 is a relative cell reference. Both reference the same cell. The difference becomes apparent when they are copied to a destination area. A formula using the **absolute cell reference** $B$20 instructs Excel to keep the cell reference B20 constant (absolute) in the formula as it copies it to the destination area. A formula using the **relative cell reference** B20 instructs Excel to adjust the cell reference as it copies it to the destination area. A cell reference with only one dollar sign before either the column or the row is called a **mixed cell reference**. Table 3–7 gives some additional examples of absolute, relative, and mixed cell references.

Table 3–7 Examples of Absolute, Relative, and Mixed Cell References

Cell Reference	Type of Reference	Meaning
$B$20	Absolute cell reference	Both column and row references remain the same when you copy this cell, because the cell references are absolute.
B$20	Mixed reference	This cell reference is mixed. The column reference changes when you copy this cell to another column because it is relative. The row reference does not change because it is absolute.
$B20	Mixed reference	This cell reference is mixed. The column reference does not change because it is absolute. The row reference changes when you copy this cell reference to another row because it is relative.
B20	Relative cell reference	Both column and row references are relative. When copied to another cell, both the column and row in the cell reference are adjusted to reflect the new location.

To Enter a Formula Containing Absolute Cell References

The following steps enter the cost of goods formula = B4*(1 − $B$21) in cell B5 using Point mode. To enter an absolute cell reference, you can type the dollar sign ($) as part of the cell reference or enter it by pressing F4 with the insertion point in or to the right of the cell reference to change to absolute.

- Press CTRL+HOME and then click cell B5.

- Type = (equal sign), click cell B4, type *(1−b21 and then press F4 to change b21 from a relative cell reference to an absolute cell reference.

- Type) to complete the formula (Figure 3–25).

Q&A

Is an absolute reference required in this formula?

No, because a mixed cell reference could have been used. The formula in cell B4 will be copied across columns, rather than down rows. So, the formula entered in cell B4 in Step 1 could have been entered as =B4*(1−$B21), rather than =B4*(1−$B$21). That is, the formula could have included the mixed cell reference $B21, rather than the absolute cell reference $B$21. When you copy a formula across columns, the row does not change anyway. The key is to ensure that column B remains constant as you copy the formula across rows. To change the absolute cell reference to a mixed cell reference, continue to press the F4 key until you get the desired cell reference.

Figure 3–25

- Click the Enter box in the formula bar to display the result, 1319724.83, in cell B5, instead of the formula (Figure 3–26).

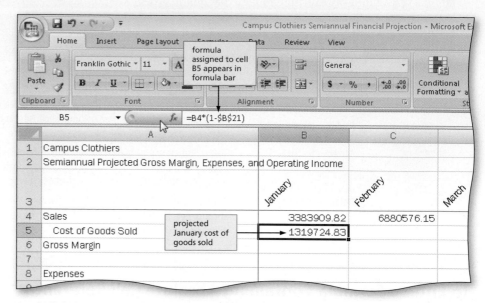

Figure 3–26

3

- Click cell B6, type = (equal sign), click cell B4, type – (minus sign), and then click cell B5.

- Click the Enter box in the formula bar to display the gross margin for January, 2064184.99, in cell B6 (Figure 3-27).

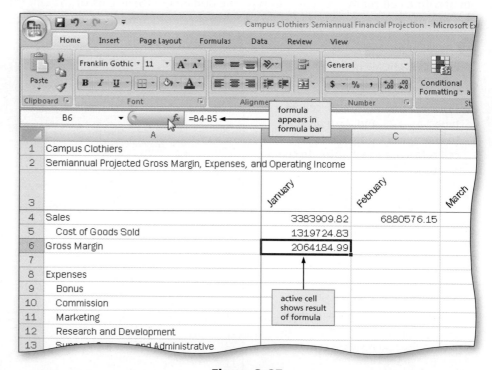

Figure 3–27

Making Decisions — The IF Function

According to the Request for New Workbook in Figure 3–2 on page EX 164, if the projected January sales in cell B4 is greater than or equal to the revenue for bonus in cell B24 (4,750,000.00), then the January bonus value in cell B9 is equal to the bonus value in cell B19 (100,000.00); otherwise, cell B9 is equal to 0. One way to assign the January bonus value in cell B9 is to check to see if the sales in cell B4 equal or exceed the revenue for bonus amount in cell B24 and, if so, then to enter 100,000.00 in cell B9. You can use this manual process for all six months by checking the values for the corresponding month.

Because the data in the worksheet changes each time a report is prepared or the figures are adjusted, however, it is preferable to have Excel assign the monthly bonus to the entries in the appropriate cells automatically. To do so, cell B9 must include a formula or function that displays 100,000.00 or 0.00 (zero), depending on whether the projected January sales in cell B4 is greater than, equal to, or less than the revenue for bonus value in cell B24.

The **IF function** is useful when you want to assign a value to a cell based on a logical test. For example, using the IF function, cell B9 can be assigned the following IF function:

The IF function instructs Excel that, if the projected January sales in cell B4 is greater than or equal to the revenue for bonus value in cell B24, then Excel should display the value 100000 in cell B19, in cell B9. If the projected January sales in cell B4 is less than the revenue for bonus value in cell B24, then Excel displays a 0 (zero) in cell B9.

The general form of the IF function is:

$$=IF(logical\_test, value\_if\_true, value\_if\_false)$$

The argument, logical_test, is made up of two expressions and a comparison operator. Each expression can be a cell reference, a number, text, a function, or a formula. Valid comparison operators, their meaning, and examples of their use in IF functions are shown in Table 3–8. The argument, value_if_true, is the value you want Excel to display in the cell when the logical test is true. The argument, value_if_false, is the value you want Excel to display in the cell when the logical test is false.

Table 3–8 Comparison Operators		
Comparison Operator	**Meaning**	**Example**
=	Equal to	=IF(H7 = 0, J6 ^ H4, L9 + D3)
<	Less than	=IF(C34 * W3 < K7, $K$6, L33 - 5)
>	Greater than	=IF(MIN(K8:K12) > 75, 1, 0)
>=	Greater than or equal to	=IF(P8 >= $H$6, J7 / V4, 7.5)
<=	Less than or equal to	=IF(G7 - G2 <= 23, L$9, 35 / Q2)
<>	Not equal to	=IF(B1 <> 0, "No","Yes")

BTW

Logical Operators in IF Functions
IF functions can use logical operators, such as AND, OR, and NOT. For example, the three IF functions =IF(AND(B3>C3, D3<C5), "OK", "Not OK") and =IF(OR(C3>G5, D2<X3), "OK", "Not OK") and =IF(NOT(A6<H7), "OK", "Not OK") use logical operators. In the first example, both logical tests must be true for the value_if_true OK to be assigned to the cell. In the second example, one or the other logical tests must be true for the value_if_true OK to be assigned to the cell. In the third example, the logical test A6<H7 must be false for the value_if_true OK to be assigned to the cell.

To Enter an IF Function

The following steps assign the IF function =IF(B4>=$B$24,$B$19,0) to cell B9. This IF function determines whether or not the worksheet assigns a bonus for January.

1

- Click cell B9. Type =if(b4>=b24, b19,0) in the cell (Figure 3–28).

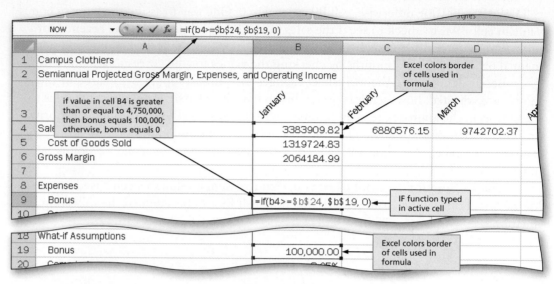

Figure 3–28

2

- Click the Enter box in the formula bar to display 0 in cell B9 (Figure 3–29), because the value in cell B4 (3383909.82) is less than the value in cell B24 (4,750,000) (Figure 3–29).

Q&A

Why does the value 0 display in cell B9?

The value that Excel displays in cell B9 depends on the values assigned to cells B4, B19, and B24. For example, if the value for January sales in cell B4 is reduced below 4,750,000.00, then the IF function in cell B9 will cause Excel to display a 0. If you change the bonus in cell B19 from 100,000.00 to another number and the value in cell B4 is greater than or equal to the value in cell B24, it will change the results in cell B9 as well. Finally, increasing the revenue for bonus in cell B24 so that it is greater than the value in cell B4 will change the result in cell B9.

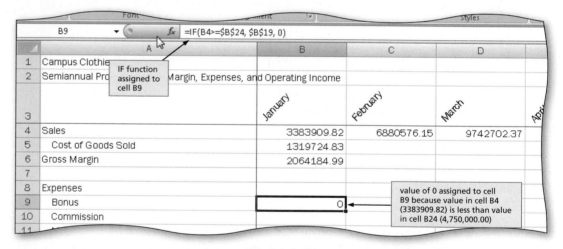

Figure 3–29

Other Ways

1. On Formulas tab on Ribbon, click Logical button, click IF

2. Click Insert Function box in formula bar, click Logical in 'Or select a category list', click IF in drop-down list, click OK button

To Enter the Remaining January Formulas

The January commission expense in cell B10 is equal to the sales in cell B4 times the commission assumption in cell B20 (3.25%). The January marketing expense in cell B11 is equal to the projected January sales in cell B4 times the marketing assumption in cell B22 (9.00%). Similar formulas determine the remaining January expenses in cells B12 and B13.

The total expenses value in cell B14 is equal to the sum of the expenses in the range B9:B13. The operating income in cell B16 is equal to the gross margin in cell B6 minus the total expenses in cell B14. The formulas are short, and therefore, they are typed in the following steps, rather than entered using Point mode.

1 Click cell B10. Type =b4*b20 and then press the DOWN ARROW key. Type =b4*b22 and then press the DOWN ARROW key. Type =b4*b23 and then press the DOWN ARROW key. Type =b4*b25 and then press the DOWN ARROW key.

2 With cell B14 selected, click the Sum button on the Home tab on the Ribbon twice. Click cell B16. Type =b6−b14 and then press the ENTER key (Figure 3–30a).

3 Press CTRL+ACCENT MARK (`) to instruct Excel to display the formulas version of the worksheet (Figure 3–30b).

4 When you are finished viewing the formulas version, press CTRL+ACCENT MARK (`) to instruct Excel to display the values version of the worksheet.

Q&A Why should I view the formulas version of the worksheet?

Viewing the formulas version (Figure 3–30b) of the worksheet allows you to check the formulas assigned to the range B5:B16. Recall that formulas were entered in lowercase. You can see that Excel converts all the formulas from lowercase to uppercase.

BTW

Replacing a Formula with a Constant
You can replace a formula with its result so it remains constant. Do the following: (1) Click the cell with the formula; (2) press F2 or click in the formula bar; (3) press F9 to display the value in the formula bar; and (4) press the ENTER key.

(a) Values Version

(b) Formulas Version

Figure 3–30

To Copy Formulas with Absolute Cell References Using the Fill Handle

The following steps show how to use the fill handle to copy the January formulas in column B to the other five months in columns C through G.

- Select the range B5:B16 and then point to the fill handle in the lower-right corner of cell B16 (Figure 3–31).

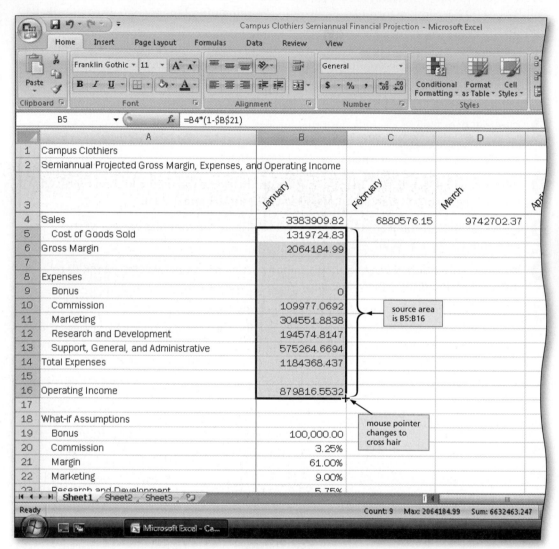

Figure 3–31

2

- Drag the fill handle to the right to select the destination area C5:G16 to copy the formulas from the source area (B5:B16) to the destination area (C5:G16) and display the calculated amounts and Auto Fill Options button (Figure 3–32).

Q&A What happens to the formulas after the copy is made?

Because the formulas in the range B5:B16 use absolute cell references, the formulas still refer to the current values in the Assumptions table when the formulas are copied to the range C5:G16.

Q&A What happened to columns B, C, and D?

As shown in Figure 3–32, as the fill handle is dragged to the right, columns B, C, and D no longer appear on the screen. Column A, however, remains on the screen, because the row titles were frozen earlier in this chapter.

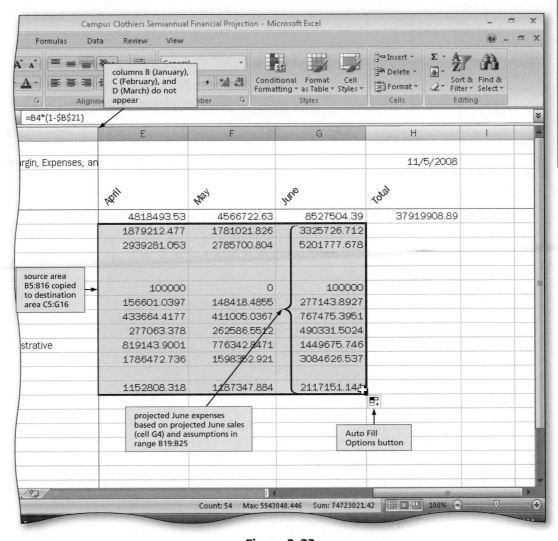

Figure 3–32

(screen labels:)
- columns B (January), C (February), and D (March) do not appear
- source area B5:B16 copied to destination area C5:G16
- projected June expenses based on projected June sales (cell G4) and assumptions in range B19:B25
- Auto Fill Options button

BTW

Error Messages
When Excel cannot calculate a formula, it displays an error message in a cell. These error messages always begin with a number sign (#). The more commonly occurring error messages are: #DIV/0! (tries to divide by zero); #NAME? (uses a name Excel does not recognize); #N/A (refers to a value not available); #NULL! (specifies an invalid intersection of two areas); #NUM! (uses a number incorrectly); #REF (refers to a cell that is not valid); #VALUE! (uses an incorrect argument or operand); and ##### (cell not wide enough to display entire entry).

To Determine Row Totals in Nonadjacent Cells

The following steps determine the row totals in column H. To determine the row totals using the Sum button, select only the cells in column H containing numbers in adjacent cells to the left. If, for example, you select the range H5:H16, Excel will display 0s as the sum of empty rows in cells H7, H8, and H15.

1 Select the range H5:H6. Hold down the CTRL key and select the range H9:H14 and cell H16 as shown in Figure 3–33.

2 Click the Sum button on the Ribbon to display the row totals in column H (Figure 3–33).

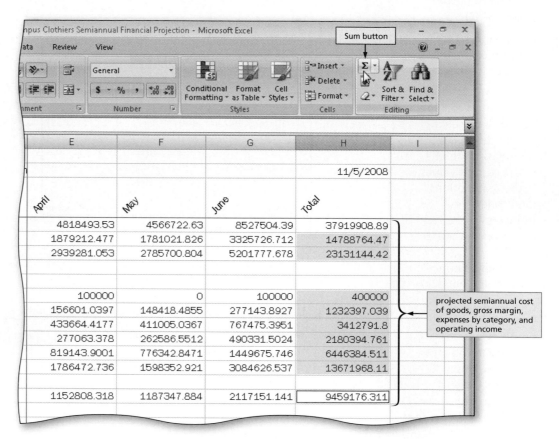

Figure 3–33

To Unfreeze the Worksheet Titles and Save the Workbook

All the text, data, and formulas have been entered into the worksheet. The following steps unfreeze the titles and save the workbook using its current file name, Campus Clothiers Semiannual Financial Projection.

1 Press CTRL+HOME to select cell B4 and view the upper-left corner of the screen.

2 Click the View tab on the Ribbon and then click the Freeze Panes button on the Ribbon to display the Freeze Panes gallery (Figure 3–34).

3 Click Unfreeze Panes in the Freeze Panes gallery to unfreeze the titles.

BTW

Toggle Commands
Many of the commands on the Ribbon, in the galleries, and the shortcut keys function as a toggle. For example, if you click the Freeze Panes command on the Freeze Panes gallery, the command changes to Unfreeze Panes the next time you view the gallery. These types of commands work like an on-off switch, or toggle.

④ Click the Home tab on the Ribbon and then click the Save button on the Quick Access Toolbar.

Q&A Why does pressing CTRL+HOME select cell B4?

When the titles are frozen and you press CTRL+HOME, Excel selects the upper-left cell of the unfrozen section of the worksheet. For example, in Step 1 of the previous steps, Excel selected cell B4. When the titles are unfrozen, then pressing CTRL+HOME selects cell A1.

BTW

Work Days
Assume that you have two dates: one in cell F3 and the other in cell F4. The date in cell F3 is your starting date and the date in cell F4 is the ending date. To calculate the work days between the two dates (excludes weekends), use the following formula: =NETWORKDAYS(F3, F4). For this function to work, make sure the Analysis ToolPak add-in is installed. You can install it on the Add-Ins page of the Excel Options dialog box.

Figure 3–34

Nested Forms of the IF Function

A **nested IF function** is one in which the action to be taken for the true or false case includes yet another IF function. The second IF function is considered to be nested, or layered, within the first. Study the nested IF function below, which determines the eligibility of a person to vote. Assume the following in this example: (1) the nested IF function is assigned to cell K12, which instructs Excel to display one of three messages in the cell; (2) cell H12 contains a person's age; and (3) cell I12 contains a Y or N, based on whether the person is registered to vote.

=IF(H12>=18, IF(I12="Y","Registered","Eligible and Not Registered"),"Not Eligible to Register")

The nested IF function instructs Excel to display one, and only one, of the following three messages in cell K12: (1) Registered; or (2) Eligible and Not Registered; or (3) Not Eligible to Register.

You can nest IF functions as deep as you want, but after you get beyond a nest of three IF functions, the logic becomes difficult to follow and alternative solutions, such as the use of multiple cells and simple IF functions, should be considered.

Formatting the Worksheet

The worksheet created thus far shows the financial projections for the six-month period, from January to June. Its appearance is uninteresting, however, even though some minimal formatting (formatting assumptions numbers, changing the column widths, and formatting the date) was performed earlier. This section will complete the formatting of the worksheet to make the numbers easier to read and to emphasize the titles, assumptions, categories, and totals.

Plan Ahead

Identify how to format various elements of the worksheet.
The worksheet will be formatted in the following manner so it appears as shown in Figure 3–35: (1) format the numbers; (2) format the worksheet title, column titles, row titles, and operating income row; and (3) format the assumptions table. Numbers in heading rows and total rows should be formatted with a currency symbol. Other dollar amounts should be formatted with a Comma style. The assumptions table should be diminished in its formatting so it does not distract from the main calculations and data in the worksheet. Assigning the data in the assumptions table a font size of 8 point would set it apart from other data formatted with a font size of 11 point.

BTW

Selecting Nonadjacent Ranges
One of the more difficult tasks to learn is selecting nonadjacent ranges. To complete this task, do not hold down the CTRL key when you select the first range because Excel will consider the current active cell to be the first selection. Once the first range is selected, hold down the CTRL key and drag through the nonadjacent ranges. If a desired range is not visible in the window, use the scroll arrows to view the range. It is not necessary to hold down the CTRL key while you scroll.

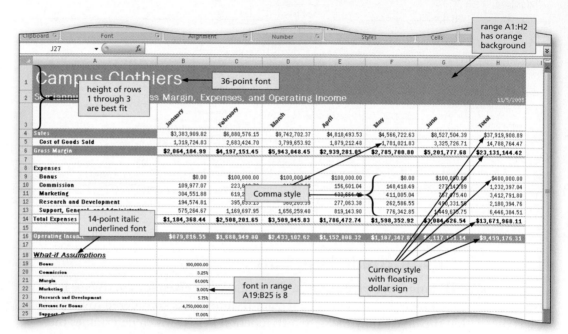

Figure 3–35

To Assign Formats to Nonadjacent Ranges

The numbers in the range B4:H16 are to be formatted as follows:

1. Assign the Currency style with a floating dollar sign to rows 4, 6, 9, 14, and 16.
2. Assign a Comma style to rows 5 and 10 through 13.

To assign a Currency style with a floating dollar sign, use the Format Cells dialog box rather than the Accounting Style button on the Ribbon, which assigns a fixed dollar sign. Also use the Format Cells dialog box to assign the Comma style, because the Comma Style button on the Ribbon assigns a format that displays a dash (-) when a cell has a value of 0. The specifications for this worksheet call for displaying a value of 0 as 0.00 (see cell B9 in Figure 3–35), rather than as a dash. To create a Comma style using the Format Cells dialog box, you can assign a Currency style with no dollar sign. The following steps assign formats to the numbers in rows 4 through 16.

1

- Select the range B4:H4.

- While holding down the CTRL key, select the nonadjacent ranges B6:H6, B9:H9, B14:H14, and B16:H16, and then release the CTRL key.

- Click the Format Cells: Number Dialog Box Launcher on the Ribbon to display the Format Cells dialog box (Figure 3–36)

Figure 3–36

2

- Click Currency in the Category list, select 2 in the Decimal places box, click $ in the Symbol list to ensure a dollar sign shows, and click the black font color ($1,234.10) in the Negative numbers list (Figure 3–37).

Q&A

Why was the particular style chosen for the negative numbers?

In accounting, negative numbers often are shown with parentheses surrounding the value rather than with a negative sign preceding the value. Thus, the format (1,234.10) in the

Figure 3–37

Negative numbers list was clicked. The data being used in this chapter contains no negative numbers. However, you must select a format for negative numbers, and you must be consistent if you are choosing different formats in a column, otherwise the decimal points may not line up.

3

- Click the OK button.

- Select the range B5:H5.

- While holding down the CTRL key, select the range B10:H13, and then release the CTRL key.

- Click the Format Cells: Number Dialog Box Launcher on the Ribbon to display the Format Cells dialog box.

- When Excel displays the Format Cells dialog box, click Currency in the Category list, select 2 in the Decimal places box, click None in the Symbol list so a dollar sign does not show, and click the black font color (1,234.10) in the Negative numbers list (Figure 3–38).

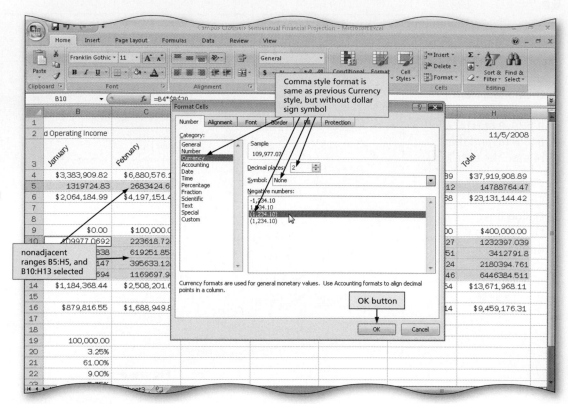

Figure 3–38

4

- Click the OK button.

- Press CTRL+HOME to select cell A1 to display the formatted numbers as shown in Figure 3–39.

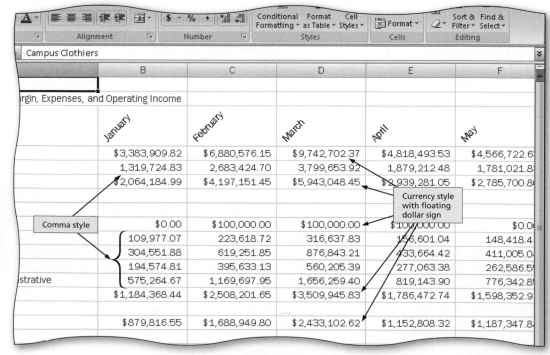

Figure 3–39

Other Ways

1. Right-click range, click Format Cells on shortcut menu, click Number tab, click category in Category list, select format, click OK button

2. Press CTRL+1, click Number tab, click category in Category list, select format, click OK button

To Format the Worksheet Titles

The following steps emphasize the worksheet titles in cells A1 and A2 by changing the font type, size, and color. The steps also format all of the row headers in column A with a Bold font style.

- Click the column A heading to select column A.

- Click the Bold button on the Ribbon to bold all of the data in column A (Figure 3–40).

Figure 3–40

- Click cell A1 to select it. Click the Font Size box arrow on the Ribbon, and then click 36 in the Font Size list.

- Click cell A2, click the Font Size box arrow, and then click 18 in the Font Size list (Figure 3–41).

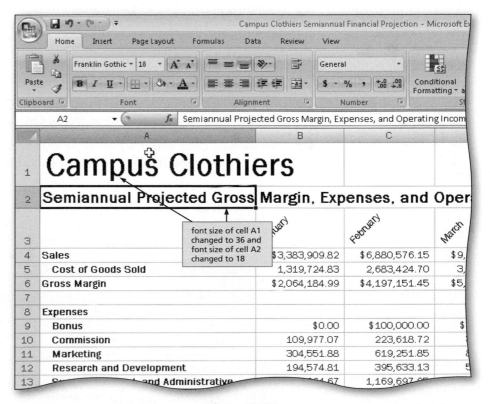

Figure 3–41

3

- Select the range A1:H2 and then click the Fill Color button arrow on the Ribbon.

- Click Orange, Accent 1 (column 5, row 1) on the Fill Color palette.

- Click the Font Color button arrow on the Ribbon and then select White, Background 1 (column 1, row 1) on the Font Color palette (Figure 3–42).

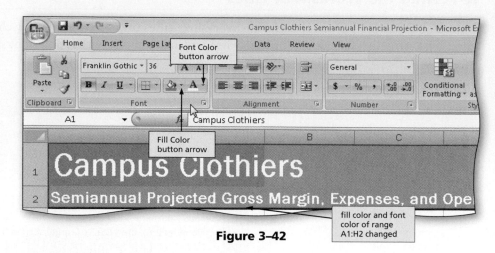

Figure 3–42

Other Ways

1. Right-click range, click Format Cells on shortcut menu, click Fill tab to color background (or click Font tab to color font), click OK button

2. Press CTRL+1, click Fill tab to color background (or click Font tab to color font), click OK button

To Assign Cell Styles to Nonadjacent Rows and Colors to a Cell

The next step to improving the appearance of the worksheet is to format the heading in row 3 and the totals in rows 4, 14, and 16. The following steps format the heading in row 3 with the Heading 3 cell style and the totals in rows 4, 14, and 16 with the Total cell style. Cell A4 also is formatted.

1 Select the range A3:H3 and apply the Heading 3 cell style.

2 Select the range A6:H6 and while holding down the CTRL key, select the ranges A14:H14 and A16:H16.

3 Apply the Total cell style.

4 Click cell A4, click the Fill Color button arrow on the Ribbon, and then click the Orange, Accent 1 color (column 5, row 1) on the Fill Color palette.

5 Click the Font Color button arrow on the Ribbon, and then click the White, Background 1 color (column 1, row 1) on the Font Color palette (Figure 3–43).

BTW

The Fill and Font Color Button
You may have noticed that the color bar at the bottom of the Fill Color and Font Color buttons on the Home tab on the Ribbon (Figure 3-42) changes to the most recently selected color. To apply this same color to a cell background or text, select a cell and then click the Fill Color button to use the color as a background or click the Font Color button to use the color as a font color.

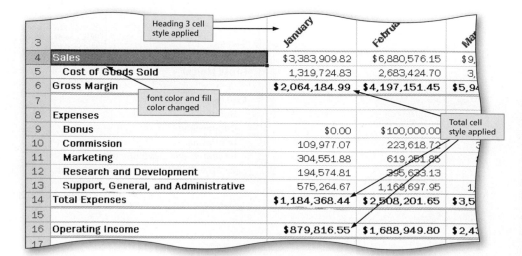

Figure 3–43

Copying a Cell's Format Using the Format Painter Button

Using the Format Painter button on the Ribbon, you can format a cell quickly by copying a cell's format to another cell or a range of cells.

To Copy a Cell's Format Using the Format Painter Button

The following steps format cells A6, A14, and the range A16:H16 using the Format Painter button.

- Select cell A4.

- Click the Format Painter button on the Ribbon and then move the mouse pointer onto the worksheet to cause the mouse pointer to change to a block plus sign with a paintbrush (Figure 3–44).

Figure 3–44

• Click cell A6 to assign the format of cell A4 to cell A6 (Figure 3–45).

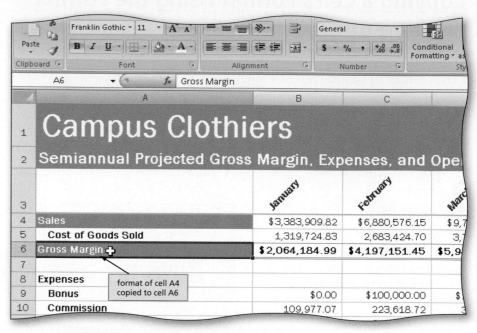

Figure 3–45

3

• With cell A6 selected, click the Format Painter button on the Ribbon and then click cell A16.

• Select the range B16:H16, click the Fill Color button on the Ribbon, and then click the Orange, Accent 1 color (column 5, row 1) on the Fill Color palette.

• Click the Font Color button on the Ribbon, and then click the Background 1 color (column 1, row 1) on the Font Color palette (Figure 3–46).

• Apply the Currency style to the range B16:G16.

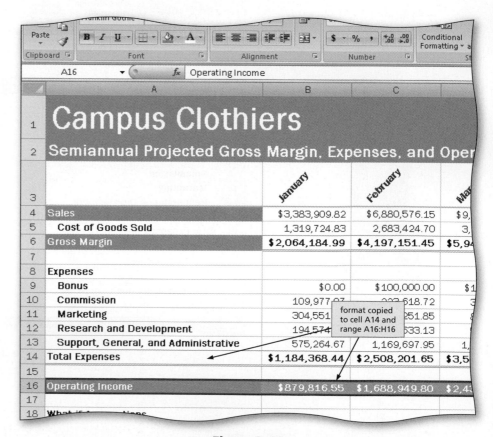

Figure 3–46

Other Ways
1. Click Copy button, select cell, click Paste button, click Paste Special command on Paste menu, click Formats, click OK button   2. Double-click Format Painter button

To Format the What-If Assumptions Table and Save the Workbook

The last step to improving the appearance of the worksheet is to format the What-If Assumptions table in the range A18:B25. The specifications in Figure 3–35 on page EX 196 require a 14-point italic underlined font for the title in cell A18 and 8-point font in the range A19:B25. The following steps format the What-If Assumptions table.

1 Scroll down to view rows 18 through 25 and then click cell A18.

2 Click the Font Size box arrow on the Ribbon and then click 14 in the Font Size list. Click the Italic button and then click the Underline button on the Ribbon.

3 Select the range A19:B25, click the Font Size button on the Ribbon, and then click 8 in the Font Size list.

4 Click cell D25 to deselect the range A19:B25 and display the What-If Assumptions table as shown in Figure 3–47.

5 Click the Save button on the Quick Access Toolbar.

Q&A What happens when I click the Italic and Underline buttons?

Recall that when you assign the italic font style to a cell, Excel slants the characters slightly to the right as shown in cell A18 in Figure 3–47. The **underline** format underlines only the characters in the cell, rather than the entire cell, as is the case when you assign a cell a bottom border.

BTW

Painting a Format to Nonadjacent Ranges
Double-click the Format Painter button on the Home tab on the Ribbon and then drag through the nonadjacent ranges to paint the formats to the ranges. Click the Format Painter button to deactivate it.

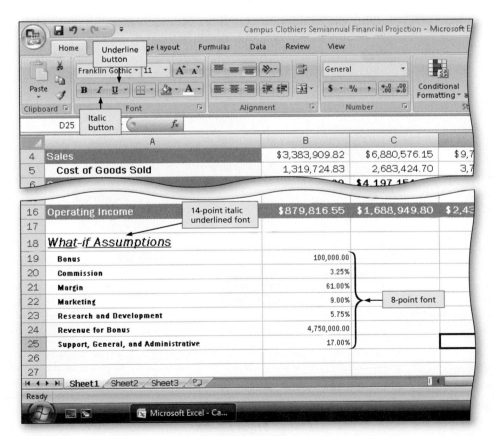

Figure 3–47

Adding a 3-D Pie Chart to the Workbook

The next step in the chapter is to draw the 3-D Pie chart on a separate sheet in the workbook, as shown in Figure 3–48. Use a **Pie chart** to show the relationship or proportion of parts to a whole. Each slice (or wedge) of the pie shows what percent that slice contributes to the total (100%).

<table>
<tr>
<td>

Plan Ahead

</td>
<td>

Specify how the chart should convey necessary information.
The 3-D Pie chart in Figure 3–48 shows the contribution of each month's projected operating income to the six-month projected operating income. The 3-D Pie chart makes it easy to evaluate the contribution of one month in comparison to the other months.

Unlike the 3-D Column chart created in Chapter 1, the 3-D Pie chart shown in Figure 3–48 is not embedded in the worksheet. Instead, the Pie chart resides on a separate sheet, called a **chart sheet**, which contains only the chart.

In this worksheet, the ranges to chart are the nonadjacent ranges B3:G3 (month names) and B16:G16 (monthly operating incomes). The month names in the range B3:G3 will identify the slices of the Pie chart; these entries are called **category names**. The range B16:G16 contains the data that determines the size of the slices in the pie; these entries are called the **data series**. Because six months are being charted, the 3-D Pie chart contains six slices.

The sketch of the 3-D Pie chart in Figure 3–3b on page EX 166 also calls for emphasizing the month of June by offsetting its slice from the main portion. A Pie chart with one or more slices offset is called an **exploded Pie chart**.

</td>
</tr>
</table>

BTW

Charts
You are aware that, when you change a value on which a chart is dependent, Excel immediately redraws the chart based on the new value. Did you know that, with bar charts, you can drag the bar in the chart in one direction or another to change the corresponding value in the worksheet, as well?

BTW

Certification
The Microsoft Certified Application Specialist (MCAS) program provides an opportunity for you to obtain a valuable industry credential – proof that you have the Excel 2007 skills required by employers. For more information, see Appendix G or visit the Excel 2007 Certification Web page (scsite.com/ex2007/cert).

BTW

Chart Items
When you rest the mouse pointer over a chart item, such as a legend, bar, or axis, Excel displays a chart tip containing the name of the item.

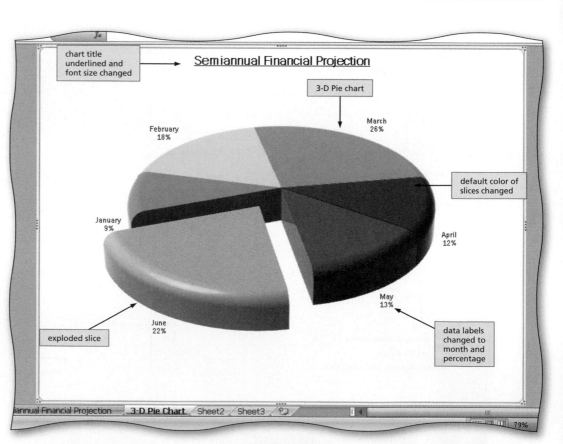

Figure 3–48

As shown in Figure 3–48, the default 3-D Pie chart also has been enhanced by rotating it, changing the colors of the slices, adding a bevel, and modifying the chart title and labels that identify the slices.

To Draw a 3-D Pie Chart on a Separate Chart Sheet

The following steps draw the 3-D Pie chart on a separate chart sheet.

①

- Select the range B3:G3.

- While holding down the CTRL key, select the range B16:G16.

- Click the Insert tab on the Ribbon.

- Click the Pie button on the Ribbon to display the Pie gallery (Figure 3–49).

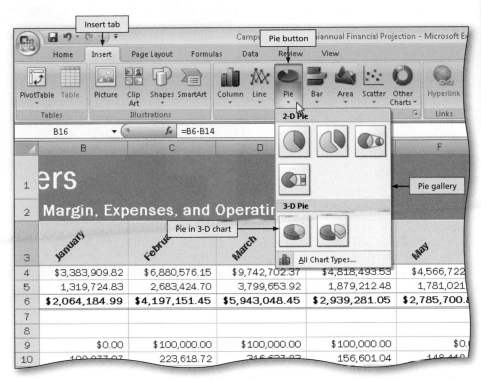

Figure 3–49

②

- Click Pie in 3-D chart in the Pie gallery.

- When Excel draws the chart, click the Move Chart button on the Ribbon to display the Move Chart dialog box (Figure 3–50).

Figure 3–50

- Click the New sheet option button and then type `3-D Pie Chart` in the New sheet name text box.

- Click the OK button to move the chart to a new chart sheet with the name 3-D Pie Chart (Figure 3–51).

Figure 3–51

Other Ways
1. Select range to chart, press F11

To Insert a Chart Title and Data Labels

The next step is to insert a chart title and labels that identify the slices. Before you can format a chart item, such as the chart title or data labels, you must select it. You can format a selected chart item using the Ribbon or shortcut menu. The following steps insert a chart title, remove the legend, and add data labels.

- Click anywhere in the chart area outside the chart.

- Click the Layout tab on the Ribbon and then click the Chart Title button.

- Click the Centered Overlay Title command in the Chart Title gallery.

- Select the text in the chart title and then type `Semiannual Financial Projection` as the new chart title (Figure 3–52).

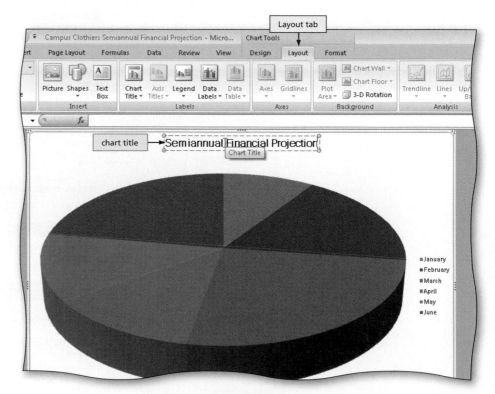

Figure 3–52

2

- Select the text in the new title and then click the Home tab on the Ribbon.

- Click the Underline button to assign an underline font style to the chart title (Figure 3–53).

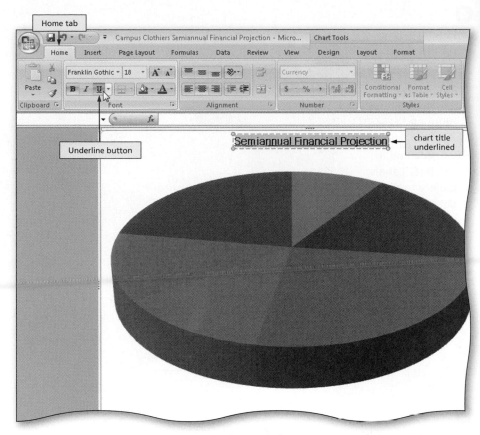

Figure 3–53

3

- Click the Layout tab on the Ribbon and then click the Legend button to display the Legend gallery.

- Point to None in the Legend gallery (Figure 3–54).

Figure 3–54

- Click None to turn off the legend on the chart.

- Click the Data Labels button on the Ribbon and then click Outside End in the Data Labels gallery to display data labels outside the chart at the end of each slice (Figure 3–55).

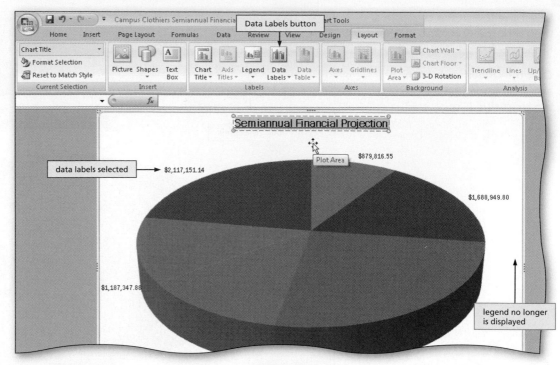

Figure 3–55

5

- If necessary, right-click any data label to select all of the data labels on the chart and to display the shortcut menu.

- Click the Format Data Labels command on the short-cut menu to display the Format Data Labels dialog box.

- If necessary, click the Series Name, Value, and Show Leader Lines check boxes to deselect them and then click the Category Name and Percentage check boxes to select them (Figure 3–56).

Figure 3–56

6
- Click the Close button to close the Format Data Labels dialog box and display the chart as shown in Figure 3–57.

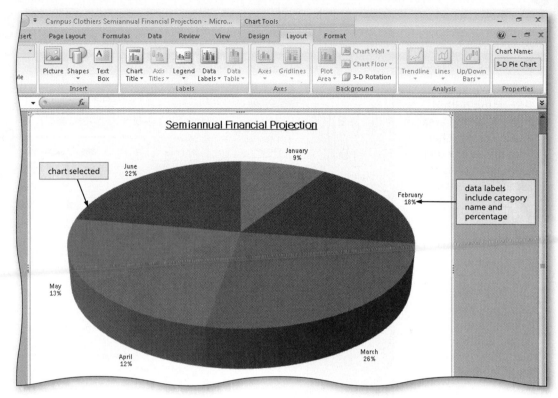

Figure 3–57

To Rotate the 3-D Pie Chart

With a three-dimensional chart, you can change the view to better show the section of the chart you are trying to emphasize. Excel allows you to control the rotation angle, elevation, perspective, height, and angle of the axes by using the Format Chart Area dialog box.

When Excel initially draws a Pie chart, it always positions the chart so that one of the dividing lines between two slices is a straight line pointing to 12 o'clock (or 0°). As shown in Figure 3–57, the line that divides the January and June slices currently is set to 0°. This line defines the rotation angle of the 3-D Pie chart.

To obtain a better view of the offset June slice, the 3-D Pie chart can be rotated 250° to the right. The following steps show how to rotate the 3-D Pie chart.

1

- Click the 3-D Rotation button on the Ribbon to display the Format Chart Area dialog box.

- Click the Increase X Rotation button in the Rotation area of the Format Chart Area dialog box until the X rotation is at 250° (Figure 3–58).

Q&A

What happens as I click the Increase X Rotation button?

Excel rotates the chart 10° in a clockwise direction each time you click the Increase X Rotation button. The Y box in the Rotation area allows you to control the tilt, or elevation, of the chart. You can tilt the chart towards or away from your view in order to enhance the view of the chart.

Figure 3–58

2

- Click the Close button in the Format Chart Area dialog box to display the rotated chart (Figure 3–59).

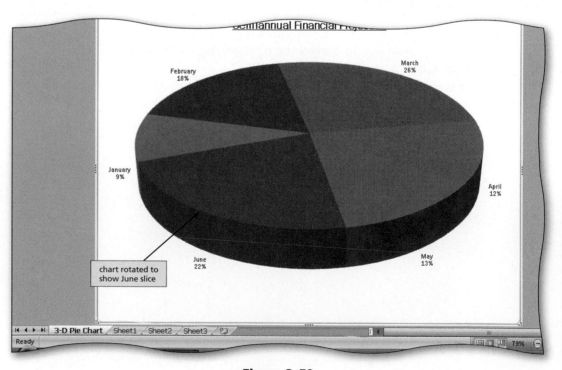

Figure 3–59

To Apply a 3-D Format to the Pie Chart

Excel allows you to apply dramatic 3-D visual effects to charts. The chart shown in Figure 3–59 could be enhanced with a bevel along the top edge. A bevel is a curve that is applied to soften the appearance of a straight edge. Excel also allows you to change the appearance of the material from which the surface of the chart appears to be constructed. The following steps apply a bevel to the chart and change the surface of the chart to a softer-looking material.

- Right-click the chart to display the shortcut menu (Figure 3–60).

Figure 3–60

- Click the Format Data Series command on the shortcut menu to display the Format Data Series dialog box and then click the 3-D Format category on the left side of the dialog box.

- Click the Top button in the Bevel area to display the Bevel gallery (Figure 3–61).

Figure 3–61

• Click the Circle bevel button (column 1, row 1) in the Bevel gallery to add a bevel to the chart.

• Type 50 pt in the top Width box in the Bevel area of the dialog box and then type 50 pt in the uppermost Height box in the Bevel area of the dialog box to increase the width and height of the bevel on the chart (Figure 3–62).

Figure 3–62

• Click the Material button in the Surface area of the Format Data Series dialog box and then point to the Soft Edge button (column 2, row 2) in the Material gallery (Figure 3–63).

Figure 3–63

5
- Click the Soft Edge button and then click the Close button in the Format Data Series dialog box (Figure 3-64).

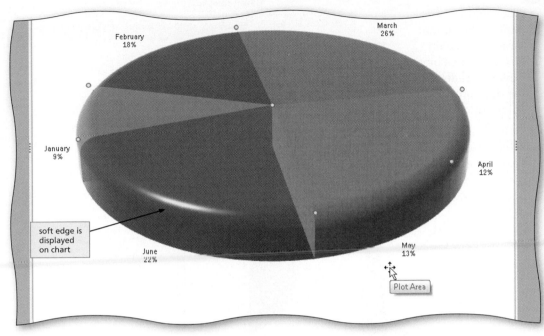

Figure 3-64

To Explode the 3-D Pie Chart and Change the Color of a Slice

The next step is to emphasize the slice representing June by **offsetting**, or exploding, it from the rest of the slices so that it stands out. The following steps explode a slice of the 3-D Pie chart and then change its color.

1
- Click the slice labeled June twice (do not double-click) to select only the June slice.

- Right-click the slice labeled June to display the shortcut menu and then point to Format Data Point (Figure 3-65).

- Click Format Data Point.

Figure 3-65

2

- When Excel displays the Format Data Point dialog box, drag the Point Explosion slider to the right until the Point Explosion box reads 28% (Figure 3–66).

Should I offset more slices?

You can offset as many slices as you want, but remember that the reason for offsetting a slice is to emphasize it. Offsetting multiple slices tends to reduce the impact on the reader and reduces the overall size of the Pie chart.

Figure 3–66

3

- Click the Fill category on the left side of the dialog box.

- Click the Solid fill option button and then click the Color button to display the color palette.

- Point to the Orange color in the Standard Colors area (Figure 3–67).

4

- Click the Orange color on the color palette and then click the Close button on the Format Data Point dialog box to change the color of the slice labeled June to orange.

Figure 3–67

To Change the Colors of the Remaining Slices

BTW

**Exploding a
3-D Pie Chart**
If you click the 3-D Pie chart so that all of the slices are selected, you can drag one of the slices to explode all of the slices.

The colors of the remaining slices also can be changed to enhance the appeal of the chart. The following steps change the color of the remaining five chart slices.

1 Click the slice labeled January twice (do not double-click) to select only the January slice.

2 Right-click the slice labeled January to display the shortcut menu and then click Format Data Point.

3 Click the Fill category on the left side of the dialog box.

4 Click the Solid fill option button and then click the Color button to display the color palette.

5 Click the Green color on the color palette and then click the Close button in the Format Data Point dialog box to change the color of the slice labeled January to green.

6 Repeat steps 1 through 5 for the remaining four slices. Assign the following colors in the Standard Colors area of the color palette to each slice: February – Yellow; March – Light Blue; April – Red; May – Blue. The completed chart appears as shown in Figure 3–68.

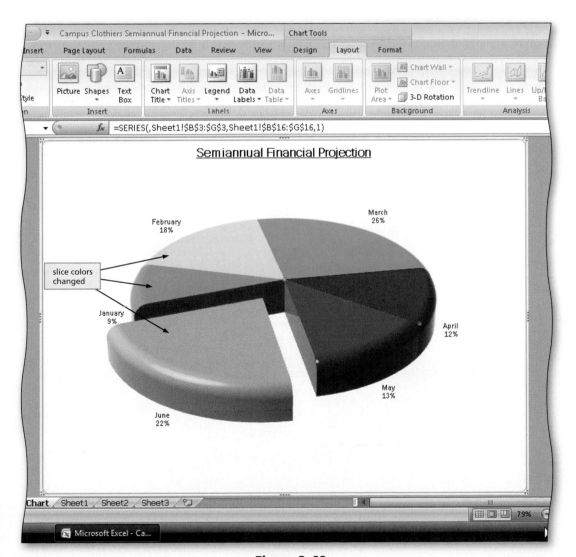

Figure 3–68

Renaming and Reordering the Sheets and Coloring Their Tabs

The final step in creating the workbook is to reorder the sheets and modify the tabs at the bottom of the screen.

To Rename and Reorder the Sheets and Color Their Tabs

The following steps rename the sheets, color the tabs, and reorder the sheets so the worksheet precedes the chart sheet in the workbook.

1

- Right-click the tab labeled 3-D Pie Chart at the bottom of the screen to display the shortcut menu.

- Point to the Tab Color command to display the color palette (Figure 3–69).

Figure 3–69

- Click Brown, Accent 2 (column 6, row 1) in the Theme Colors area to change the color of the tab to brown.

- Double-click the tab labeled Sheet1 at the bottom of the screen.

- Type `Semiannual Financial Projection` as the new sheet name and then press the ENTER key.

- Right-click the tab and then click Tab Color on the shortcut menu.

- Point to the Orange, Accent 1 (column 5, row 1) color in the Theme Colors area of the palette (Figure 3–70).

3

- Click Orange, Accent 1 (column 5, row 1) in the Theme Colors area to change the color of the tab to orange.

- Drag the Semiannual Financial Projection tab to the left in front of the 3-D Pie Chart tab to rearrange the sequence of the sheets and then click cell E18 (Figure 3–71).

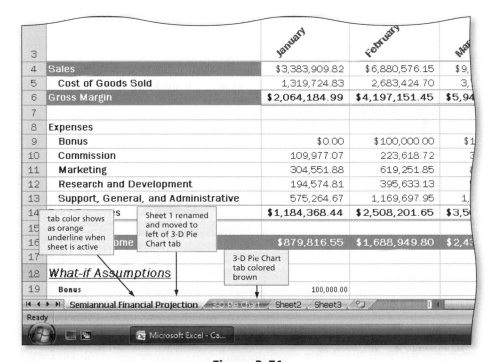

Figure 3–70

Figure 3–71

Other Ways

1. To rename sheet, right-click sheet tab, click Rename on shortcut menu

2. To move sheet, right-click sheet tab, click Move or Copy on shortcut menu

BTW

Checking Spelling
Unless you first select a range of cells or an object before starting the spell checker, Excel checks the selected worksheet, including all cell values, cell comments, embedded charts, text boxes, buttons, and headers and footers.

Checking Spelling, Saving, Previewing, and Printing the Workbook

With the workbook complete, this section checks spelling, saves, previews, and then prints the workbook. Each set of steps concludes with saving the workbook to ensure that the latest changes are saved.

To Check Spelling in Multiple Sheets

By default, the spell checker checks the spelling only in the selected sheets. It will check all the cells in the selected sheets, unless you select a range of two or more cells. Before checking the spelling, the following steps select the 3-D Pie Chart sheet so that the entire workbook is checked for spelling errors.

1 With the Semiannual Financial Projection sheet active, press CTRL+HOME to select cell A1. Hold down the CTRL key and then click the 3-D Pie Chart tab.

2 Click the Review tab on the Ribbon and then click the Spelling button on the Ribbon.

3 Correct any errors and then click the OK button when the spell check is complete.

4 Click the Save button on the Quick Access Toolbar.

BTW

Printing in Black and White
You can speed up the printing process and save ink if you print worksheets with color in black and white. To print a worksheet in black and white on a color printer, do the following: (1) Click the Page Setup Dialog Box Launcher on the Page Layout tab on the Ribbon, click the Sheet tab, and then click 'Black and white' in the Print area. (2) Click the Preview button to see that Excel has removed the colored backgrounds, click the Close button, and then click the OK button. You are now ready to print economically, in black and white.

To Preview and Print the Workbook

After checking the spelling, the next step is to preview and print the sheets. As with spelling, Excel previews and prints only the selected sheets. In addition, because the worksheet is too wide to print in portrait orientation, the orientation must be changed to landscape. The following steps adjust the orientation and scale, preview the workbook, and then print the workbook.

1 Ready the printer. If both sheets are not selected, hold down the CTRL key and then click the tab of the inactive sheet.

2 Click the Page Layout tab on the Ribbon and then click the Page Setup Dialog Box Launcher. Click the Page tab and then click Landscape. Click Fit to in the Scaling area.

3 Click the Print Preview button in the Page Setup dialog box. When the preview of the first of the selected sheets appears, click the Next Page button at the top of the Print Preview window to view the next sheet. Click the Previous Page button to redisplay the first sheet.

4 Click the Print button at the top of the Print Preview window. When Excel displays the Print dialog box, click the OK button to print the worksheet and chart (Figure 3–72).

5 Right-click the Semiannual Financial Projection tab. Click Ungroup Sheets on the shortcut menu to deselect the 3-D Pie Chart tab.

6 Click the Save button on the Quick Access Toolbar.

BTW

Quick Reference
For a table that lists how to complete the tasks covered in this book using the mouse, Ribbon, shortcut menu, and keyboard, see the Quick Reference Summary at the back of this book, or visit the Excel 2007 Quick Reference Web page (scsite.com/ex2007/qr).

Campus Clothiers
Semiannual Projected Gross Margin, Expenses, and Operating Income   3/21/2007

	January	February	March	April	May	June	Total
Sales	$3,383,909.82	$6,880,576.15	$9,742,702.37	$4,818,493.53	$4,566,722.63	$8,527,504.39	$37,919,908.89
Cost of Goods Sold	1,319,724.83	2,683,424.70	3,799,653.92	1,879,212.48	1,781,021.83	3,325,726.71	14,788,764.47
Gross Margin	$2,064,184.99	$4,197,151.45	$5,943,048.45	$2,939,281.05	$2,785,700.80	$5,201,777.68	$23,131,144.42
Expenses							
Bonus	$0.00	$100,000.00	$100,000.00	$100,000.00	$0.00	$100,000.00	$400,000.00
Commission	109,977.07	223,618.72	316,637.83	156,601.04	148,418.49	277,143.89	1,232,397.04
Marketing	304,551.88	619,251.85	876,843.21	433,664.42	411,005.04	767,475.40	3,412,791.80
Research and Development	194,574.81	395,633.13	560,205.39	277,063.38	262,586.55	490,331.50	2,180,394.76
Support, General, and Administrative	575,264.67	1,169,697.95	1,656,259.40	819,143.90	776,342.85	1,449,675.75	6,446,384.51
Total Expenses	$1,184,368.44	$2,508,201.65	$3,509,945.83	$1,786,472.74	$1,598,352.92	$3,084,626.54	$13,671,968.11
Operating Income	$879,816.55	$1,688,949.80	$2,433,102.62	$1,152,808.32	$1,187,347.88	$2,117,151.14	$9,459,176.31

What-If Assumptions

Bonus	100,000.00
Commission	3.25%
Margin	61.00%
Marketing	9.00%
Research and Development	5.75%
Revenue for Bonus	4,750,000.00
Support, General, and Administrative	17.00%

(a) Worksheet

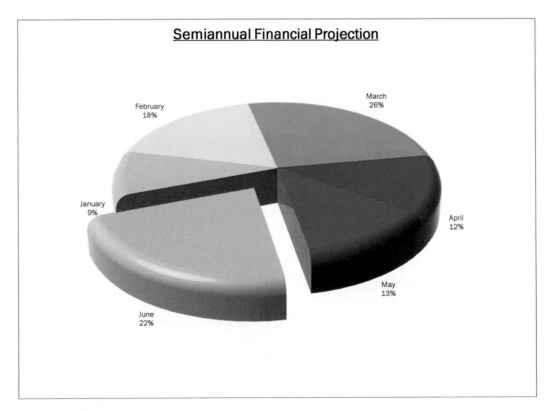

(b) 3-D Pie Chart

Figure 3–72

BTW

Zooming
You can use the Zoom In and Zoom Out buttons on the status bar to zoom from 10% to 400% to reduce or enlarge the display of the worksheet.

Changing the View of the Worksheet

With Excel, you easily can change the view of the worksheet. For example, you can magnify or shrink the worksheet on the screen. You also can view different parts of the worksheet through window panes.

To Shrink and Magnify the View of a Worksheet or Chart

You can magnify (zoom in) or shrink (zoom out) the appearance of a worksheet or chart by using the Zoom button on the View tab on the Ribbon. When you magnify a worksheet, Excel enlarges the view of the characters on the screen, but displays fewer columns and rows. Alternatively, when you shrink a worksheet, Excel is able to display more columns and rows. Magnifying or shrinking a worksheet affects only the view; it does not change the window size or printout of the worksheet or chart. The following steps shrink and magnify the view of the worksheet.

1

- If cell A1 is not active, press CTRL+HOME.

- Click the View tab on the Ribbon and then click the Zoom button on the Ribbon to display a list of Magnifications in the Zoom dialog box (Figure 3–73).

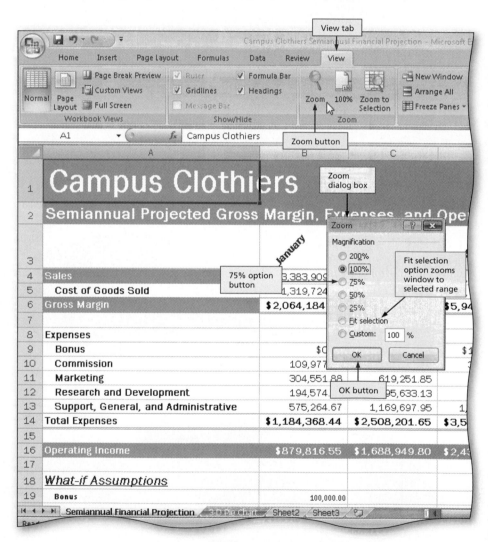

Figure 3–73

2

- Click 75% and then click the OK button to shrink the display of the worksheet to 75% of its normal display (Figure 3–74).

Figure 3–74

3

- Click the Zoom In button on the status bar until the worksheet displays at 100% (Figure 3–75).

Figure 3–75

To Split a Window into Panes

When working with a large worksheet, you can split the window into two or four panes to view different parts of the worksheet at the same time. Splitting the Excel window into four panes at cell D7 allows you to view all four corners of the worksheet easily. The following steps split the Excel window into four panes.

- Select cell D7, the intersection of the four proposed panes.

- If necessary, click the View tab on the Ribbon and then point to the Split button on the Ribbon (Figure 3–76).

Figure 3–76

2

- Click the Split button to divide the window into four panes.

- Use the scroll arrows to show the four corners of the worksheet at the same time (Figure 3–77).

Q&A

What is shown in the four panes?

The four panes in Figure 3–77 are used to show the following: (1) range A1:C6 in the upper-left pane; (2) range G1:I6 in the upper-right pane; (3) range A14:C26 in the lower-left pane; and (4) range G14:I26 in the lower-right pane. The vertical split bar is the vertical bar going up and down the middle of the window. The horizontal split bar is the horizontal bar going across the middle of the window. If you use the scroll bars below the window and to the right of the window to scroll the window, you will see that the panes split by the horizontal split bar scroll together vertically. The panes split by the vertical split bar scroll together horizontally. To resize the panes, drag either split bar to the desired location in the window.

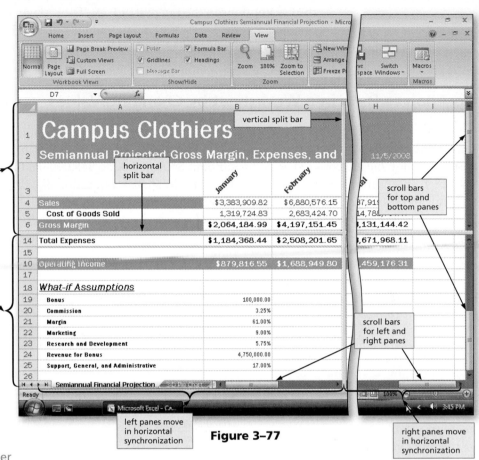

Figure 3–77

Other Ways

1. Drag horizontal split box and vertical split box to desired locations

To Remove the Panes from the Window

1 Position the mouse pointer at the intersection of the horizontal and vertical split bars.

2 When the mouse pointer changes to a four-headed arrow, double-click to remove the four panes from the window.

What-If Analysis

The automatic recalculation feature of Excel is a powerful tool that can be used to analyze worksheet data. Using Excel to scrutinize the impact of changing values in cells that are referenced by a formula in another cell is called **what-if analysis** or **sensitivity analysis**. When new data is entered, Excel not only recalculates all formulas in a worksheet, but also redraws any associated charts.

BTW

Window Panes
If you want to split the window into two panes, rather than four, drag the vertical split box to the far left of the window or horizontal split box to the top of the window (Figure 3–78 on the next page). You also can drag the center of the four panes in any direction to change the size of the panes.

In the workbook created in this chapter, many of the formulas are dependent on the assumptions in the range B19:B25. Thus, if you change any of the assumption values, Excel immediately recalculates all formulas. Excel redraws the 3-D Pie chart as well, because it is based on these numbers.

To Analyze Data in a Worksheet by Changing Values

A what-if question for the worksheet in Chapter 3 might be *what* would happen to the semiannual operating income in cell H16 *if* the Bonus, Commission, Support, General, and Administrative assumptions in the What-If Assumptions table are changed as follows: Bonus $100,000.00 to $75,000.00; Commission 3.25% to 2.25%; Support, General, and Administrative 17.00% to 14.50%? To answer a question like this, you need to change only the first, second, and seventh values in the What-If Assumptions table as shown in the following steps. The steps also divide the window into two vertical panes. Excel instantaneously recalculates the formulas in the worksheet and redraws the 3-D Pie chart to answer the question.

- Use the vertical scroll bar to move the window so cell A6 is in the upper-left corner of the screen.

- Drag the vertical split box from the lower-right corner of the screen to the left so that the vertical split bar is positioned as shown in Figure 3–78.

- Use the right scroll arrow to view the totals in column H in the right pane.

- Enter 75000 in cell B19, 2.25 in cell B20, and 14.50 in cell B25 (Figure 3–78), which causes the semiannual operating income in cell H16 to increase from $9,459,176.31 to $10,886,373.12.

Figure 3–78

To Goal Seek

If you know the result you want a formula to produce, you can use **goal seeking** to determine the value of a cell on which the formula depends. The following steps close and reopen the Campus Clothiers Semiannual Financial Projection workbook. They then show how to use the Goal Seek command on the Data tab on the Ribbon to determine the Support, General, and Administrative percentage in cell B25 that will yield a semiannual operating income of $10,500,000 in cell H16, rather than the original $9,459,176.31.

1

- Close the workbook without saving changes and then reopen it.

- Drag the vertical split box so that the vertical split bar is positioned as shown in Figure 3–79.

- Show column H in the right pane.

- Click cell H16, the cell that contains the semiannual operating income.

- Click the Data tab on the Ribbon and then click the What-If Analysis button on the Ribbon to display the What-If Analysis menu (Figure 3–79).

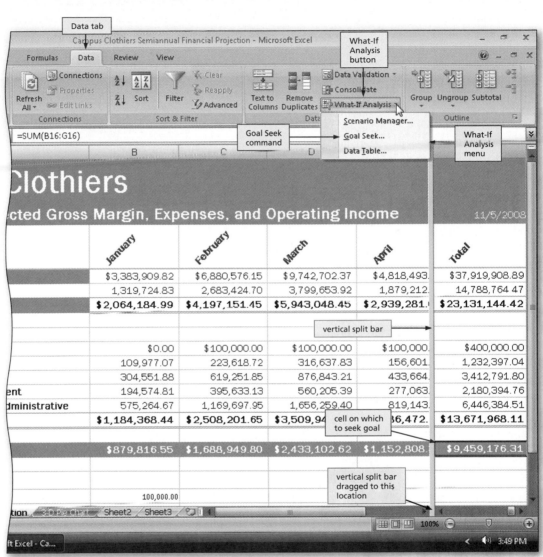

Figure 3–79

2

- Click Goal Seek to display the Goal Seek dialog box with the Set cell box set to the selected cell, H16.

- When Excel displays the Goal Seek dialog box, click the To value text box, type 10,500,000 and then click the By changing cell box.

- Scroll down so row 4 is at the top of the screen.

- Click cell B25 on the worksheet to assign cell B25 to the By changing cell box (Figure 3–80).

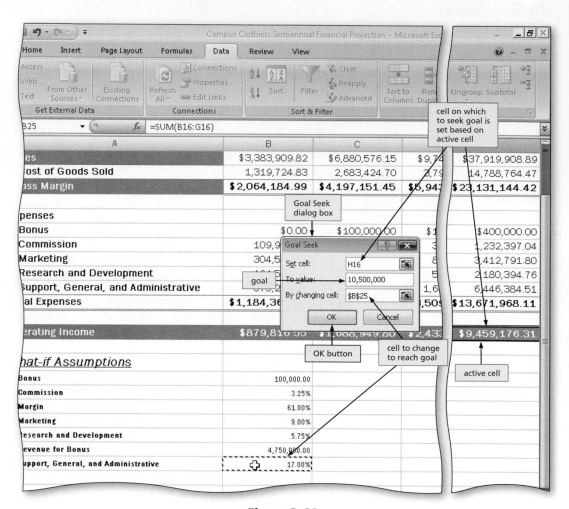

Figure 3–80

3
- Click the OK button to goal seek for the value $10,500,000.00 in cell H16 (Figure 3–81).

Q&A

What happens when I click the OK button?

Excel immediately changes cell H16 from $9,459,176.31 to the desired value of $10,500,000.00. More importantly, Excel changes the Support, General, and Administrative assumption in cell B25 from 17.00% to 14.26% (Figure 3–81). Excel also displays the Goal Seek Status dialog box. If you click the OK button, Excel keeps the new values in the worksheet. If you click the Cancel button, Excel redisplays the original values.

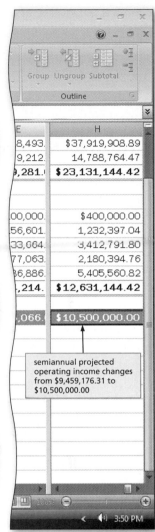

Figure 3–81

4
- Click the Cancel button in the Goal Seek Status dialog box.

Other Ways

1. Press ALT+T, G

Goal Seeking

Goal seeking assumes you can change the value of only one cell referenced directly or indirectly to reach a specific goal for a value in another cell. In this example, to change the semiannual operating income in cell H16 to $10,500,000.00, the Support, General, and Administrative percentage in cell B25 must decrease by 2.74% from 17.00% to 14.26%.

You can see from this goal seeking example that the cell to change (cell B25) does not have to be referenced directly in the formula or function. For example, the semiannual operating income in cell H16 is calculated by the function =SUM(B16:G16). Cell B25 is not referenced in this function. Instead, cell B25 is referenced in the formulas in rows 9 through 13, on which the monthly operating incomes in row 16 are based. Excel thus is capable of goal seeking on the semiannual operating income by varying the value for the Support, General, and Administrative assumption.

BTW

Undoing What You Did
The Undo button is ideal for returning the worksheet to its original state after you have changed the values in a worksheet to answer a what-if question. To view the original worksheet after answering a what-if question, click the Undo button on the Quick Access Toolbar for each value you changed.

To Quit Excel

To quit Excel, complete the following steps.

1 Click the Close button on the title bar.

2 If the Microsoft Excel dialog box is displayed, click the No button.

Chapter Summary

In this chapter you learned how to work with large worksheets that extend beyond the window, how to use the fill handle to create a series, new formatting techniques, about the difference between absolute cell references and relative cell references, how to use the IF function, how to rotate text in a cell, freeze titles, change the magnification of the worksheet, show different parts of the worksheet at the same time through multiple panes, create a 3-D Pie chart, and improve the appearance of a 3-D Pie chart. This chapter also introduced you to using Excel to do what-if analysis by changing values in cells and goal seeking. The items listed below include all the new Excel skills you have learned in this chapter.

1. Rotate Text and Use the Fill Handle to Create a Series of Month Names (EX 169)
2. Increase Column Widths and Enter Row Titles (EX 173)
3. Copy a Range of Cells to a Nonadjacent Destination Area (EX 175)
4. Insert a Row (EX 177)
5. Enter Numbers with Format Symbols (EX 181)
6. Freeze Column and Row Titles (EX 182)
7. Enter and Format the System Date (EX 184)
8. Enter a Formula Containing Absolute Cell References (EX 187)
9. Enter an IF Function (EX 190)
10. Copy Formulas with Absolute Cell References Using the Fill Handle (EX 192)
11. Unfreeze the Worksheet Titles and Save the Workbook (EX 194)
12. Assign Formats to Nonadjacent Ranges (EX 196)
13. Format the Worksheet Titles (EX 199)
14. Copy a Cell's Format Using the Format Painter Button (EX 201)
15. Draw a 3-D Pie Chart on a Separate Chart Sheet (EX 205)
16. Insert a Chart Title and Data Labels (EX 206)
17. Rotate the 3-D Pie Chart (EX 209)
18. Apply a 3-D Format to the Pie Chart (EX 211)
19. Explode the 3-D Pie Chart and Change the Color of a Slice (EX 213)
20. Rename and Reorder the Sheets and Color Their Tabs (EX 216)
21. Check Spelling in Multiple Sheets (EX 218)
22. Shrink and Magnify the View of a Worksheet or Chart (EX 220)
23. Split a Window into Panes (EX 222)
24. Analyze Data in a Worksheet by Changing Values (EX 224)
25. Goal Seek (EX 225)

 If you have a SAM user profile, you may have access to hands-on instruction, practice, and assessment. Log in to your SAM account (http://sam2007.course.com) to launch any assigned training activities or exams that relate to the skills covered in this chapter.

Learn It Online

Learn It Online is a series of online student exercises that test your knowledge of chapter content and key terms.

Instructions: To complete the Learn It Online exercises, start your browser, click the Address bar, and then enter the Web address scsite.com/off2007/learn. When the Office 2007 Learn It Online page is displayed, click the link for the exercise you want to complete and then read the instructions.

Chapter Reinforcement TF, MC, and SA
A series of true/false, multiple choice, and short answer questions that test your knowledge of the chapter content.

Flash Cards
An interactive learning environment where you identify chapter key terms associated with displayed definitions.

Practice Test
A series of multiple choice questions that test your knowledge of chapter content and key terms.

Who Wants To Be a Computer Genius?
An interactive game that challenges your knowledge of chapter content in the style of a television quiz show.

Wheel of Terms
An interactive game that challenges your knowledge of chapter key terms in the style of the television show *Wheel of Fortune*.

Crossword Puzzle Challenge
A crossword puzzle that challenges your knowledge of key terms presented in the chapter.

Apply Your Knowledge

Reinforce the skills and apply the concepts you learned in this chapter.

Understanding Logical Tests and Absolute Cell Referencing
Instructions Part 1: Determine the truth value (true or false) of the following logical tests, given the following cell values: X4 = 25; Y3 = 28; K7 = 110; Z2 = 15; and Q9 = 35. Enter true or false.

a. Y3 < X4   Truth value: _____

b. Q9 = K7   Truth value: _____

c. X4 + 15 * Z2 / 5 <> K7   Truth value: _____

d. K7 / Z2 > X4 − Y3   Truth value: _____

e. Q9 * 2 − 42 < (X4 + Y3 − 8) / 9   Truth value: _____

f. K7 + 300 <= X4 * Z2 + 10   Truth value: _____

g. Q9 + K7 > 2 * (Q9 + 25)   Truth value: _____

h. Y3 = 4 * (Q9 / 5)   Truth value: _____

Instructions Part 2: Write cell K23 as a relative reference, absolute reference, mixed reference with the row varying, and mixed reference with the column varying.

_____ _____ _____ _____

Instructions Part 3: Start Excel. Open the workbook Apply 3-1 Absolute Cell References. See the inside back cover of this book for instructions for downloading the Data Files for Students, or see your instructor for information on accessing the files required in this book. You will recreate the numerical grid pictured in Figure 3–82 on the next page.

Continued >

Apply Your Knowledge *continued*

Perform the following tasks:

1. Enter a formula in cell C7 that multiplies cell C2 times the sum of cells C3 through C6. Write the formula so that when you copy it to cells D7 and E7, cell C2 remains absolute. Verify your formula by checking it with the values found in cells C7, D7, and E7 in Figure 3–82.

2. Enter a formula in cell F3 that multiplies cell B3 times the sum of cells C3 through E3. Write the formula so that when you copy the formula to cells F4, F5, and F6, cell B3 remains absolute. Verify your formula by checking it with the values found in cells F3, F4, F5, and F6 in Figure 3–82.

3. Enter a formula in cell C8 that multiplies cell C2 times the sum of cells C3 through C6. Write the formula so that when you copy the formula to cells D8 and E8, Excel adjusts all the cell references according to the destination cells. Verify your formula by checking it with the values found in cells C8, D8, and E8 in Figure 3–82.

4. Enter a formula in cell G3 that multiplies cell B3 times the sum of cells C3, D3, and E3. Write the formula so that when you copy the formula to cells G4, G5, and G6, Excel adjusts all the cell references according to the destination cells. Verify your formula by checking it with the values found in cells G3, G4, G5, and G6 in Figure 3–82.

5. Change the document properties, as specified by your instructor. Change the worksheet header with your name, course number, and other information requested by your instructor. Save the workbook using the file name, Apply 3-1 Absolute Cell References Complete, and submit the revised workbook as requested by your instructor.

Figure 3–82

Extend Your Knowledge

Extend the skills you learned in this chapter and experiment with new skills. You may need to use Help to complete the assignment.

Nested IF Functions and More About the Fill Handle

Instructions Part 1: Start Excel. You will use nested IF functions to determine values for sets of data.

Perform the following tasks:

1. Enter the following IF function in cell C1:

=IF(B1="CA","West", IF(B1="NJ","East", IF(B1="IL","Midwest","State Error")))

2. Use the fill handle to copy the nested IF function down through cell C7. Enter the following data in the cells in the range B1:B7 and then write down the results that display in cells C1 through C7 for each set. Set 1: B1 = CA; B2 = NY; B3 = NJ; B4 = MI; B5 = IL; B6 = CA; B7 = IL. Set 2: B1= WI; B2 = NJ; B3 = IL; B4 = CA; B5 = NJ; B6 = NY; B7 = CA.

Set 1 Results: _____

Set 2 Results: _____

Instructions Part 2: Start Excel. Open the workbook Extend 3-1 Create Series. See the inside back cover of this book for instructions for downloading the Data Files for Students, or see your instructor for information on accessing the files required in this book.

Perform the following tasks:

1. Use the fill handle on one column at a time to propagate the fourteen series through row 16 as shown in Figure 3–83. For example, in column A, select cell A2 and drag the fill handle down to cell A16. In column C, hold down the CTRL key to repeat Monday through cell C16. In column D, select the range D2:D3 and drag the fill handle down to cell D16. Likewise, in columns F and I through K, select the two adjacent cells in rows 2 and 3 before dragging the fill handle down to the corresponding cell in row 16.

2. Select cell D21. While holding down the CTRL key, one at a time drag the fill handle three cells to the right, to the left, up, and down to generate four series of numbers beginning with zero and incremented by one.

3. Select cell I21. Point to the cell border so that the mouse pointer changes to a plus sign with four arrows. Drag the mouse pointer down to cell I22 to move the contents of cell I21 to cell I22.

4. Select cell I22. Point to the cell border so that the mouse pointer changes to a plus sign with four arrows. While holding down the CTRL key, drag the mouse pointer to cell M22 to copy the contents of cell I22 to cell M22.

5. Select cell M21. Drag the fill handle in to the center of cell M21 so that the cell is shaded in order to delete the cell contents.

6. Change the document properties, as specified by your instructor. Change the worksheet header with your name,

	B	C	D	E	F	G	H	I	J	K	L	M	N	O	P
1				Using the Magical Fill Handle											
2	Monday	Monday	Mon	January	Jan	1	Version 1	1st Year	-1	1.00%	0.2	2007			
3	Tuesday	Monday	Tue	February	Feb	2	Version 2	2nd Year	-3	3.00%	0.4	2008			
4	Wednesda	Monday	Wed	March	Mar	3	Version 3	3rd Year	-5	5.00%	0.6	2009			
5	Thursday	Monday	Thu	April	Apr	4	Version 4	4th Year	-7	7.00%	0.8	2010			
6	Friday	Monday	Fri	May	May	5	Version 5	5th Year	-9	9.00%	1	2011			
7	Saturday	Monday	Sat	June	Jun	6	Version 6	6th Year	-11	11.00%	1.2	2012			
8	Sunday	Monday	Sun	July	Jul	7	Version 7	7th Year	-13	13.00%	1.4	2013			
9	Monday	Monday	Mon	August	Aug	8	Version 8	8th Year	-15	15.00%	1.6	2014			
10	Tuesday	Monday	Tue	September	Sep	9	Version 9	9th Year	-17	17.00%	1.8	2015			
11	Wednesda	Monday	Wed	October	Oct	10	Version 10	10th Year	-19	19.00%	2	2016			
12	Thursday	Monday	Thu	November	Nov	11	Version 11	11th Year	-21	21.00%	2.2	2017			
13	Friday	Monday	Fri	December	Dec	12	Version 12	12th Year	-23	23.00%	2.4	2018			
14	Saturday	Monday	Sat	January	Jan	13	Version 13	13th Year	-25	25.00%	2.6	2019			
15	Sunday	Monday	Sun	February	Feb	14	Version 14	14th Year	-27	27.00%	2.8	2020			
16	Monday	Monday	Mon	March	Mar	15	Version 15	15th Year	-29	29.00%	3	2021			
17															
18			-3												
19			-2												
20			-1												
21	-2	-1	0		1	2	3								
22			1					Move				Move			
23			2												
24			3												
25															

Figure 3–83

course number, and other information requested by your instructor. Save the workbook using the file name, Extend 3-1 Create Series Complete, and submit the revised workbook as requested by your instructor.

STUDENT ASSIGNMENTS

Make It Right

Analyze a workbook and correct all errors and/or improve the design.

Inserting Rows, Moving a Range, and Correcting Formulas in a Worksheet

Instructions: Start Excel. Open the workbook Make It Right 3-1 e-MusicPro.com Annual Projected Net Income. See the inside back cover of this book for instructions for downloading the Data Files for Students, or see your instructor for information on accessing the files required for this book. Correct the following design and formula problems (Figure 3–84a) in the worksheet.

(a) Before

(b) After

Figure 3–84

1. The Royalty in cell C3 is computed using the formula =B9*B3 (Royalties % × Sales). Similar formulas are used in cells C4 and C5. The formula in cell C3 was entered and copied to cells C4 and C5. Although the result in cell C3 is correct, the results in cells C4 and C5 are incorrect. Edit the formula in cell C3 by changing cell B9 to an absolute cell reference. Copy the corrected formula in cell C3 to cells C4 and C5. After completing the copy, click the Auto Fill Options button arrow that displays below and to the right of cell C5 and choose Fill Without Formatting.

2. The Royalty Bonus amounts in cells D3, D4, and D5 are computed using the IF function. The Royalty Bonus should equal the amount in cell B10 ($50,000) if the corresponding Sales in column B is greater than or equal to $2,750,000. If the corresponding Sales in column B is less than $2,750,000, then the Royalty Bonus is zero ($0). The IF function in cell D3 was entered and

copied to cells D4 and D5. The current IF functions in cells D3, D4, and D5 are incorrect. Edit and correct the IF function in cell D3. Copy the corrected formula in cell D3 to cells D4 and D5. After completing the copy, click the Auto Fill Options button arrow that displays below and to the right of cell D5 and choose Fill Without Formatting.

3. The Manufacturing Costs in cell E3 is computed using the formula =B11*B3 (Manu. Costs % x Sales). The formula in cell E3 was entered and copied to cells E4 and E5. Although the result in cell E3 is correct, the results in cells E4 and E5 are incorrect. Edit and correct the formula in cell E3 by changing cell B11 to an absolute cell reference. Copy the corrected formula in cell E3 to cells E4 and E5. After completing the copy, click the Auto Fill Options button arrow that displays below and to the right of cell E5 and choose Fill Without Formatting.

4. Change the design of the worksheet by moving the Assumptions table in the range A8:B11 to the range A1:B4 as shown in Figure 3–84b. To complete the move, insert five rows above row 1 and then drag the Assumptions table to the range A1:B4. Use Figure 3–84b to verify that Excel automatically adjusted the cell references based on the move. Use the Undo button and Redo button on the Quick Access Toolbar to move the Assumptions table back and forth while the results of the formulas remain the same.

5. Change the document properties, as specified by your instructor. Change the worksheet header with your name, course number, and other information requested by your instructor. Save the workbook using the file name, Make It Right 3-1 e-MusicPro.com Annual Projected Net Income Complete, and submit the revised workbook as requested by your instructor.

In the Lab

Create a workbook using the guidelines, concepts, and skills presented in this chapter. Labs are listed in order of increasing difficulty.

Lab 1: Eight-Year Financial Projection

Problem: Your supervisor in the Finance department at Salioto Auto Parts has asked you to create a worksheet that will project the annual gross margin, expenses, total expenses, operating income, income taxes, and net income for the next ten years based on the assumptions in Table 3–9. The desired worksheet is shown in Figure 3–85 on the next page. In Part 1 you will create the worksheet. In Part 2 you will create a chart to present the data, shown in Figure 3–86 on page 236. In Part 3 you will use Goal Seek to analyze three different sales scenarios.

Table 3–9 Salioto Auto Parts Financial Projection Assumptions	
Units Sold in Prior Year	11,459,713
Unit Cost	$13.40
Annual Sales Growth	4.50%
Annual Price Decrease	4.25%
Margin	39.25%

Continued >

In the Lab *continued*

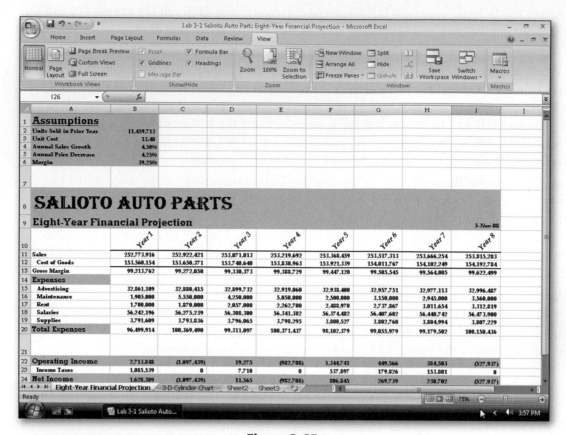

Figure 3–85

Instructions Part 1:

1. Start Excel. Apply the Apex theme to the worksheet by using the Themes button on the Page Layout tab on the Ribbon. Bold the entire worksheet by selecting the entire worksheet and using the Bold button on the Home tab on the Ribbon.

2. Enter the worksheet title Salioto Auto Parts in cell A8 and the subtitle Eight-Year Financial Projection in cell A9. Format the worksheet title in cell A8 to 36-point Algerian (or a similar font). Format the worksheet subtitle in cell A9 to 20-point Rockwell (or a similar font). Enter the system date in cell I9 using the NOW function. Format the date to the 14-Mar-01 style.

3. Change the following column widths: A = 25.00 characters; B through I = 15.00 characters. Change the heights of rows 7, 10, and 21 to 42.00 points.

4. Enter the eight column titles Year 1 through Year 8 in the range B10:I10 by entering Year 1 in cell B10 and then dragging cell B10's fill handle through the range C10:I10. Format cell B10 as follows: (a) increase the font size to 14; (b) center and italicize; and (c) rotate its contents 45°. Use the Format Painter button to copy the format assigned to cell B10 to the range C10:I10.

5. Enter the row titles in the range A11:A24. Change the font in cells A14, A20, A22, and A24 to 14-point Rockwell (or a similar font). Add thick bottom borders to the ranges B10:I10 and B12:I12.

6. Enter the table title Assumptions in cell A1. Enter the assumptions in Table 3-9 in the range A2:B6. Use format symbols when entering the numbers. Change the font size of the table title to 14-point Rockwell and underline it.

7. Select the range B11:I24 and then click the Format Cells: Number Dialog Box Launcher on the Home tab on the Ribbon to display the Format Cells dialog box. Use the Number category in the Format Cells dialog box to assign the Comma style with no decimal places and negative numbers enclosed in parentheses to the range B11:I24.

8. Complete the following entries:

   a. Year 1 Sales (cell B11) = Units Sold in Prior Year * (Unit Cost / (1 − Margin)) or =B2 * (B3 / (1 − B6))

   b. Year 2 Sales (cell C11) = Year 1 Sales * (1 + Annual Sales Growth) * (1 − Annual Price Decrease) or =B11 * (1 + $B$4) * (1 − $B$5)

   c. Copy cell C11 to the range D11:I11.

   d. Year 1 Cost of Goods (cell B12) = Year 1 Sales − (Year 1 Sales * Margin) or =B11 * (1 − $B$6)

   e. Copy cell B12 to the range C12:I12.

   f. Gross Margin (cell B13) = Year 1 Sales − Year 1 Cost of Goods or =B11 − B12

   g. Copy cell B13 to the range C13:I13.

   h. Year 1 Advertising (cell B15) = 500 + 13% * Year 1 Sales or =500 + 13% * B11

   i. Copy cell B15 to the range C15:I15.

   j. Maintenance (row 16): Year 1 = 1,905,000; Year 2 = 5,550,000; Year 3 = 4,250,000; Year 4 = 5,050,000; Year 5 = 2,500,000; Year 6 = 3,150,000; Year 7 = 2,945,000; and Year 8 = 3,560.000.

   k. Year 1 Rent (cell B17) = 1,700,000

   l. Year 2 Rent (cell C17) = Year 1 Rent + 10% * Year 1 Rent or =B17 * (1 + 10%)

   m. Copy cell C17 to the range D17:I17.

   n. Year 1 Salaries (cell B18) = 22.25% * Year 1 Sales or =22.25% * B11

   o. Copy cell B18 to the range C18:I18.

   p. Year 1 Supplies (cell B19) = 1.5% * Year 1 Sales or =1.5% * B11

   q. Copy cell B19 to the range C19:I19.

   r. Year 1 Total Expenses (cell B20) or =SUM(B15:B19)

   s. Copy cell B20 to the range C20:I20.

   t. Year 1 Operating Income (cell B22) = Year 1 Gross Margin − Year 1 Total Expenses or =B13 − B20

   u. Copy cell B22 to the range C22:I22.

   v. Year 1 Income Taxes (cell B23): If Year 1 Operating Income is less than 0, then Year 1 Income Taxes equal 0; otherwise Year 1 Income Taxes equal 40% * Year 1 Operating Income or =IF(B22 < 0, 0, 40% * B22)

   w. Copy cell B23 to the range C23:I23.

   x. Year 1 Net Income (cell B24) = Year 1 Operating Income − Year 1 Income Taxes or =B22 − B23

   y. Copy cell B24 to the range C24:I24.

9. Change the background colors as shown in Figure 3-85. Use Orange (column 3 under Standard Colors) for the background colors.

10. Zoom to: (a) 200%; (b) 75%; (c) 25%; and (d) 100%.

11. Change the document properties, as specified by your instructor. Change the worksheet header with your name, course number, and other information requested by your instructor. Save the workbook using the file name, Lab 3-1 Salioto Auto Parts Eight-Year Financial Projection.

12. Preview the worksheet. Use the Page Setup button to fit the printout on one page in landscape orientation. Preview the formulas version (CTRL+`) of the worksheet in landscape orientation using the Fit to option. Press CTRL+` to instruct Excel to display the values version of the worksheet. Save the workbook again and close the workbook.

13. Submit the workbook as requested by your instructor.

Instructions Part 2:

1. Start Excel. Open the workbook Lab 3-1 Salioto Auto Parts Eight-Year Financial Projection.

2. Use the nonadjacent ranges B10:I10 and B24:I24 to create a 3-D Cylinder chart. Draw the chart by clicking the Column button on the Insert tab on the Ribbon. When the Column gallery is displayed, click the Clustered Cylinder chart type (column 1, row 2). When the chart is displayed, click the Move Chart button on the Ribbon to move the chart to a new sheet.

Continued >

In the Lab *continued*

3. Select the legend on the right side of the chart and delete it. Add the chart title by clicking the Layout tab on the Ribbon, then clicking the Chart Title button. Click Above Chart in the Chart Title gallery. Format the chart title as shown in Figure 3–86.

4. To change the color of the cylinders, click one of the cylinders and use the Shape Fill button on the Format tab on the Ribbon. To change the color of the wall, click the wall behind the cylinders and use the Shape Fill button on the Format tab on the Ribbon. Use the same procedure to change the color of the base of the wall.

5. Rename the sheet tabs Eight-Year Financial Projection and 3-D Cylinder Chart. Rearrange the sheets so that the worksheet is leftmost, and color their tabs as shown in Figure 3–86.

6. Click the Eight-Year Financial Projection tab to display the worksheet. Save the workbook using the same file name (Lab 3-1 Salioto Auto Parts Eight-Year Financial Projection) as defined in Part 1. Submit the workbook as requested by your instructor.

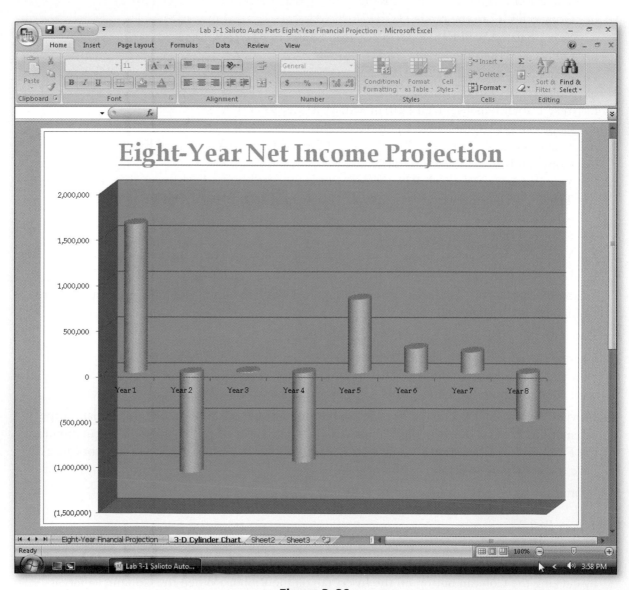

Figure 3–86

Instructions Part 3:

1. Start Excel. Open the workbook Lab 3-1 Salioto Auto Parts Eight-Year Financial Projection. Do not save the workbook in this part. Divide the window into two panes by dragging the horizontal split box between rows 6 and 7. Use the scroll bars to show both the top and bottom of the worksheet. Using the numbers in columns 2 and 3 of Table 3-10, analyze the effect of changing the annual sales growth (cell B4) and annual price decrease (cell B5) on the net incomes in row 24. The resulting answers are in column 4 of Table 3-10. Submit the workbook or results of the what-if analysis for each case as requested by your instructor.

Table 3–10 Salioto Auto Parts Data to Analyze and Results			
Case	Annual Sales Growth	Annual Price Decrease	Year 8 Resulting Net Income in Cell I24
1	7.45%	5.25%	174,568
2	12.75%	−3.00%	6,677,903
3	−7.25%	1.65%	(3,552,156)

2. Close the workbook without saving it, and then reopen it. Use the What-If Analysis button on the Data tab on the Ribbon to goal seek. Determine a margin (cell B6) that would result in a Year 8 net income of $2,000,000 (cell I24). You should end up with a margin of 40.68% in cell B6. Submit the workbook with the new values or the results of the goal seek as requested by your instructor. Do not save the workbook with the latest changes.

In the Lab

Lab 2: Modifying a Weekly Payroll Worksheet

Problem: As a summer intern at Britney's Music Emporium, you have been asked to modify the weekly payroll report shown in Figure 3–87a on the next page. The workbook, Lab 3-2 Britney's Music Emporium Weekly Payroll Report, is included with the Data Files for Students. See the inside back cover of this book for instructions for downloading the Data Files for Students, or see your instructor for information on accessing the files required for this book.

The major modifications to the payroll report to be made in this exercise include: (1) reformatting the worksheet; (2) adding computations of time-and-a-half for hours worked greater than 40; (3) adding calculations to charge no federal tax in certain situations; (4) adding Social Security and Medicare deductions; (5) adding and deleting employees; and (6) changing employee information. The final payroll report is shown in Figure 3–87b on the next page.

STUDENT ASSIGNMENTS

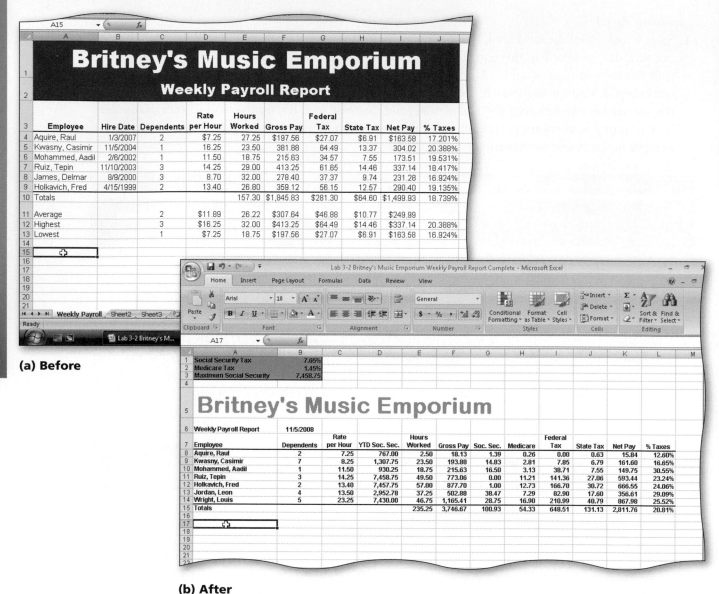

(a) Before

(b) After

Figure 3–87

Instructions Part 1:

1. Start Excel. Open the workbook, Lab 3-2 Britney's Music Emporium Weekly Payroll Report and then save the workbook using the file name Lab 3-2 Britney's Music Emporium Weekly Payroll Report Complete.

2. Select the worksheet by clicking the Select All button. Click the Clear button on the Home tab on the Ribbon and then click Clear Formats on the Clear menu to clear the formatting. Bold the entire worksheet.

3. Delete rows 11 through 13 to remove the statistics below the Totals row. Change all the row heights back to the default height (12.75).

4. Insert four rows above row 1 by selecting rows 1 through 4, right-clicking the selection, and clicking Insert on the shortcut menu.

5. Change the row heights as follows: row 5 = 48.00; rows 6 and 7 = 25.50. One at a time, select cells D7, E7, and G7. For each cell, press the F2 key and then the ENTER key to display the column headings on multiple rows. Center the range B7:J7.

6. Delete column B by right-clicking the column heading and clicking Delete on the shortcut menu.

7. Insert a new column between columns C and D. Change the column widths as follows: A = 25.00; D = 13.00; and E through K = 9.71. Enter the new column D title **YTD Soc. Sec.** in cell D7.

8. Insert two new columns between columns F and G. Enter the new column G title **Soc. Sec.** in cell G7. Enter the new column H title **Medicare** in cell H7.

9. Enhance the worksheet title in cell A5 by using a 36-point light blue Arial Rounded MT Bold (or a similar font) font style as shown in Figure 3–87b.

10. Assign the NOW function to cell B6 and format it to the 3/14/2001 style.

11. Delete employee James, Delmar (row 12). Change Raul Aquire's (row 8) hours worked to 2.5. Change Casimir Kwasny's (row 9) number of dependents to 7 and rate per hour to $8.25. Change Tepin Ruiz's (row 11) hours worked to 49.5 and Fred Holkavich's (row 12) hours worked to 57.

12. Freeze column A and rows 1 through 7 by selecting cell B8, clicking the Freeze Panes button on the View tab on the Ribbon, and then clicking Freeze Panes on the Freeze Panes menu.

13. In column D, enter the YTD Soc. Sec. values listed in Table 3–11.

14. Insert two new rows immediately above the Totals row. Add the new employee data as listed in Table 3–12.

Table 3–11 The Britney Music Emporium's YTD Social Security Values

Employee	YTD Soc. Sec.
Aquire, Raul	767.00
Kwasny, Casimir	1307.75
Mohammed, Aadil	930.25
Ruiz, Tepin	7458.75
Holkavich, Fred	7457.75

Table 3–12 The Britney Music Emporium's New Employee Data

Employee	Dependents	Rate per Hour	YTD Soc. Sec.	Hours Worked
Jordan, Leon	4	13.50	2952.78	37.25
Wright, Louis	5	23.25	7430.00	46.75

15. Center the range B6:B14. Use the Currency category in the Format Cells dialog box to assign a Comma style (no dollar signs) with two decimal places and negative numbers within parentheses to the range C8:K15. Assign a Percent style and two decimal places to the range L8:L15. Draw a thick bottom border in the ranges A7:L7 and A14:L14.

16. As shown in Figure 3–87b, enter and format the Social Security (7.65% with a maximum of $7,458.75) and Medicare tax (1.45%) information in the range A1:B3. Use format symbols where applicable.

17. Change the formulas to determine the gross pay in column F and the federal tax in column I as follows:

   a. In cell F8, enter an IF function that applies the following logic and then copy it to the range F9:F14. If Hours Worked <= 40, then Rate per Hour * Hours Worked, otherwise Rate per Hour * Hours Worked + 0.5 * Rate per Hour * (Hours Worked − 40) or =IF(E8 <= 40, C8 * E8, C8 * E8 + 0.5 * C8 *(E8 − 40))

   b. In cell I8, enter the IF function that applies the following logic and then copy it to the range I9:I14. If (Gross Pay − Dependents * 22.09 > 0, then 20% * (Gross Pay − Dependents * 22.09), otherwise 0 or =IF(F8 − B8 * 22.09 > 0, 20% * (F8 − B8 * 22.09), 0)

Continued >

In the Lab *continued*

18. An employee pays Social Security tax only if his or her YTD Soc. Sec. in column D is less than the Maximum Social Security value in cell B3. Use the following logic to determine the Social Security tax for Raul Aquire in cell G8 and then copy it to the range G9:G14.

    Soc. Sec. (cell G8): If Social Security Tax * Gross Pay + YTD Soc. Sec. > Maximum Social Security, then Maximum Social Security − YTD Soc. Sec., otherwise Social Security Tax * Gross Pay or =IF($B$1 * F8 + D8 >= $B$3, $B$3 − D8, $B$1 * F8)

19. In cell H8, enter the following formula and then copy it to the range H9:H14:

    Medicare (cell H8) = Medicare Tax * Gross Pay or =$B$2 * F8

20. In cell K8, enter the following formula and copy it to the range K9:K14:

    Net Pay (K8) = Gross Pay − (Soc. Sec. + Medicare + Federal Tax + State Tax) or =F8 − (G8 + H8 + I8 + J8)

21. In cell L8, enter the following formula and copy it to the range L9:L14:

    % Taxes (cell L8) = (Soc. Sec. + Medicare + Federal Tax + State Tax) / Gross Pay or =(G8 + H8 + I8 + J8) / F8

22. Use the Range Finder (double-click cell) to verify the new totals as shown in row 15 in Figure 3–87b. Unfreeze the worksheet by clicking the Freeze Panes button on the View tab on the Ribbon, and then clicking Unfreeze Panes on the Freeze Panes menu.

23. Preview the worksheet. Use the Page Setup button to change the orientation to landscape and fit the report on one page.

24. Change the document properties, as specified by your instructor. Change the worksheet header with your name, course number, and other information requested by your instructor. Save the workbook.

25. Use the Zoom button on the View tab on the Ribbon to change the view of the worksheet. One by one, select all the percents on the Zoom dialog box. When you are done, return the worksheet to 100% magnification.

26. Preview the formulas version (CTRL+`) in landscape orientation. Close the worksheet without saving the latest changes.

27. Submit the workbook as requested by your instructor.

Instructions Part 2: Start Excel. Open Lab 3-2 Britney's Music Emporium Weekly Payroll Report Complete. Do not save the workbook in this part. Using the numbers in Table 3–13, analyze the effect of changing the Medicare tax in cell B2. The first case should result in a total Medicare tax in cell H15 of $106.78. The second case should result in a total Medicare tax of $166.73. Close the workbook without saving changes. Submit the results of the what-if analysis as requested by your instructor.

Table 3–13 The Britney Music Emporium's Medicare Tax Cases	
Case	**Medicare Tax**
1	2.85%
2	4.45%

Instructions Part 3: Submit results for this part as requested by your instructor.

1. Start Excel. Open Lab 3-2 Britney's Music Emporium Weekly Payroll Report Complete. Select cell F8. Write down the formula that Excel displays in the formula bar. Select the range C8:C14. Point to the border surrounding the range and drag the selection to the range D17:D23. Click cell F8, and write down the formula that Excel displays in the formula bar below the one you wrote down earlier. Compare the two formulas. What can you conclude about how Excel responds when you move cells involved in a formula? Click the Undo button on the Quick Access Toolbar.

2. Right-click the range C8:C14 and then click Delete on the shortcut menu. When Excel displays the Delete dialog box, click Shift cells left and then click the OK button. What does Excel display in cell F8? Click cell F8 and then point to the Trace Error button that is displayed to the left of the cell. Write down the ScreenTip that is displayed. Click the Undo button on the Quick Access Toolbar.

3. Right-click the range C8:C14 and then click Insert on the shortcut menu. When Excel displays the Insert dialog box, click Shift cells right and then click the OK button. What does Excel display in the formula bar when you click cell F8? What does Excel display in the formula bar when you click cell G8? What can you conclude about how Excel responds when you insert cells next to cells involved in a formula? Close the workbook without saving the changes.

In the Lab

Lab 3: Analysis of Indirect Expense Allocations

Problem: Your classmate works part time as a consultant for RockieView Resort and Spa. She has asked you to assist her in creating an indirect expense allocation worksheet (Figure 3–88) that will help the resort and spa administration better evaluate the profit centers described in Table 3–14 on the next page.

Figure 3–88

Continued >

In the Lab *continued*

Table 3–14 RockieView Resort and Spa Worksheet Data

	Banquet Room	Business Center	Children's Game Room	Conference Rooms	Gift Shop	Lounge	Restaurant	Spa
Total Net Revenue	345819	192190	52750	212300	112100	622350	615350	92900
Cost of Sales	19750	16235	12900	55250	42100	115400	175000	42150
Direct Expenses	9245	9245	7250	19300	37400	101000	115600	24800
Square Footage	10500	875	1425	6250	1325	7500	6700	2750

Instructions Part 1: Do the following to create the worksheet shown in Figure 3–88.

1. Apply the Solstice theme to the worksheet. Bold the entire worksheet by selecting the entire worksheet and using the Bold button on the Ribbon.

2. Change the following column widths: A = 28.00; B through I = 13.00; J = 14.00.

3. Enter the worksheet titles in cells A1 and A2 and the system date in cell J2. Format the date to the 14-Mar-01 style.

4. Enter the column titles, row titles, and the first three rows of numbers in Table 3–14 in rows 3 through 6. Center and italicize the column headings in the range B3:J3. Add a thick bottom border to the range B3:J3. Sum the individual rows 4, 5, and 6 in the range J4:J6.

5. Enter the Square Footage row in Table 3–14 with the comma format symbol in row 16. Sum row 16 in cell J16. Use the Format Painter button to format cell J16. Change the height of row 16 to 39.00. Vertically center the range A16:J16 through the use of the Format Cells dialog box.

6. Enter the remaining row titles in the range A7:A17 as shown in Figure 3–88. Increase the font size in cells A7, A14, and A15 to 16 point.

7. Copy the row titles in range A8:A13 to the range A18:A23. Enter the numbers shown in the range B18:B23 of Figure 3–88 with format symbols.

8. The planned indirect expenses in the range B18:B23 are to be prorated across the profit center as follows: Administrative (row 8), Energy (row 10), and Marketing (row 13) on the basis of Total Net Revenue (row 4); Depreciation (row 9), Insurance (row 11), and Maintenance (row 12) on the basis of Square Footage (row 16). Use the following formulas to accomplish the prorating:

   a. Banquet Room Administrative (cell B8) = Administrative Expenses * Banquet Room Total Net Revenue / Resort Total Net Revenue or =$B$18 * B4 / $J$4

   b. Banquet Room Depreciation (cell B9) = Depreciation Expenses * Banquet Room Square Footage / Total Square Footage or =$B$19 * B16 / $J$16

   c. Banquet Room Energy (cell B10) = Energy Expenses * Banquet Room Total Net Revenue / Resort Total Net Revenue or =$B$20 * B4 / $J$4

   d. Banquet Room Insurance (cell B11) = Insurance Expenses * Banquet Room Square Feet / Total Square Footage or =$B$21 * B16 / $J$16

   e. Banquet Room Maintenance (cell B12) = Maintenance Expenses * Banquet Room Square Footage / Total Square Footage or =$B$22 * B16 / $J$16

   f. Banquet Room Marketing (cell B13) = Marketing Expenses * Banquet Room Total Net Revenue / Resort Total Net Revenue or =$B$23 * B4 / $J$4

   g. Banquet Room Total Indirect Expenses (cell B14) = SUM(B8:B13)

   h. Banquet Room Net Income (cell B15) = Total Net Revenue − (Cost of Sales + Direct Expenses + Total Indirect Expenses) or =B4 − (B5 + B6 + B14)

   i. Copy the range B8:B15 to the range C8:I15.

   j. Sum the individual rows 8 through 15 in the range J8:J15.

9. Add a thick bottom border to the range B13:J13. Assign the Currency style with two decimal places and show negative numbers in parentheses to the following ranges: B4:J4; B8:J8; and B14:J15. Assign the Comma style with two decimal places and show negative numbers in parentheses to the following ranges: B5:J6 and B9:J13.

10. Change the font in cell A1 to 48-point Britannic Bold (or a similar font). Change the font in cell A2 to 22-point Britannic Bold (or a similar font). Change the font in cell A17 to 18-point italic Britannic Bold.

11. Use the background color blue and the font color white for the ranges A1:J2; A7; A15:J15; and A17:B23 as shown in Figure 3–88.

12. Rename the Sheet1 sheet, Analysis of Indirect Expenses, and color its tab blue.

13. Update the document properties with your name, course number, and name for the workbook. Change the worksheet header with your name, course number, and other information requested by your instructor. Save the workbook using the file name, Lab 3-3 RockieView Resort and Spa Indirect Expenses Allocations.

14. Preview the worksheet. Use the Page Setup button to change the orientation to landscape and fit the report on one page. Preview the formulas version (CTRL+`) of the worksheet in landscape orientation using the Fit to option button in the Page Setup dialog box. Press CTRL+` to show the values version of the worksheet. Save the workbook again.

15. Divide the window into four panes and show the four corners of the worksheet. Remove the four panes. Close the workbook but do not save the workbook.

Instructions Part 2: Start Excel. Open Lab 3-3 RockieView Resort and Spa Indirect Expenses Allocations. Draw a 3-D Pie chart (Figure 3–89) on a separate sheet that shows the contribution of each category of indirect expense to the total indirect expenses. That is, chart the nonadjacent ranges A8:A13 (category names) and J8:J13 (data series). Show labels that include category names and percentages. Do not show the legend or leader lines. Format the 3-D Pie chart as shown in Figure 3–89. Rename the chart sheet 3-D Pie Chart and color the tab red. Move the chart tab to the right of the worksheet tab. Save the workbook using the file name, Lab 3-3 RockieView Resort and Spa Indirect Expenses Allocations. Submit the workbook as requested by your instructor.

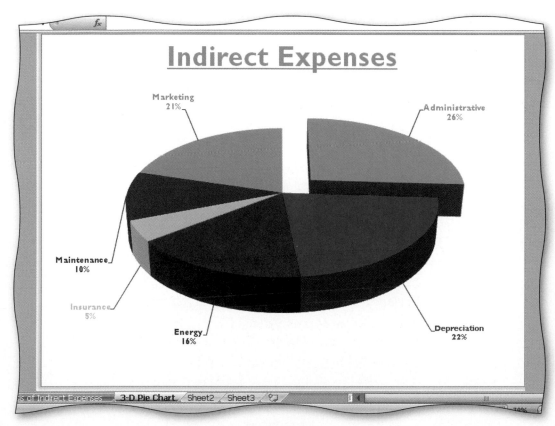

Figure 3–89

Continued >

In the Lab *continued*

Instructions Part 3:   Start Excel. Open Lab 3-3 RockieView Resort and Spa Indirect Expenses Allocations.

1. Using the numbers in Table 3–15, analyze the effect of changing the planned indirect expenses in the range B18:B23 on the net incomes for each profit center. You should end with the following totals in cell J15: Case 1 = $892,684.00 and Case 2 = $869,634.00. Submit the workbook or results for each case as requested by your instructor.

2. Use the What-If Analysis button on the Data tab on the Ribbon to goal seek. Determine a planned indirect Administrative

Table 3–15 RockieView Resort and Spa Indirect Expense Allocations What-If Data		
	Case 1	Case 2
Administrative	234000	210000
Depreciation	123500	152000
Energy	67750	48000
Insurance	26200	53000
Maintenance	42000	38000
Marketing	57000	72500

expense (cell B18) that would result in a total net income of $1,200,000 (cell J15). You should end up with a planned indirect Administrative expense of $50,159 in cell B18. Submit the workbook with the new values or the results of the goal seek as requested by your instructor.

Cases and Places

Apply your creative thinking and problem solving skills to design and implement a solution.

● EASIER   ●● MORE DIFFICULT

● 1: Five-Year Sales Projections

You have been asked to develop a worksheet for Millennium Steel that shows annual growth for the next five years based on the prior year's sales and growth data. Include an embedded exploded 3-D Pie chart that shows the contribution of each year to the total gross margin. The data and general layout of the worksheet, including the totals, are shown in Table 3–16.

Table 3–16 Millennium Steel Sales Data and General Layout						
	Year 1	**Year 2**	**Year 3**	**Year 4**	**Year 5**	**Total**
Sales	Formula A ———————————————————————→					—
Cost of Goods	Formula B ———————————————————————→					—
Gross Margin	Formula C ———————————————————————→					—
Assumptions						
Prior Year's Sales	35234500					
Annual Growth Rate	−1.75%	12.35%	5.00%	−1.25%	8.75%	
Annual Cost Rate	41.25%	44.00%	33.00%	43.75%	34.25%	
Premium	2.90%	3.10%	4.95%	2.50%	4.50%	

Enter the formulas shown in Table 3–17 in the locations shown in Table 3–16. Copy formulas A, B, and C to the remaining years. The gross margin for the five years should equal $118,986,982.

Table 3–17 Millennium Steel Sales Projection Formulas
Formula A = Prior Year's Sales * (1 + Annual Growth Rate)
Formula B = IF(Annual Growth Rate < 0, Sales * (Annual Cost Rate + Premium), Sales * Annual Cost Rate)
Formula C = Sales − Cost of Goods

   Use the concepts and techniques developed in the first three projects to create and format the worksheet and embedded 3-D Pie chart.
   Use the Goal Seek command to determine the Year 1 annual growth rate that will generate a total gross margin of $125,000,000. You should end up with a Year 1 annual growth rate of 2.35%. Submit the workbook and results of the goal seek as requested by your instructor.

● 2: Bimonthly Projected Earnings and Expenditures

The *Chesterton Trib* is a small newspaper that publishes stories of local interest. Revenues are earned from subscriptions and the sale of advertising space. A fixed percentage of the Net Revenue is spent on marketing, payroll, commissions (advertising sales only), production costs, and reportorial expenses. The editor has summarized the paper's expenditures over the past year and the anticipated income from subscriptions and advertising on a bimonthly basis as shown in Table 3–18.
   With the data, you have been asked to prepare a worksheet for the next shareholder's meeting showing total revenues, total expenditures, and operating incomes for each bimonthly period. Include a 3-D Cylinder chart on a separate sheet that compares the six bimonthly operating incomes. Use the concepts and techniques presented in this project to create and format the worksheet and chart.

STUDENT ASSIGNMENTS

Table 3–18 Chesterton Trib Bimonthly Projected Earnings and Expenditures

Revenue	February	April	June	August	October	December
Subscriptions	12178.30	8391.50	15714.50	16340.10	12567.25	12800.15
Advertising	4130.20	6425.00	4123.15	5023.30	7015.75	9273.20
Assumptions						
Marketing	15.60%					
Payroll	21.50%					
Commissions on Advertising	3.25%					
Production Costs	12.50%					
Reportorial Expenses	5.00%					

One shareholder lobbied to reduce marketing expenditures by 3% and payroll costs by 5%. Perform a what-if-analysis reflecting the proposed changes in expenditure assumptions. The reduction in expenditures should result in a total operating income of $59,696.91 or an increase of $9,118.59. Submit the workbook and results of the what-if analysis as requested by your instructor.

•• 3: Projected Used-Truck Savings

Cousin Abe and Aunt Esther own a paint company. Their good friend Billie Bob is retiring after 35 years of delivering the morning newspaper. Billie Bob has offered them the opportunity to take his place next year. The job requires, however, that they own a truck. They need to save enough money over the next six months to buy a $10,000 used truck.

They have job orders at their paint company for the next six months: $22,150 in July, $22,480 in August, $32,900 in September, $31,200 in October, $45,301 in November, and $32,190 in December. Each month, they spend 34.55% of the job order income on material, 3.00% on rollers and brushes, 4.75% on their retirement account, and 39.5% on food and clothing. The remaining profits (orders − total expenses) will be put aside for the used truck. Aunt Esther's retired parents have agreed to provide a bonus of $250 whenever the monthly profit exceeds $2,000. Use the concepts and techniques presented in this project to create and format the worksheet.

Cousin Abe has asked you to create a worksheet that shows orders, expenses, profits, bonuses, and savings for the next six months, and totals for each category. Aunt Esther would like to save for another used truck for $17,000. She has asked you to (a) perform a what-if analysis to determine the effect on the savings by reducing the percentage spent on material to 25% (answer total savings = $16,084.49), and (b) with the original assumptions, goal seek to determine what percentage of profits to spend on food and clothing if $15,000 is needed for the used truck (answer = 29.165%). Submit the workbook and results of the what-if analysis as requested by your instructor.

•• 4: College Expense and Resource Projections

Make It Personal

Attending college with limited resources can be a trying experience. One way to alleviate some of the financial stress is to plan ahead. Develop a worksheet following the general layout in Table 3–19 that shows the projected expenses and resources for four years of college. Use the formulas listed in Table 3–20 and the concepts and techniques presented in this project to create the worksheet.

Table 3–19 College Expense and Resource Projections

Expenses	Freshman	Sophomore	Junior	Senior	Total
Room & Board	$6,125.00	Formula A	⟶		—
Tuition & Books	8,750.00	Formula A	⟶		—
Clothes	750.00	Formula A	⟶		—
Entertainment	1,025.00	Formula A	⟶		—
Miscellaneous	675.00	Formula A	⟶		—
Total Expenses	—	—	—	—	—

Resources	Freshman	Sophomore	Junior	Senior	Total
Savings	Formula B	⟶			—
Parents	Formula B	⟶			—
Job	Formula B	⟶			—
Loans	Formula B	⟶			—
Scholarships	Formula B	⟶			—
Total Resources	—	—	—	—	—

Assumptions	
Savings	10.00%
Parents	20.00%
Job	10.00%
Loans	30.00%
Scholarships	30.00%
Annual Rate Increase	7.50%

After creating the worksheet: (a) perform what-if analysis by changing the percents of the resource assumptions; (b) perform a what-if analysis to determine the effect on the resources by increasing the Annual Rate Increase to 9%; and (c) with the original assumptions, goal seek to determine what the Annual Rate Increase would be for the total expenses to be $100,000. Submit the workbook and results of the what-if analysis as requested by your instructor.

Table 3–20 College Expense and Resource Projections Formulas

Formula A = Prior Year's Expense * (1 + Annual Rate Increase)

Formula B = Total Expenses for Year * Corresponding Assumption

•• 5: Cost of Storing Radio Isotopes

Working Together

A government agency plans to conduct experiments that will result in some radioactive waste. Although the isotopes will break apart into atoms of other elements over time, agency watchdogs are concerned about containment costs while the material still is radioactive. The agency director has asked your group to prepare a worksheet showing the amount of radioactive material remaining, containment costs, estimated agency appropriations, and the percentage of appropriations that will be spent on containment every year for the next decade. The director has outlined the desired worksheet as shown in Table 3–21 on the next page.

Continued >

Cases and Places *continued*

These formulas have been supplied:

Formula A: Amount Remaining = Original Amount × 0.5 (Number of Years Stored / Half-Life)

Formula B: Containment Costs = Containment Cost Per Kilogram × Total Amount Remaining

Formula C: Estimated Appropriations = Appropriations × (1 + Estimated Yearly Increase) (Number of Years Stored / Half-Life)

Formula D: Percentage Spent on Containment = Containment Costs / Estimated Appropriations

The director has asked your group to include a function that prints "Acceptable" below the percentage spent on containment whenever the percentage is less than 1%, otherwise print "Not Acceptable."

Have each member of your team submit a sketch of the proposed worksheet and then implement the best one. Use the concepts and techniques presented in this project to create and format the worksheet. Submit the sketches and workbook as requested by your instructor.

Table 3–21 Cost of Storing Radioactive Isotopes

	Number of Years Stored				
Number of Years Stored	1	2	3	....	10
Amount of Isotope X Remaining (in kg)	Formula A				⟶
Amount of Isotope Y Remaining (in kg)	Formula A				⟶
Total Remaining (in kg)	—	—	—	....	—
Containment Costs	Formula B				⟶
Estimated Appropriations	Formula C				⟶
Percentage Spent on Containment	Formula D				⟶
	Message				⟶

Assumptions

Original Amount of Isotope X Remaining (in kg)	650
Half-Life of Isotope X (in years)	1
Containment Cost per Kilogram	1000
Estimated Yearly Increase	10.00%
Original Amount of Isotope Y Remaining (in kg)	3000
Half-Life of Isotope Y (in years)	0.45
Appropriations	6000000

Web Feature
Creating Web Pages Using Excel

Objectives

You will have mastered the material in this Web feature when you can:

- Customize the Quick Access Toolbar
- Publish a worksheet and chart as a Web page
- Display Web pages published in Excel in a browser
- Complete file management tasks within Excel

Web Feature Introduction

Excel provides fast, easy methods for saving workbooks as Web pages that can be stored on the World Wide Web, a company's intranet, or a local hard disk. A user then can display the workbook using a browser, rather than Excel.

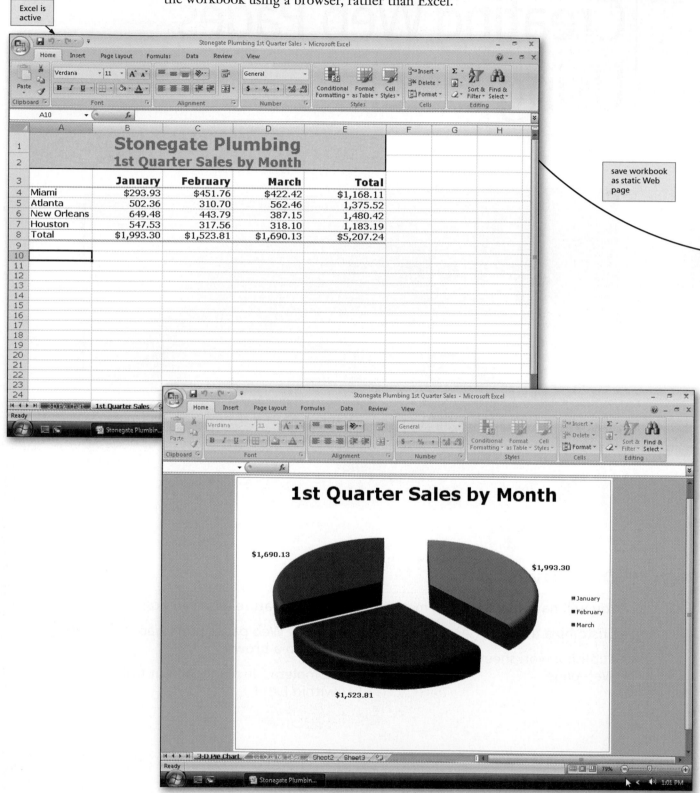

(a) Workbook Viewed in Excel

Figure 1

Project — Workbook with Chart Saved as a Web Page

Figure 1a shows the workbook for Stonegate Plumbing's 1st quarter sales by month. The chief financial officer for the company requests that the information in the worksheet, including the chart, be made available on the company's intranet for others in the company to view. In order to accomplish this task, you must save the workbook as a Web page.

You can save a workbook, or a portion of a workbook, as a Web page. The saved **Web page** is a snapshot of the workbook. It is similar to a printed report in that you can view it, but you cannot modify it. In the browser window, the workbook appears as it would in Microsoft Excel, including sheet tabs that you can click to switch between worksheets. As illustrated in Figure 1, this Web feature shows you how to save a workbook (Figure 1a) as a Web page (Figure 1b) and view it using your browser.

When you use the Save As command on the Office Button menu and choose to save a workbook as a Web page, Excel allows you to **publish workbooks**, which is the process of making a workbook available to others; for example, on the World Wide Web or on a

(b) Static Web Page Viewed in Browser

BTW

Web Folders and FTP Locations
You can save any type of file to a Web folder or on an FTP location, just as you would save to a folder on your hard disk. Web folders and FTP locations are particularly useful because they appear as standard folders in Windows Explorer or in the Address bar list. For additional information, see Appendix D.

company's intranet. If you have access to a Web server, you can publish Web pages by saving them on a Web server or on an FTP location. To learn more about publishing Web pages on a Web server or on an FTP location using Microsoft Office applications, refer to Appendix D.

This Web feature illustrates how to create and save the Web pages on a USB flash drive, rather than on a Web server. This feature also demonstrates how to preview a workbook as a Web page and create a new folder using the Save As dialog box.

Overview

As you read through this Web feature, you will learn how to create the worksheet shown in Figure 1 on pages EX 250 and 251 by performing these general tasks:

- Save a Workbook as a Web page
- Preview the Workbook in a Web browser
- Complete file management tasks within Excel

Using Web Page Preview and Saving an Excel Workbook as a Web Page

At any time during the construction of a workbook, you can preview it as a Web page by using the Web Page Preview command. The Web Page Preview command is not available on the Ribbon, but you can add the command to the Quick Access Toolbar. When you invoke the Web Page Preview command, it starts your browser and displays the active sheet in the workbook as a Web page. If the preview is acceptable, then you can save the workbook as a Web page.

To Add a Button to the Quick Access Toolbar

Many commands available in Excel are not included on any of the tabs on the Ribbon. You can, however, add such commands to the Quick Access Toolbar. One such command allows you to preview a document in a Web browser. This command, Web Page Preview, needs to be added to the Quick Access Toolbar so that the Web page can be previewed. The following steps add the Web Page Preview command to the Quick Access Toolbar.

- Connect a USB flash drive with the Data Files for Students on it to one of the computer's USB ports.

- Start Excel and then open the workbook, Stonegate Plumbing 1st Quarter Sales, from the Data Files for Students.

- Click the Customize Quick Access Toolbar button to display the Customize Quick Access Toolbar menu (Figure 2).

Figure 2

- Click the More
  Commands
  command on the
  Customize Quick
  Access Toolbar menu.

- When the Excel
  Options dialog box
  is displayed, click the
  'Choose commands
  from' box arrow to
  display the 'Choose
  commands from' list
  (Figure 3).

Figure 3

- Click Commands Not
  in the Ribbon in the
  'Choose commands
  from' list to display a
  list of commands not
  in the Ribbon
  (Figure 4).

Figure 4

● Scroll to the bottom of the list, click Web Page Preview, and then click the Add button to add the button to the Quick Access Toolbar (Figure 5).

Figure 5

● Click the OK button to close the Excel Options dialog box and display the Quick Access Toolbar with the Web Page Preview button added to it (Figure 6).

Will the Web Page Preview command be on the Quick Access Toolbar the next time that I start Excel?

Yes. When you change the Quick Access Toolbar, the changes remain even after you restart Excel. If you share a computer with somebody else or if the Quick Access Toolbar becomes cluttered, Excel allows you to remove commands from the Quick Access Toolbar. The Web Page Preview button is removed from the Quick Access Toolbar later in this Web feature.

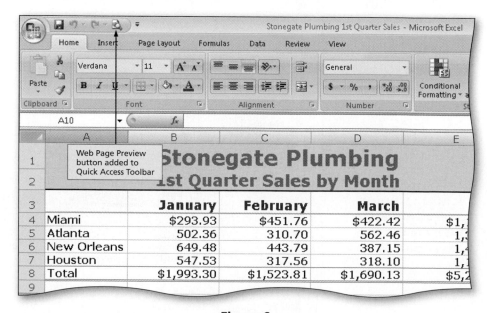

Figure 6

To Preview the Web Page

The following steps preview the Web page version of the workbook in a browser.

1

- Click the Web Page Preview button on the Quick Access Toolbar to display the Web page in your browser. If the security warning appears in the Information bar at the top of the Web page, click its Close button.

- If necessary, click the Maximize button on your browser's title bar (Figure 7).

Q&A

What happens when I click the Web Page Preview button?

Excel starts your browser. The browser displays a preview of how the 1st Quarter Sales sheet will appear as a Web page (Figure 7). The Web page preview in the browser is nearly identical to the display of the worksheet in Excel. A highlighted browser button appears on the Windows Vista taskbar indicating it is active. The Excel button on the Windows Vista taskbar no longer is highlighted.

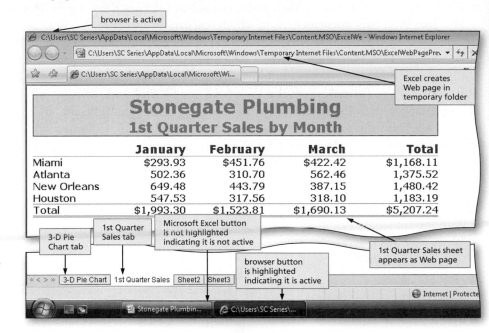

Figure 7

2

- Click the 3-D Pie Chart tab at the bottom of the Web page to display the 3-D Pie chart in the browser (Figure 8).

3

- After viewing the Web page preview of the Stonegate Plumbing 1st Quarter Sales workbook, click the Close button on the right side of the browser title bar to close the browser and make Excel active again.

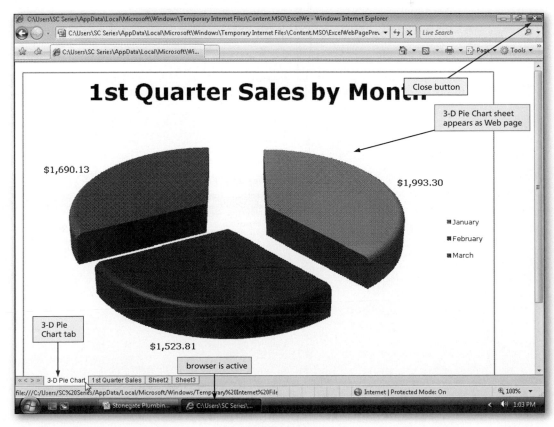

Figure 8

To Save an Excel Workbook as a Web Page in a Newly Created Folder

Once the preview of the workbook as a Web page is acceptable, you can save the workbook as a Web page so that others can view it using a Web browser, such as Internet Explorer or Mozilla Firefox.

Two Web page formats exist in which you can save workbooks. Both formats convert the contents of the workbook into HTML (HyperText Markup Language), which is a language browsers can interpret. One format is called **Single File Web Page format**, which saves all of the components of the Web page in a single file with an .mht extension. This format is useful particularly for e-mailing workbooks in HTML format. The second format, called **Web Page format**, saves the Web page in a file and some of its components in a folder. This format is useful if you need access to the components, such as images, that make up the Web page.

Experienced users organize the files saved on a storage medium, such as a USB flash drive or hard disk, by creating folders. They then save related files in a common folder. Excel allows you to create folders before saving a file using the Save As dialog box. The following steps create a new folder on the USB flash drive and save the workbook as a Web page in the new folder.

1

- With the Stonegate Plumbing 1st Quarter Sales workbook open, click the Office Button.

- Click Save As on the Office Button menu to display the Save As dialog box (Figure 9).

Figure 9

2

• Type Stonegate Plumbing 1st Quarter Sales Web Page in the File name box.

• Click the 'Save as type' box arrow and then click Single File Web Page.

• Click the Address bar arrow, select UDISK 2.0 (E:) (your USB flash drive name and letter may be different), and then click the New Folder button to create a new folder.

• When Excel displays the new folder with the name New Folder, type Web Feature in the text box (Figure 10).

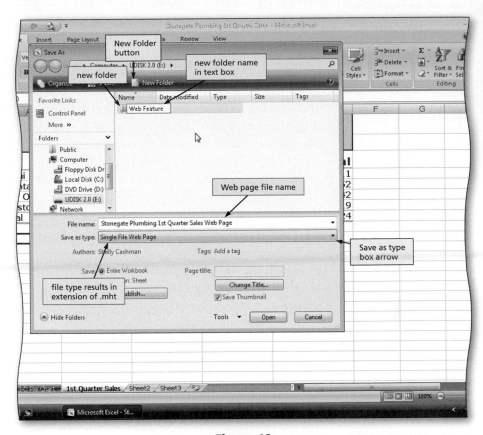

Figure 10

3

• Press the ENTER key. If the Microsoft Office Excel dialog box appears, click the Yes button.

Q&A What does Excel do when I press the ENTER key?

Excel automatically selects the new folder named Web Feature in the Address bar (Figure 11). The Entire Workbook option button in the Save area instructs Excel to save all sheets in the workbook as Web pages.

4

• Click the Save button in the Save As dialog box to save the workbook in a single file in HTML format in the Web Feature folder on the USB flash drive.

• If the Microsoft Office Excel dialog box is displayed, click the Yes button.

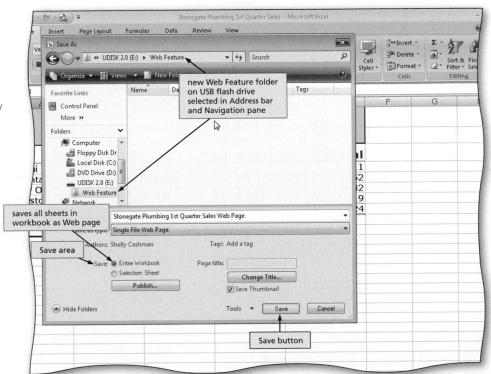

Figure 11

BTW

Creating Links
You can add hyperlinks to an Excel workbook before you save it as a Web page. The hyperlinks in the Excel workbook can link to a Web page, a location in a Web page, or an e-mail address that automatically starts the viewer's e-mail program.

Saving Workbooks as Web Pages

The Save As dialog box changes when you select Single File Web Page, which is in MHTML format, in the 'Save as type' box. When you use the Single File Web Page format, a Save area appears in the dialog box. Within the Save area are two option buttons and a Publish button (Figure 11). You can select only one of the option buttons. The Entire Workbook option button is selected by default. This indicates Excel will save all the active sheets (1st Quarter Sales and 3-D Pie Chart) in the workbook as a Web page. The alternative is the Selection: Sheet option button. If you select this option, Excel will save only the active sheet (the one that currently is displaying in the Excel window) in the workbook. The Publish button in the Save As dialog box in Figure 11 is an alternative to the Save button. It allows you to customize the Web page further.

If you have access to a Web server and it allows you to save files in a Web folder, then you can save the Web page directly on the Web server by clicking the Network icon in the Folders list in the Save As dialog box (Figure 11). If you have access to a Web server that allows you to save on an FTP site, then you can select the FTP site below FTP locations in the Address bar just as you select any folder in which to save a file. To learn more about publishing Web pages in a Web folder or on an FTP location using Office applications, refer to Appendix D.

After Excel saves the workbook in Step 4, it displays the MHTML file in the Excel window. Excel can continue to display the workbook in HTML format, because, within the MHTML file that it created, it also saved the Excel formats that allow it to display the MHTML file in Excel.

Viewing Source Code
To view the HTML source code for a Web page created in Excel, use your browser to display the Web page, click the Page button and then click View Source.

To Reset the Quick Access Toolbar and Quit Excel

The necessary work with the Excel workbook is complete. The following steps remove the Web Page Preview button from the Quick Access Toolbar and quit Excel.

1 Click the Customize the Quick Access Toolbar button on the Ribbon.

2 Click the More Commands command.

3 When the Excel Options dialog box is displayed, click the Reset button. If the Reset Customizations dialog box is displayed, click the Yes button.

4 Click the OK button in the Excel Options dialog box to close it.

5 Click the Close button on the Microsoft Excel title bar.

Q&A

Do I need to remove the button from the Quick Access Toolbar?

No. For consistency, in this book the Quick Access Toolbar is reset after the added buttons no longer are needed. If you share a computer with others, you should reset the Quick Access Toolbar when you are finished using the computer.

File Management Tools in Excel

In the previous set of steps, Excel automatically navigates to the new folder name in the Save in box when you press the ENTER key after typing the new folder name (Figure 11 on page EX 257). It actually was not necessary to create a new folder earlier in this Web feature; the Web page could have been saved on the USB flash drive in the same manner files were saved on the USB flash drive in the previous projects. Creating a new folder, however, allows you to organize your work.

Finally, once you create a folder, you can right-click it while the Save As dialog box is active and perform many file management tasks directly in Excel (Figure 12). For example, once the shortcut menu appears, you can rename the selected folder, delete it, copy it, display its properties, and perform other file management functions.

BTW

Quick Reference
For a table that lists how to complete the tasks covered in this book using the mouse, Ribbon, shortcut menu, and keyboard, see the Quick Reference Summary at the back of this book, or visit the Excel 2007 Quick Reference Web page (scsite.com/ex2007/qr).

BTW

Certification
The Microsoft Certified Application Specialist (MCAS) program provides an opportunity for you to obtain a valuable industry credential – proof that you have the Excel 2007 skills required by employers. For more information, see Appendix G or visit the Excel 2007 Certification Web page (scsite.com/ex2007/cert).

Figure 12

Excel Web Feature

To View and Manipulate the Web Page Using a Browser

With the Web page saved in the Web Feature folder on the USB flash drive, you can now view it using a browser, as shown in the following steps.

- If necessary, connect the USB flash drive with the Data Files for Students to one of the computer's USB ports.

- Click the Start button on the Windows Vista taskbar, click All Programs on the Start menu, and then click Internet Explorer in the All Programs list.

- When the Internet Explorer window opens, type e:\web feature\ stonegate plumbing 1st quarter sales web page.mht in the Address box and then press the ENTER key to display the Web page in your browser (Figure 13). (Your USB flash drive may have a different name and letter.)

- If the Internet Explorer dialog box appears, click the OK button, right-click the first Internet Explorer button on the Windows Vista taskbar, and then click Close on the shortcut menu. If a security warning appears in the Information bar at the top of the Web page, click its Close button.

Figure 13

2

- Click the 3-D Pie Chart sheet tab at the bottom of the window to display the 3-D Pie chart in your browser (Figure 14). If the security warning appears in the Information bar at the top of the Web page, click its Close button.

- Use the scroll arrows to display the lower portion of the chart.

Q&A

What are the benefits of using a browser to view a workbook?

You can see from Figures 13 and 14 that a Web page is an ideal way to distribute information to a large group of people. For example, the Web page could be published on a Web server connected to the Internet and made available to anyone with a computer, browser, and the address of the Web page. It also can be e-mailed easily, because the Web page resides in a single file, rather than in a file and folder. Publishing a workbook as a Web page, therefore, is an excellent alternative to distributing printed copies of the workbook.

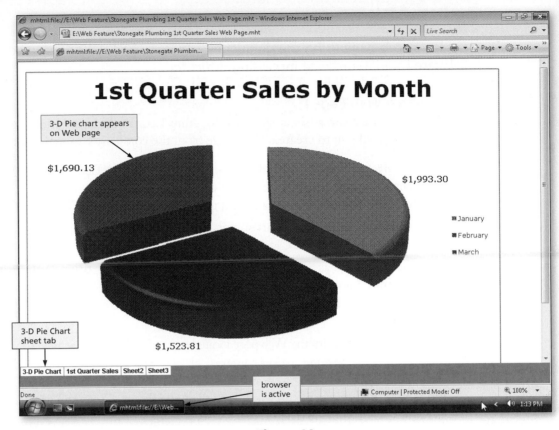

Figure 14

3

- Click the Close button on the right side of the browser title bar to close the browser.

Feature Summary

This Web feature introduced you to customizing the Quick Access Toolbar, previewing a workbook as a Web page, creating a new folder on a USB flash drive, and publishing and viewing a Web page. The items listed below include all the new Office 2007 skills you have learned in this Web feature.

1. Add a Button to the Quick Access Toolbar (EX 252)
2. Preview the Web Page (EX 255)
3. Save an Excel Workbook as a Web Page in a Newly Created Folder (EX 256)
4. View and Manipulate the Web Page Using a Browser (EX 260)

If you have a SAM user profile, you may have access to hands-on instruction, practice, and assessment. Log in to your SAM account (http://sam2007.course.com) to launch any assigned training activities or exams that relate to the skills covered in this feature.

In the Lab

Create a Web page using the guidelines, concepts, and skills presented in this Web feature. Labs are listed in order of increasing difficulty.

1 Creating a Web Page I

Problem: You are a spreadsheet specialist for Aunt Leona's Pizza, a national chain of pizzerias. Your manager has asked you to create a Web page from the company's annual sales workbook.

Instructions Part 1: Start Excel and open the Lab WF-1 Aunt Leonas Pizza Annual Sales workbook from the Data Files for Students. Perform the following tasks:

1. Add the Web Page Preview command to the Quick Access Toolbar.

2. Review the worksheet and chart so you have an idea of what the workbook contains. Preview the workbook as a Web page. Close the browser.

3. Save the workbook as a single file Web page in a new folder titled Web Feature Exercises using the file name, Lab WF-1 Aunt Leonas Pizza Annual Sales Web Page. Make sure you select Entire Workbook in the Save area before you click the Save button. Reset the Quick Access Toolbar and then quit Excel.

4. Start your browser. With the Web page located on the USB flash drive, type `e:\web feature exercises\ lab wf-1 aunt leonas pizza annual sales web page.mht` in the Address box (your USB flash drive may have a different name and letter). When the browser displays the Web page, click the tabs at the bottom of the window to view the sheets. Close the browser. Submit the assignment as requested by your instructor.

In the Lab

2 Creating a Web Page II

Problem: You work part-time as a spreadsheet analyst for What-a-Racket Tennis Club. You have been asked to create a Web page from the workbook that the company uses to project membership dues and payroll expenses.

Instructions Part 1: Start Excel and open the Lab WF-2 What-a-Racket Tennis Club Projections workbook from the Data Files for Students. Perform the following tasks:

1. Add the Web Page Preview command to the Quick Access Toolbar.

2. Review the 3-D Bar Chart sheet and the Projected Expenses sheet in Excel. Preview the workbook as a Web page. Close the browser.

3. Save the workbook as a Web page (select Web Page in the Save as type box) in the Web Feature Exercises folder using the file name, Lab WF-2 What-a-Racket Tennis Club Projections Web Page. Make sure you select Entire Workbook in the Save area before you click the Save button. Reset the Quick Access Toolbar and then quit Excel. Saving the workbook as a Web page, rather than a single file Web page, will result in an additional folder being added to the Web Feature Exercises folder.

4. Start your browser. Type `e:\web feature exercises\lab wf-2 what-a-racket tennis club projections web page.htm` in the Address box (your USB flash drive may have a different name and letter). When the browser displays the Web page, click the tabs at the bottom of the window to view the sheets. Close the browser. Submit the assignment as requested by your instructor.

In the Lab

3 File Management within Excel

Problem: Your manager at What-a-Racket Tennis Club has asked you to teach her to complete basic file management tasks from within Excel.

Instructions: Start Excel and click the Open command on the Office Button menu. When Excel displays the Open dialog box, create a new folder called In the Lab 3. Click the Back to button to reselect the drive in the Address bar. Use the shortcut menu to complete the following tasks: (1) rename the In the Lab 3 folder to In the Lab 3A; (2) show the properties of the In the Lab 3A folder; and (3) delete the In the Lab 3A folder.

Appendix A
Project Planning Guidelines

Using Project Planning Guidelines

The process of communicating specific information to others is a learned, rational skill. Computers and software, especially Microsoft Office 2007, can help you develop ideas and present detailed information to a particular audience.

Using Microsoft Office 2007, you can create projects such as Word documents, Excel spreadsheets, Access databases, and PowerPoint presentations. Computer hardware and productivity software such as Microsoft Office 2007 minimizes much of the laborious work of drafting and revising projects. Some communicators handwrite ideas in notebooks, others compose directly on the computer, and others have developed unique strategies that work for their own particular thinking and writing styles.

No matter what method you use to plan a project, follow specific guidelines to arrive at a final product that presents information correctly and effectively (Figure A–1). Use some aspects of these guidelines every time you undertake a project, and others as needed in specific instances. For example, in determining content for a project, you may decide that a bar chart communicates trends more effectively than a paragraph of text. If so, you would create this graphical element and insert it in an Excel spreadsheet, a Word document, or a PowerPoint slide.

Determine the Project's Purpose

Begin by clearly defining why you are undertaking this assignment. For example, you may want to track monetary donations collected for your club's fundraising drive. Alternatively, you may be urging students to vote for a particular candidate in the next election. Once you clearly understand the purpose of your task, begin to draft ideas of how best to communicate this information.

Analyze your Audience

Learn about the people who will read, analyze, or view your work. Where are they employed? What are their educational backgrounds? What are their expectations? What questions do they have?

PROJECT PLANNING GUIDELINES

1. DETERMINE THE PROJECT'S PURPOSE
Why are you undertaking the project?

2. ANALYZE YOUR AUDIENCE
Who are the people who will use your work?

3. GATHER POSSIBLE CONTENT
What information exists, and in what forms?

4. DETERMINE WHAT CONTENT TO PRESENT TO YOUR AUDIENCE
What information will best communicate the project's purpose to your audience?

Figure A–1

Design experts suggest drawing a mental picture of these people or finding photographs of people who fit this profile so that you can develop a project with the audience in mind.

By knowing your audience members, you can tailor a project to meet their interests and needs. You will not present them with information they already possess, and you will not omit the information they need to know.

Example: Your assignment is to raise the profile of your college's nursing program in the community. How much do they know about your college and the nursing curriculum? What are the admission requirements? How many of the applicants admitted complete the program? What percent pass the state Boards?

Gather Possible Content

Rarely are you in a position to develop all the material for a project. Typically, you would begin by gathering existing information that may reside in spreadsheets or databases. Web sites, pamphlets, magazine and newspaper articles, and books could provide insights of how others have approached your topic. Personal interviews often provide perspectives not available by any other means. Consider video and audio clips as potential sources for material that might complement or support the factual data you uncover.

Determine What Content to Present to your Audience

Experienced designers recommend writing three or four major ideas you want an audience member to remember after reading or viewing your project. It also is helpful to envision your project's endpoint, the key fact you wish to emphasize. All project elements should lead to this ending point.

As you make content decisions, you also need to think about other factors. Presentation of the project content is an important consideration. For example, will your brochure be printed on thick, colored paper or transparencies? Will your PowerPoint presentation be viewed in a classroom with excellent lighting and a bright projector, or will it be viewed on a notebook computer monitor? Determine relevant time factors, such as the length of time to develop the project, how long readers will spend reviewing your project, or the amount of time allocated for your speaking engagement. Your project will need to accommodate all of these constraints.

Decide whether a graph, photograph, or artistic element can express or emphasize a particular concept. The right hemisphere of the brain processes images by attaching an emotion to them, so audience members are more apt to recall these graphics long term rather than just reading text.

As you select content, be mindful of the order in which you plan to present information. Readers and audience members generally remember the first and last pieces of information they see and hear, so you should put the most important information at the top or bottom of the page.

Summary

When creating a project, it is beneficial to follow some basic guidelines from the outset. By taking some time at the beginning of the process to determine the project's purpose, analyze the audience, gather possible content, and determine what content to present to the audience, you can produce a project that is informative, relevant, and effective.

Appendix B

Introduction to Microsoft Office 2007

What Is Microsoft Office 2007?

Microsoft Office 2007 is a collection of the more popular Microsoft application software. It is available in Basic, Home and Student, Standard, Small Business, Professional, Ultimate, Professional Plus, and Enterprise editions. Each edition consists of a group of programs, collectively called a suite. Table B-1 lists the suites and their components. **Microsoft Office Professional Edition 2007** includes these six programs: Microsoft Office Word 2007, Microsoft Office Excel 2007, Microsoft Office Access 2007, Microsoft Office PowerPoint 2007, Microsoft Office Publisher 2007, and Microsoft Office Outlook 2007. The programs in the Office suite allow you to work efficiently, communicate effectively, and improve the appearance of the projects you create.

Table B–1

	Microsoft Office Basic 2007	Microsoft Office Home & Student 2007	Microsoft Office Standard 2007	Microsoft Office Small Business 2007	Microsoft Office Professional 2007	Microsoft Office Ultimate 2007	Microsoft Office Professional Plus 2007	Microsoft Office Enterprise 2007
Microsoft Office Word 2007	✓	✓	✓	✓	✓	✓	✓	✓
Microsoft Office Excel 2007	✓	✓	✓	✓	✓	✓	✓	✓
Microsoft Office Access 2007					✓	✓	✓	✓
Microsoft Office PowerPoint 2007		✓	✓	✓	✓	✓	✓	✓
Microsoft Office Publisher 2007				✓	✓	✓	✓	✓
Microsoft Office Outlook 2007	✓		✓				✓	✓
Microsoft Office OneNote 2007		✓				✓		
Microsoft Office Outlook 2007 with Business Contact Manager				✓	✓	✓		
Microsoft Office InfoPath 2007						✓	✓	✓
Integrated Enterprise Content Management						✓	✓	✓
Electronic Forms						✓	✓	✓
Advanced Information Rights Management and Policy Capabilities						✓	✓	✓
Microsoft Office Communicator 2007							✓	✓
Microsoft Office Groove 2007						✓		✓

Microsoft has bundled additional programs in some versions of Office 2007, in addition to the main group of Office programs. Table B–1 on the previous page lists the components of the various Office suites.

In addition to the Office 2007 programs noted previously, Office 2007 suites can contain other programs. Microsoft Office OneNote 2007 is a digital notebook program that allows you to gather and share various types of media, such as text, graphics, video, audio, and digital handwriting. Microsoft Office InfoPath 2007 is a program that allows you to create and use electronic forms to gather information. Microsoft Office Groove 2007 provides collaborative workspaces in real time. Additional services that are oriented toward the enterprise solution also are available.

Office 2007 and the Internet, World Wide Web, and Intranets

Office 2007 allows you to take advantage of the Internet, the World Wide Web, and intranets. The Microsoft Windows operating system includes a **browser**, which is a program that allows you to locate and view a Web page. The Windows browser is called Internet Explorer.

One method of viewing a Web page is to use the browser to enter the Web address for the Web page. Another method of viewing a Web page is clicking a hyperlink. A **hyperlink** is colored or underlined text or a graphic that, when clicked, connects to another Web page. Hyperlinks placed in Office 2007 documents allow for direct access to a Web site of interest.

An **intranet** is a private network, such as a network used within a company or organization for internal communication. Like the Internet, hyperlinks are used within an intranet to access documents, pages, and other destinations on the intranet. Unlike the Internet, the materials on the network are available only for those who are part of the private network.

Online Collaboration Using Office

Organizations that, in the past, were able to make important information available only to a select few, now can make their information accessible to a wider range of individuals who use programs such as Office 2007 and Internet Explorer. Office 2007 allows colleagues to use the Internet or an intranet as a central location to view documents, manage files, and work together.

Each of the Office 2007 programs makes publishing documents on a Web server as simple as saving a file on a hard disk. Once placed on the Web server, users can view and edit the documents and conduct Web discussions and live online meetings.

Using Microsoft Office 2007

The various Microsoft Office 2007 programs each specialize in a particular task. This section describes the general functions of the more widely used Office 2007 programs, along with how they are used to access the Internet or an intranet.

Microsoft Office Word 2007

Microsoft Office Word 2007 is a full-featured word processing program that allows you to create many types of personal and business documents, including flyers, letters, resumes, business documents, and academic reports.

Word's AutoCorrect, spelling, and grammar features help you proofread documents for errors in spelling and grammar by identifying the errors and offering suggestions for corrections as you type. The live word count feature provides you with a constantly updating word count as you enter and edit text. To assist with creating specific documents, such as a business letter or resume, Word provides templates, which provide a formatted document before you type the text of the document. Quick Styles provide a live preview of styles from the Style gallery, allowing you to preview styles in the document before actually applying them.

Word automates many often-used tasks and provides you with powerful desktop publishing tools to use as you create professional looking brochures, advertisements, and newsletters. SmartArt allows you to insert interpretive graphics based on document content.

Word makes it easier for you to share documents for collaboration. The Send feature opens an e-mail window with the active document attached. The Compare Documents feature allows you easily to identify changes when comparing different document versions.

Word 2007 and the Internet   Word makes it possible to design and publish Web pages on the Internet or an intranet, insert a hyperlink to a Web page in a word processing document, as well as access and search the content of other Web pages.

Microsoft Office Excel 2007

Microsoft Office Excel 2007 is a spreadsheet program that allows you to organize data, complete calculations, graph data, develop professional looking reports, publish organized data to the Web, and access real-time data from Web sites.

In addition to its mathematical functionality, Excel 2007 provides tools for visually comparing data. For instance, when comparing a group of values in cells, you can set cell backgrounds with bars proportional to the value of the data in the cell. You can also set cell backgrounds with full-color backgrounds, or use a color scale to facilitate interpretation of data values.

Excel 2007 provides strong formatting support for tables with the new Style Preview gallery.

Excel 2007 and the Internet   Using Excel 2007, you can create hyperlinks within a worksheet to access other Office documents on the network or on the Internet. Work-sheets saved as static, or unchanging Web pages can be viewed using a browser. The person viewing static Web pages cannot change them.

In addition, you can create and run queries that retrieve information from a Web page and insert the information directly into a worksheet.

Microsoft Office Access 2007

Microsoft Office Access 2007 is a comprehensive database management system (DBMS). A **database** is a collection of data organized in a manner that allows access, retrieval, and use of that data. Access 2007 allows you to create a database; add, change, and delete data in the database; sort data in the database; retrieve data from the database; and create forms and reports using the data in the database.

Access 2007 and the Internet   Access 2007 lets you generate reports, which are summaries that show only certain data from the database, based on user requirements.

Microsoft Office PowerPoint 2007

Microsoft Office PowerPoint 2007 is a complete presentation graphics program that allows you to produce professional looking presentations. With PowerPoint 2007, you can create informal presentations using overhead transparencies, electronic presentations using a projection device attached to a personal computer, formal presentations using 35mm slides or a CD, or you can run virtual presentations on the Internet.

PowerPoint 2007 and the Internet   PowerPoint 2007 allows you to publish presentations on the Internet or other networks.

Microsoft Office Publisher 2007

Microsoft Office Publisher 2007 is a desktop publishing program (DTP) that allows you to design and produce professional quality documents (newsletters, flyers, brochures, business cards, Web sites, and so on) that combine text, graphics, and photographs. Desktop publishing software provides a variety of tools, including design templates, graphic manipulation tools, color schemes or libraries, and various page wizards and templates. For large jobs, businesses use desktop publishing software to design publications that are **camera ready**, which means the files are suitable for production by outside commercial printers. Publisher 2007 also allows you to locate commercial printers, service bureaus, and copy shops willing to accept customer files created in Publisher.

Publisher 2007 allows you to design a unique image, or logo, using one of more than 45 master design sets. This, in turn, permits you to use the same design for all your printed documents (letters, business cards, brochures, and advertisements) and Web pages. Publisher includes 70 coordinated color schemes; 30 font schemes; more than 10,000 high-quality clip art images; 1,500 photographs; 1,000 Web-art graphics; 340 animated graphics; and hundreds of unique Design Gallery elements (quotations, sidebars, and so on). If you wish, you also can download additional images from the Microsoft Office Online Web page on the Microsoft Web site.

Publisher 2007 and the Internet   Publisher 2007 allows you easily to create a multipage Web site with custom color schemes, photographic images, animated images, and sounds.

Microsoft Office Outlook 2007

Microsoft Office Outlook 2007 is a powerful communications and scheduling program that helps you communicate with others, keep track of your contacts, and organize your schedule. Outlook 2007 allows you to view a To-Do bar containing tasks and appointments from your Outlook calendar. Outlook 2007 allows you to send and receive electronic mail (e-mail) and permits you to engage in real-time communication with family, friends, or coworkers using instant messaging. Outlook 2007 also provides you with the means to organize your contacts, and you can track e-mail messages, meetings, and notes with a particular contact. Outlook's Calendar, Contacts, Tasks, and Notes components aid in this organization. Contact information is available from the Outlook Calendar, Mail, Contacts, and Task components by accessing the Find a Contact feature. **Personal information management (PIM)** programs such as Outlook provide a way for individuals and workgroups to organize, find, view, and share information easily.

Microsoft Office 2007 Help

At any time while you are using one of the Office programs, you can interact with **Microsoft Office 2007 Help** for that program and display information about any topic associated with the program. Several categories of help are available. In all programs, you can access Help by pressing the F1 key on the keyboard. In Publisher 2007 and Outlook 2007, the Help window can be opened by clicking the Help menu and then selecting Microsoft Office Publisher or Outlook Help command, or by entering search text in the 'Type a question for help' text box in the upper-right corner of the program window. In the other Office programs, clicking the Microsoft Office Help button near the upper-right corner of the program window opens the program Help window.

The Help window in all programs provides several methods for accessing help about a particular topic, and has tools for navigating around Help. Appendix C contains detailed instructions for using Help.

Collaboration and SharePoint

While not part of the Microsoft Office 2007 suites, SharePoint is a Microsoft tool that allows Office 2007 users to share data using collaborative tools that are integrated into the main Office programs. SharePoint consists of Windows SharePoint Services, Office SharePoint Server 2007, and, optionally, Office SharePoint Designer 2007.

Windows SharePoint Services provides the platform for collaboration programs and services. Office SharePoint Server 2007 is built on top of Windows SharePoint Services. The result of these two products is the ability to create SharePoint sites. A SharePoint site is a Web site that provides users with a virtual place for collaborating and communicating with their colleagues while working together on projects, documents, ideas, and information. Each member of a group with access to the SharePoint site has the ability to contribute to the material stored there. The basic building blocks of SharePoint sites are lists and libraries. Lists contain collections of information, such as calendar items, discussion points, contacts, and links. Lists can be edited to add or delete information. Libraries are similar to lists, but include both files and information about files. Types of libraries include document, picture, and forms libraries.

The most basic type of SharePoint site is called a Workspace, which is used primarily for collaboration. Different types of Workspaces can be created using SharePoint to suit different needs. SharePoint provides templates, or outlines of these Workspaces, that can be filled in to create the Workspace. Each of the different types of Workspace templates contain a different collection of lists and libraries, reflecting the purpose of the Workspace. You can create a Document Workspace to facilitate collaboration on documents. A Document Workspace contains a document library for documents and supporting files, a Links list that allows you to maintain relevant resource links for the document, a Tasks list for listing and assigning To-Do items to team members, and other links as needed. Meeting Workspaces allow users to plan and organize a meeting, with components such as Attendees, Agenda, and a Document Library. Social Meeting Workspaces provide a place to plan social events, with lists and libraries such as Attendees, Directions, Image/Logo, Things To Bring, Discussions, and Picture Library. A Decision Meeting Workspace is a Meeting Workspace with a focus on review and decision-making, with lists and libraries such as Objectives, Attendees, Agenda, Document Library, Tasks, and Decisions.

Users also can create a SharePoint site called a WebParts page, which is built from modules called WebParts. WebParts are modular units of information that contain a title bar and content that reflects the type of WebPart. For instance, an image WebPart would contain a title bar and an image. WebParts allow you quickly to create and modify a SharePoint site, and allow for the creation of a unique site that can allow users to access and make changes to information stored on the site.

Large SharePoint sites that include multiple pages can be created using templates as well. Groups needing more refined and targeted sharing options than those available with SharePoint Server 2007 and Windows SharePoint Services can add SharePoint Designer 2007 to create a site that meets their specific needs.

Depending on which components have been selected for inclusion on the site, users can view a team calendar, view links, read announcements, and view and edit group documents and projects. SharePoint sites can be set up so that documents are checked in and out, much like a library, to prevent multiple users from making changes simultaneously. Once a SharePoint site is set up, Office programs are used to perform maintenance of the site. For example, changes in the team calendar are updated using Outlook 2007, and changes that users make in Outlook 2007 are reflected on the SharePoint site. Office 2007 programs include a Publish feature that allows users easily to save file updates to a SharePoint site. Team members can be notified about changes made to material on the site either by e-mail or by a news feed, meaning that users do not have to go to the site to check to see if anything has been updated since they last viewed or worked on it. The search feature in SharePoint allows users quickly to find information on a large site.

Appendix C
Microsoft Office Excel 2007 Help

Using Microsoft Office Excel 2007 Help

This appendix shows how to use Microsoft Office Excel Help. At any time while you are using one of the Microsoft Office 2007 programs, you can use Office Help to display information about all topics associated with the program. This appendix uses Microsoft Office Excel 2007 to illustrate the use of Office Help. Help in other Office 2007 programs responds in a similar fashion.

In Office 2007, Help is presented in a window that has Web browser-style navigation buttons. Each Office 2007 program has its own Help home page, which is the starting Help page that is displayed in the Help window. If your computer is connected to the Internet, the contents of the Help page reflect both the local help files installed on the computer and material from Microsoft's Web site. As shown in Figure C–1, two methods for accessing Excel's Help are available:

1. Microsoft Office Excel Help button near the upper-right corner of the Excel window
2. Function key F1 on the keyboard

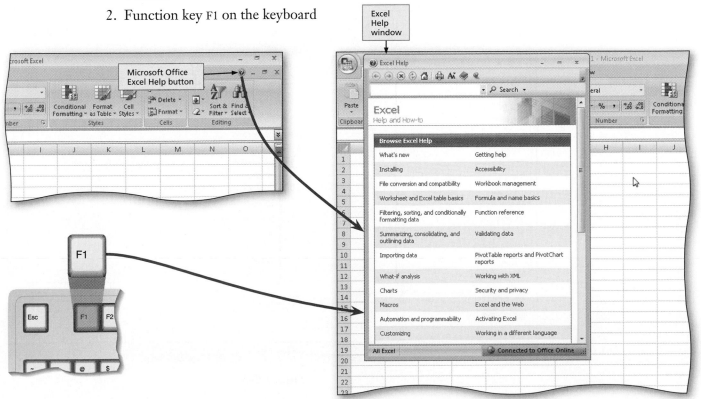

Figure C–1

To Open the Excel Help Window

The following steps open the Excel Help window and maximize the window.

1

- Start Microsoft Excel, if necessary. Click the Microsoft Office Excel Help button near the upper-right corner of the Excel window to open the Excel Help window (Figure C–2).

Figure C–2

2

- Click the Maximize button on the Help title bar to maximize the Help window (Figure C–3).

Figure C–3

The Excel Help Window

The Excel Help window provides several methods for accessing help about a particular topic, and also has tools for navigating around Help. Methods for accessing Help include searching the help content installed with Excel, or searching the online Office content maintained by Microsoft.

Figure C–3 shows the main Excel Help window. To navigate Help, the Excel Help window includes search features that allow you to search on a word or phrase about which you want help; the Connection Status button, which allows you to control where Excel Help searches for content; toolbar buttons; and links to major Help categories.

Search Features

You can perform Help searches on words or phrases to find information about any Excel feature using the 'Type words to search for' text box and the Search button (Figure C–4a). Click the 'Type words to search for' text box and then click the Search button or press the ENTER key to initiate a search of Excel Help.

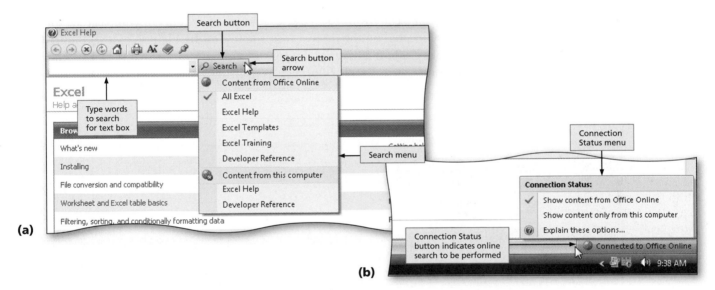

Figure C–4

Excel Help offers the user the option of searching the online Help Web pages maintained by Microsoft or the offline Help files placed on your computer when you install Excel. You can specify whether Excel Help should search online or offline from two places: the Connection Status button on the status bar of the Excel Help window, or the Search button arrow on the toolbar. The Connection Status button indicates whether Help currently is set up to work with online or offline information sources. Clicking the Connection Status button provides a menu with commands for selecting online or offline searches (Figure C–4b). The Connection Status menu allows the user to select whether help searches will return content only from the computer (offline), or content from the computer and from Office Online (online).

Clicking the Search button arrow also provides a menu with commands for an online or offline search (Figure C–4a). These commands determine the source of information that Help searches for during the current Help session only. For example, assume that your preferred search is an offline search because you often do not have Internet access. You would set Connection Status to 'Show content only from this computer'. When you have Internet access, you can select an online search from the Search menu to search Office Online for information for your current search session only. Your search will use the Office Online resources until you quit Help. The next time you start Help, the Connection Status once again will be offline. In addition to setting the source of information that Help searches for during the current Help session, you can use the Search menu to further target the current search to one of four subcategories of online Help: Excel Help, Excel Templates, Excel Training, and Developer Reference. The local search further can target one subcategory, Developer Reference.

In addition to searching for a word or string of text, you can use the links provided on the Browse Excel Help area (Figure C–3) on page APP 10 to search for help on a topic. These links direct you to major help categories. From each major category, subcategories are available to further refine your search.

Finally, you can use the Table of Contents for Excel Help to search for a topic the same way you would in a hard copy book. The Table of Contents is accessed via a toolbar button.

Toolbar Buttons

You can use toolbar buttons to navigate through the results of your search. The toolbar buttons are located on the toolbar near the top of the Help Window (Figure C–5). The toolbar buttons contain navigation buttons as well as buttons that perform other useful and common tasks in Excel Help, such as printing.

Figure C–5

The Excel Help navigation buttons are the Back, Forward, Stop, Refresh, and Home buttons. These five buttons behave like the navigation buttons in a Web browser window. You can use the Back button to go back one window, the Forward button to go forward one window, the Stop button to stop loading the current page, and the Home button to redisplay the Help home page in the Help window. Use the Refresh button to reload the information requested into the Help window from its original source. When getting Help information online, this button provides the most current information from the Microsoft Help Web site.

The buttons located to the right of the navigation buttons — Print, Change Font Size, Show Table of Contents, and Not on Top — provide you with access to useful and common commands. The Print button prints the contents of the open Help window. The Change Font Size button customizes the Help window by increasing or decreasing the size of its text. The Show Table of Contents button opens a pane on the left side of the Help window that shows the Table of Contents for Excel Help. You can use the Table of Contents for Excel Help to navigate through the contents of Excel Help much as you would use the Table of Contents in a book to search for a topic. The Not On Top button is an example of a toggle button, which is a button that can be switched back and forth between two states. It determines how the Excel Help window behaves relative to other windows. When clicked, the Not On Top button changes to Keep On Top. In this state, it does not allow other windows from Excel or other programs to cover the Excel Help window when those windows are the active windows. When in the Not On Top state, the button allows other windows to be opened or moved on top of the Excel Help window.

You can customize the size and placement of the Help window. Resize the window using the Maximize and Restore buttons, or by dragging the window to a desired size. Relocate the Help window by dragging the title bar to a new location on the screen.

Searching Excel Help

Once the Excel Help window is open, several methods exist for navigating Excel Help. You can search for help by using any of the three following methods from the Help window:

1. Enter search text in the 'Type words to search for' text box
2. Click the links in the Help window
3. Use the Table of Contents

To Obtain Help Using the Type Words to Search for Text Box

Assume for the following example that you want to know more about watermarks. The following steps use the 'Type words to search for' text box to obtain useful information about watermarks by entering the phrase, conditional formatting, as search text. The steps also navigate in the Excel Help window.

1

- **Type** conditional formatting in the 'Type words to search for' text box at the top of the Excel Help window.

- Click the Search button arrow to display the Search menu.

- If it is not selected already, click All Excel on the Search menu to select the command. If All Excel is already selected, click the Search button arrow again to close the Search menu.

Q&A

Why select All Excel on the Search menu?

Selecting All Excel on the Search menu ensures that Excel Help will search all possible sources for information on your search term. It will produce the most complete search results.

Figure C–6

- Click the Search button to display the search results (Figure C–7).

Q&A Why do my results differ?

If you do not have an Internet connection, your results will reflect only the content of the Help files on your computer. When searching for help online, results also can change as material is added, deleted, and updated on the online Help Web pages maintained by Microsoft.

Q&A Why were my search results not very helpful?

When initiating a search, keep in mind to check the spelling of the search text; and to keep your search very specific, with fewer than seven words, to return the most accurate results.

Figure C–7

- Click the 'Add, change, or clear conditional formats' link to open the Help document associated with the link in the Help window (Figure C–8).

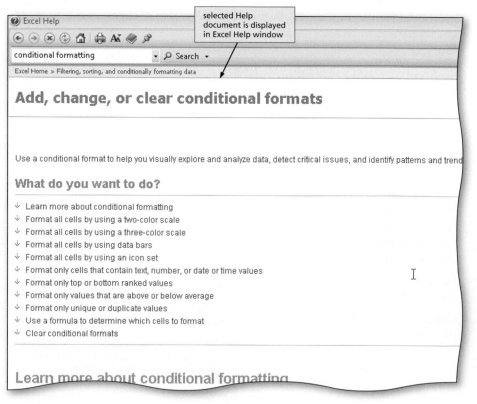

Figure C–8

4
- Click the Home button on the taskbar to clear the search results and redisplay the Excel Help home page (Figure C–9).

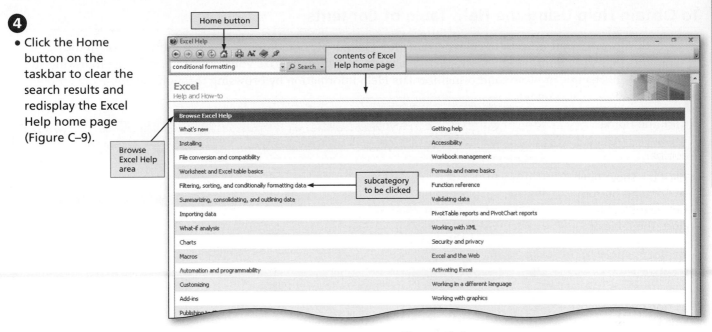

Home button

contents of Excel Help home page

Browse Excel Help area

subcategory to be clicked

Figure C–9

To Obtain Help Using the Help Links

If your topic of interest is listed in the Browse Excel Help area, you can click the link to begin browsing Excel Help categories instead of entering search text. You browse Excel Help just like you would browse a Web site. If you know in which category to find your Help information, you may wish to use these links. The following steps find the Add, change, or clear conditional formats Help information using the category link from the Excel Help home page.

1
- Click the 'Filtering, sorting, and conditionally formatting data' link to open the Filtering, sorting, and conditionally formatting data page.

- Click the 'Add, change, or clear conditional formats' link to open the Help document associated with the link (Figure C–10).

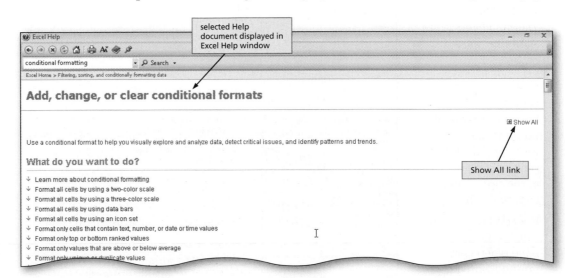

selected Help document displayed in Excel Help window

Show All link

Figure C–10

Q&A

What does the Show All link do?

In many Help documents, additional information about terms and features is available by clicking a link in the document to display additional information in the Help document. Clicking the Show All link opens all the links in the Help document that expand to additional text.

To Obtain Help Using the Help Table of Contents

A third way to find Help in Excel is through the Help Table of Contents. You can browse through the Table of Contents to display information about a particular topic or to familiarize yourself with Excel. The following steps access the Add, change, or clear conditional formats Help information by browsing through the Table of Contents.

- Click the Home button on the toolbar.

- Click the Show Table of Contents button on the toolbar to open the Table of Contents pane on the left side of the Help window. If necessary, click the Maximize button on the Help title bar to maximize the window (Figure C–11).

Figure C–11

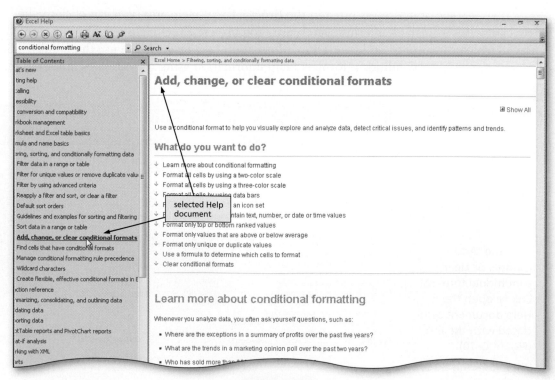

- Click the 'Filtering, sorting, and conditionally formatting data' link in the Table of Contents pane to view a list of Help subtopics.

- Click the 'Add, change, or clear conditional formats' link in the Table of Contents pane to view the selected Help document in the right pane (Figure C–12).

Q&A

How do I remove the Table of Contents pane when I am finished with it?

The Show Table of Contents button acts as a toggle switch. When the Table of Contents pane is visible, the button changes to Hide Table of Contents. Clicking it hides the Table of Contents pane and changes the button to Show Table of Contents.

Figure C–12

Obtaining Help while Working in Excel

Often you may need help while working on a document without already having the Help window open. For example, you may be unsure about how a particular command works, or you may be presented with a dialog box that you are not sure how to use. Rather than opening the Help window and initiating a search, Excel Help provides you with the ability to search directly for help.

Figure C–13 shows one option for obtaining help while working in Excel. If you want to learn more about a command, point to the command button and wait for the Enhanced ScreenTip to appear. If the Help icon appears in the Enhanced ScreenTip, press the F1 key while pointing to the command to open the Help window associated with that command.

Figure C–13

Figure C–14 shows a dialog box with a Get help button in it. Pressing the F1 key while the dialog box is displayed opens a Help window. The Help window contains help about that dialog box, if available. If no help file is available for that particular dialog box, then the main Help window opens.

Figure C–14

Use Help

1 Obtaining Help Using Search Text

Instructions: Perform the following tasks using Excel Help.

1. Use the 'Type words to search for' text box to obtain help about landscape printing. Use the Connection Status menu to search online help if you have an Internet connection.

2. Click 'Print landscape or portrait' in the list of links in the search results. Double-click the Microsoft Office Excel Help window title bar to maximize it. Read and print the information. At the top of the printout, write down the number of links Excel Help found.

3. Use the Search menu to search for help offline. Repeat the search from Step 1. At the top of the printout, write down the number of links that Excel Help found searching offline. Submit the printouts as specified by your instructor.

4. Use the 'Type words to search for' text box to search for information online about adjusting cell width. Click the 'Change column width and row height' link in the search results. If necessary, maximize the Microsoft Office 2007 Excel Help window. Read and print the contents of the window. Close the Microsoft Office Excel Help window. Submit the printouts as specified by your instructor.

5. For each of the following words and phrases, click one link in the search results, click the Show All link, and then print the page: pie charts; formulas; print preview; Ribbon; data sorting; and accounting format. Submit the printouts as specified by your instructor.

2 Expanding on Excel Help Basics

Instructions: Use Excel Help to better understand its features and answer the questions listed below. Answer the questions on your own paper, or submit the printed Help information as specified by your instructor.

1. Use Help to find out how to customize the Help window. Change the font size to the smallest option and then print the contents of the Microsoft Office Excel Help window. Change the font size back to its original setting. Close the window.

2. Press the F1 key. Search for information about tables, restricting the search results to Excel Templates. Print the first page of the Search results. You must be working online to restrict the results to Excel templates.

3. Search for information about tables, restricting the search results to Excel Help files. Print the first page of the Search results.

4. Use Excel Help to find out what happened to the Office Assistant, a feature in the previous version of Excel. Print out the Help document that contains the answer.

Appendix D

Publishing Office 2007 Web Pages to a Web Server

With the Office 2007 programs, you use the Save As command on the Office Button menu to save a Web page to a Web server using one of two techniques: Web folders or File Transfer Protocol. A **Web folder** is an Office shortcut to a Web server. **File Transfer Protocol (FTP)** is an Internet standard that allows computers to exchange files with other computers on the Internet.

You should contact your network system administrator or technical support staff at your Internet access provider to determine if their Web server supports Web folders, FTP, or both, and to obtain necessary permissions to access the Web server. If you decide to publish Web pages using a Web folder, you must have the Office Server Extensions (OSE) installed on your computer.

Using Web Folders to Publish Office 2007 Web Pages

When publishing to a Web folder, someone first must create the Web folder before you can save to it. If you are granted permission to create a Web folder, you must obtain the Web address of the Web server, a user name, and possibly a password that allows you to access the Web server. You also must decide on a name for the Web folder. Table D–1 explains how to create a Web folder.

Office 2007 adds the name of the Web folder to the list of current Web folders. You can save to this folder, open files in the folder, rename the folder, or perform any operations you would to a folder on your hard disk. You can use your Office 2007 program or Windows Explorer to access this folder. Table D–2 explains how to save to a Web folder.

Table D–1 Creating a Web Folder

1. Click the Office Button and then click Save As or Open.

2. When the Save As dialog box (or Open dialog box) appears, click the Tools button arrow, and then click Map Network Drive... When the Map Network Drive dialog box is displayed, click the 'Connect to a Web site that you can use to store your documents and pictures' link.

3. When the Add Network Location Wizard dialog box appears, click the Next button. If necessary, click Choose a custom network location. Click the Next button. Click the View examples link, type the Internet or network address, and then click the Next button. Click 'Log on anonymously' to deselect the check box, type your user name in the User name text box, and then click the Next button. Enter the name you want to call this network place and then click the Next button. Click to deselect the 'Open this network location when I click Finish' check box, and then click the Finish button.

Table D–2 Saving to a Web Folder

1. Click the Office Button, click Save As.

2. When the Save As dialog box is displayed, type the Web page file name in the File name text box. Do not press the ENTER key.

3. Click the Save as type box arrow and then click Web Page to select the Web Page format.

4. Click Computer in the Navigation pane.

5. Double-click the Web folder name in the Network Location list.

6. If the Enter Network Password dialog box appears, type the user name and password in the respective text boxes and then click the OK button.

7. Click the Save button in the Save As dialog box.

Using FTP to Publish Office 2007 Web Pages

When publishing a Web page using FTP, you first must add the FTP location to your computer before you can save to it. An FTP location, also called an **FTP site**, is a collection of files that reside on an FTP server. In this case, the FTP server is the Web server.

To add an FTP location, you must obtain the name of the FTP site, which usually is the address (URL) of the FTP server, and a user name and a password that allows you to access the FTP server. You save and open the Web pages on the FTP server using the name of the FTP site. Table D–3 explains how to add an FTP site.

Office 2007 adds the name of the FTP site to the FTP locations list in the Save As and Open dialog boxes. You can open and save files using this list. Table D–4 explains how to save to an FTP location.

Table D–3 Adding an FTP Location
1. Click the Office Button and then click Save As or Open.
2. When the Save As dialog box (or Open dialog box) appears, click the Tools button arrow, and then click Map Network Drive... When the Map Network Drive dialog box is displayed, click the 'Connect to a Web site that you can use to store your documents and pictures' link.
3. When the Add Network Location Wizard dialog box appears, click the Next button. If necessary, click Choose a custom network location. Click the Next button. Click the View examples link, type the Internet or network address, and then click the Next button. If you have a user name for the site, click to deselect 'Log on anonymously' and type your user name in the User name text box, and then click Next. If the site allows anonymous logon, click Next. Type a name for the location, click Next, click to deselect the 'Open this network location when I click Finish' check box, and click Finish. Click the OK button.
4. Close the Save As or the Open dialog box.

Table D–4 Saving to an FTP Location
1. Click the Office Button and then click Save As.
2. When the Save As dialog box is displayed, type the Web page file name in the File name text box. Do not press the ENTER key.
3. Click the Save as type box arrow and then click Web Page to select the Web Page format.
4. Click Computer in the Navigation pane.
5. Double-click the name of the FTP site in the Network Location list.
6. When the FTP Log On dialog box appears, enter your user name and password and then click the OK button.
7. Click the Save button in the Save As dialog box.

Appendix E
Customizing Microsoft Office Excel 2007

This appendix explains how to change the screen resolution in Windows Vista to the resolution used in this book. It also describes how to customize the Excel window by changing the Ribbon, Quick Access Toolbar, and the color scheme.

Changing Screen Resolution

Screen resolution indicates the number of pixels (dots) that the computer uses to display the letters, numbers, graphics, and background you see on the screen. When you increase the screen resolution, Windows displays more information on the screen, but the information decreases in size. The reverse also is true: as you decrease the screen resolution, Windows displays less information on the screen, but the information increases in size.

The screen resolution usually is stated as the product of two numbers, such as 1024×768 (pronounced "ten twenty-four by seven sixty-eight"). A 1024×768 screen resolution results in a display of 1,024 distinct pixels on each of 768 lines, or about 786,432 pixels. The figures in this book were created using a screen resolution of 1024×768.

The screen resolutions most commonly used today are 800×600 and 1024×768, although some Office specialists set their computers at a much higher screen resolution, such as 2048×1536.

To Change the Screen Resolution

The following steps change the screen resolution from 1280×1024 to 1024×768. Your computer already may be set to 1024×768 or some other resolution.

- If necessary, minimize all programs so that the Windows Vista desktop appears.

- Right-click the Windows Vista desktop to display the Windows Vista desktop shortcut menu (Figure E–1).

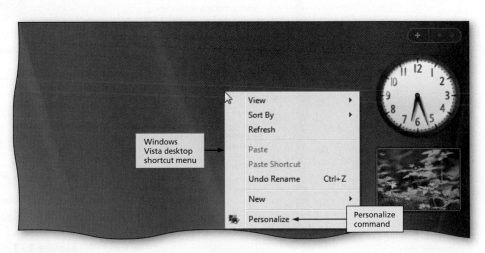

Figure E–1

2

- Click Personalize on the shortcut menu to open the Personalize window.

- Click Display Settings in the Personalization window to display the Display Settings dialog box (Figure E–2).

Figure E–2

3

- Drag the slider in the Resolution area so that the screen resolution changes to 1024 × 768 (Figure E–3).

Figure E–3

4

- Click the OK button to change the screen resolution from 1280 × 1024 to 1024 × 768 (Figure E–4).

Figure E–4

5

- Click the Yes button in the Display Settings dialog box to accept the new screen resolution (Figure E–5).

Q&A

What if I do not want to change the screen resolution after seeing it applied after I click the OK button?

You either can click the No button in the inner Display Settings dialog box, or wait for the timer to run out, at which point Windows Vista will revert to the original screen resolution.

- Click the Close button to close the Personalization Window.

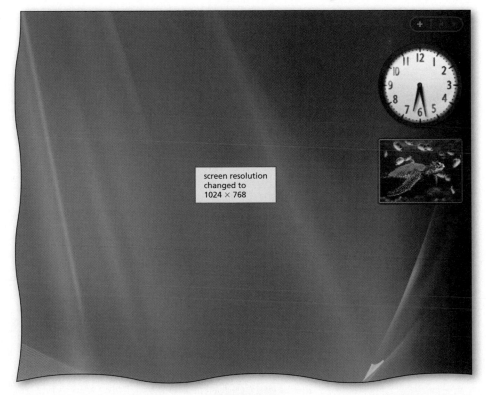

Figure E–5

Screen Resolution and the Appearance of the Ribbon in Office 2007 Programs

Changing the screen resolution affects how the Ribbon appears in Office 2007 programs. Figure E–6 shows the Word Ribbon at the screen resolutions of 800 × 600, 1024 × 768, and 1280 × 1024. All of the same commands are available regardless of screen resolution. Word, however, makes changes to the groups and the buttons within the groups to accommodate the various screen resolutions. The result is that certain commands may need to be accessed differently depending on the resolution chosen. A command that is visible on the Ribbon and available by clicking a button at one resolution may not be visible and may need to be accessed using its group button at a different resolution.

Figure E–6

Comparing the three Ribbons, notice changes in content and layout of the groups and galleries. In some cases, the content of a group is the same in each resolution, but the layout of the group differs. For example, the same buttons appear in the Font and Paragraph groups in the three resolutions, but the layouts differ. The buttons are displayed in three rows at the 800 × 600 resolution, and in two rows in the 1024 × 768 and 1280 × 1024 resolutions. In other cases, the content and layout are the same across the resolution, but the level of detail differs with the resolution. In the Clipboard group, when the resolution increases to 1280 × 1024, the names of all the buttons in the group appear in addition to the buttons themselves. At the lower resolution, only the buttons appear.

Changing resolutions also can result in fewer commands being visible in a group. Comparing the Editing groups, notice that the group at the 800 × 600 resolution consists of an Editing button, while at the higher resolutions, the group has three buttons visible. The commands that are available on the Ribbon at the higher resolutions must be accessed using the Editing button at the 800 × 600 resolution.

Changing resolutions results in different amounts of detail being available at one time in the galleries on the Ribbon. The Styles gallery in the three resolutions presented show different numbers of styles. At 800 × 600, you can scroll through the gallery three styles at a time, at 1024 × 768, you can scroll through the gallery four styles at a time, and at 1280 × 1024, you can scroll through the gallery six styles at a time.

Customizing the Excel Window

When working in Excel, you may want to make your working area as large as possible. One option is to minimize the Ribbon. You also can modify the characteristics of the Quick Access Toolbar, customizing the toolbar's commands and location to better suit your needs.

To Minimize the Ribbon in Excel

The following steps minimize the Ribbon.

- Start Excel.

- Maximize the Excel window, if necessary.

- Click the Customize Quick Access Toolbar button on the Quick Access Toolbar to display the Customize Quick Access Toolbar menu (Figure E–7).

Figure E–7

- Click Minimize the Ribbon on the Quick Access Toolbar menu to cause the Ribbon to display just the tabs (Figure E–8).

Figure E–8

Other Ways

1. Double-click the active Ribbon tab
2. Press CTRL+F1

Customizing and Resetting the Quick Access Toolbar

The Quick Access Toolbar, located to the right of the Office Button by default, provides easy access to some of the more frequently used commands in Excel (Figure E–7). By default, the Quick Access Toolbar contains buttons for the Save, Undo, and Redo commands. Customize the Quick Access Toolbar by changing its location in the window and by adding additional buttons to reflect which commands you would like to be able to access easily.

To Change the Location of the Quick Access Toolbar

The following steps move the Quick Access Toolbar to below the Ribbon.

- Double-click the Home tab to redisplay the Ribbon.

- Click the Customize Quick Access Toolbar button on the Quick Access Toolbar to display the Customize Quick Access Toolbar menu (Figure E–9).

Figure E–9

● Click Show Below the Ribbon on
the Quick Access Toolbar menu
to move the Quick Access Toolbar
below the Ribbon (Figure E–10).

Figure E–10

To Add Commands to the Quick Access Toolbar Using the Customize Quick Access Toolbar Menu

Some of the more commonly added commands are available for selection from the Customize Quick Access Toolbar menu. The following steps add the Quick Print button to the Quick Access Toolbar.

● Click the Customize Quick Access
Toolbar button to display the
Customize Quick Access Toolbar
menu (Figure E–11).

Figure E–11

• Click Quick Print on the Quick Access Toolbar menu to add the Quick Print button to the Quick Access Toolbar (Figure E–12).

Figure E–12

To Add Commands to the Quick Access Toolbar Using the Shortcut Menu

Commands also can be added to the Quick Access Toolbar from the Ribbon. Adding an existing Ribbon command that you use often to the Quick Access Toolbar makes the command immediately available, regardless of which tab is active.

• Click the Review tab on the Ribbon to make it the active tab.

• Right-click the Spelling button on the Review tab to display a shortcut menu (Figure E–13).

Figure E–13

2

- Click Add to Quick Access Toolbar on the shortcut menu to add the Spelling button to the Quick Access Toolbar (Figure E–14).

Figure E–14

To Add Commands to the Quick Access Toolbar Using Excel Options

Some commands do not appear on the Ribbon. They can be added to the Quick Access Toolbar using the Excel Options dialog box.

1

- Click the Office Button to display the Office Button menu (Figure E–15).

Figure E–15

2

• Click the Excel
Options button on
the Office Button
menu to display the
Excel Options dialog
box (Figure E–16).

Figure E–16

3

• Click Customize in
the left pane.

• Click the 'Choose
commands from'
box arrow to
display the 'Choose
commands from'
list.

• Click Commands Not
in the Ribbon in the
'Choose commands
from' list.

• Scroll to display the
Web Page Preview
command.

• Click Web Page
Preview to select it
(Figure E–17).

Figure E–17

4

• Click the Add button to add the Web Page Preview button to the list of buttons on the Quick Access Toolbar (Figure E–18).

Figure E–18

5

• Click the OK button to add the Web Page Preview button to the Quick Access Toolbar (Figure E–19).

Figure E–19

Other Ways
1. Click Customize Quick Access Toolbar button, click More Commands, select commands to add, click Add button, click OK button

To Remove a Command from the Quick Access Toolbar

1

- Right-click the Web Page Preview button on the Quick Access Toolbar to display a shortcut menu (Figure E–20).

Figure E–20

2

- Click Remove from Quick Access Toolbar on the shortcut menu to remove the button from the Quick Access Toolbar (Figure E–21).

Figure E–21

Other Ways

1. Click Customize Quick Access Toolbar button, click More Commands, click the command you wish to remove in the Customize Quick Access Toolbar list, click Remove button, click OK button

2. If the command appears on the Customize Quick Access Toolbar menu, click the Customize Quick Access Toolbar button, click the command you wish to remove

To Reset the Quick Access Toolbar

1

- Click the Customize Quick Access Toolbar button on the Quick Access Toolbar.

- Click More Commands on the Quick Access Toolbar menu to display the Excel Options Dialog box.

- Click the 'Show Quick Access Toolbar below the Ribbon' check box to deselect it (Figure E–22).

Figure E–22

- Click the Reset button, click the Yes button in the dialog box that appears, and then click the OK button in the Excel Options dialog box, to reset the Quick Access Toolbar to its original position to the right of the Office Button, with the original three buttons (Figure E–23).

Figure E–23

Changing the Excel Color Scheme

The Microsoft Excel window can be customized by selecting a color scheme other than the default blue one. Three color schemes are available in Excel.

To Change the Excel Color Scheme

The following steps change the color scheme.

1

- Click the Office Button to display the Office Button menu.

- Click the Excel Options button on the Office Button menu to display the Excel Options dialog box.

- If necessary, click Popular in the left pane. Click the Color scheme box arrow to display a list of color schemes (Figure E–24).

Figure E–24

2

- Click Silver in the list.

- Click the OK button to change the color scheme to silver (Figure E–25).

 How do I switch back to the default color scheme?

Follow the steps for changing the Excel color scheme, and select Blue from the list of color schemes.

Figure E–25

Appendix F

Steps for the Windows XP User

For the XP User of this Book

For most tasks, no differences exist between using Excel under the Windows Vista operating system and using Excel under the Windows XP operating system. With some tasks, however, you will see some differences, or need to complete the tasks using different steps. This appendix shows how to Start Excel, Save a Workbook, Open a Workbook, and Insert a Picture while using Microsoft Office under Windows XP. The tasks can be accomplished in other Office programs in a similar fashion.

To Start Excel

The following steps, which assume Windows is running, start Excel based on a typical installation. You may need to ask your instructor how to start Excel for your computer.

1

- Click the Start button on the Windows taskbar to display the Start menu.

- Point to All Programs on the Start menu to display the All Programs submenu.

- Point to Microsoft Office on the All Programs submenu to display the Microsoft Office submenu (Figure F–1).

Figure F–1

- Click Microsoft Office Excel 2007 to start Word and display a new workbook in the Excel window (Figure F–2).

- If the Excel window is not maximized, click the Maximize button next to the Close button on its title bar to maximize the window.

- If the worksheet window in Excel is not maximized, click the Maximize button next to the Close button on its title bar to maximize the worksheet window within Excel (Figure F-2).

Figure F–2

Other Ways
1. Double-click Excel icon on desktop, if one is present 2. Click Microsoft Office Excel 2007 on Start menu

To Save a Workbook

After editing, you should save the document. The following steps save a document on a USB flash drive using the file name, Walk and Rock Music 1st Quarter Sales.

- With a USB flash drive connected to one of the computer's USB ports, click the Save button on the Quick Access Toolbar to display the Save As dialog box (Figure F–3).

Q&A

Do I have to save to a USB flash drive?

No. You can save to any device or folder. A **folder** is a specific location on a storage medium. You can save to the default folder or a different folder. You also can create your own folders, which is explained later in this book.

Figure F–3

2

- Type the name of your file (Walk and Rock Music 1st Quarter Sales in this example) in the File name text box to change the file name. Do not press the ENTER key after typing the file name (Figure F–4).

Q&A

What characters can I use in a file name?

A file name can have a maximum of 255 characters, including spaces. The only invalid characters are the backslash (\), slash (/), colon (:), asterisk (*), question mark (?), quotation mark ("), less than symbol (<), greater than symbol (>), and vertical bar (|).

Figure F–4

3

- Click the Save in box arrow to display a list of available drives and folders (Figure F–5).

Q&A

Why is my list of files, folders, and drives arranged and named differently from those shown in the figure?

Your computer's configuration determines how the list of files and folders is displayed and how drives are named. You can change the save location by clicking shortcuts on the **My Places bar**.

Q&A

How do I save the file if I am not using a USB flash drive?

Use the same process, but be certain to select your device in the Save in list.

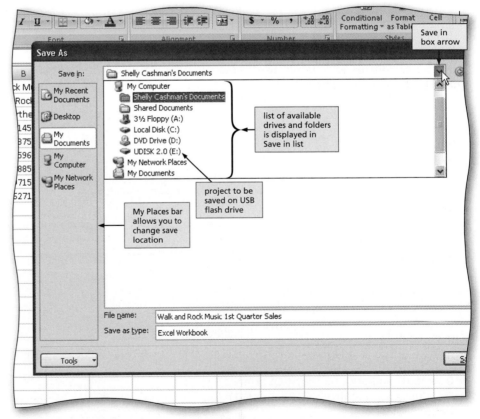

Figure F–5

4

- Click UDISK 2.0 (E:) in the Save in list to select the USB flash drive, Drive E in this case, as the new save location (Figure F–6).

- Click the Save button to save the workbook.

Q&A

What if my USB flash drive has a different name or letter?

It is very likely that your USB flash drive will have a different name and drive letter and be connected to a different port. Verify the device in your Save in list is correct.

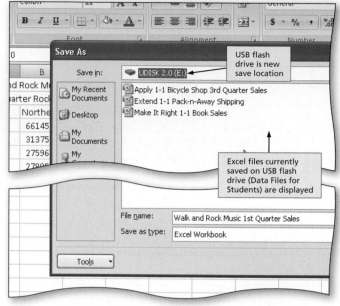

Figure F–6

Other Ways

1. Click Office Button, click Save, type file name, select drive or folder, click Save button

2. Press CTRL+S or press SHIFT+F12, type file name, select drive or folder, click Save button

To Open a Workbook

The following steps open the Walk and Rock Music 1st Quarter Sales file from the USB flash drive.

1

- With your USB flash drive connected to one of the computer's USB ports, click the Office Button to display the Office Button menu.

- Click Open on the Office Button menu to display the Open dialog box.

- If necessary, click the Look in box arrow and then click UDISK 2.0 (E:) to select the USB flash drive, Drive E in this case, in the Look in list as the new open location.

- Click Walk and Rock Music 1st Quarter Sales to select the file name (Figure F–7).

- Click the Open button to open the workbook.

Q&A

How do I open the file if I am not using a USB flash drive?

Use the same process, but be certain to select your device in the Look in list.

Figure F–7

Other Ways

1. Click Office Button, double-click file name in Recent Documents list

2. Press CTRL+O, select file name, press ENTER

To Insert a Picture

The following steps insert a picture, which, in this example, is located on a USB flash drive.

1 Click Insert on the Ribbon to display the Insert tab.

2 Click the Insert Picture from File button on the Insert tab to display the Insert Picture dialog box.

3 With your USB flash drive connected to one of the computer's USB ports, if necessary, click the Look in box arrow and then click UDISK 2.0 (E:) to select the USB flash drive, Drive E in this case, in the Look in list as the device that contains the picture.

4 Select the file name of the picture file.

5 Click the Insert button in the dialog box to insert the picture in the current worksheet.

Appendix G
Microsoft Business Certification Program

What Is the Microsoft Business Certification Program?

The Microsoft Business Certification Program enables candidates to show that they have something exceptional to offer – proved expertise in Microsoft Office 2007 programs. The two certification tracks allow candidates to choose how they want to exhibit their skills, either through validating skills within a specific Microsoft product or taking their knowledge to the next level and combining Microsoft programs to show that they can apply multiple skill sets to complete more complex office tasks. Recognized by businesses and schools around the world, more than 3 million certifications have been obtained in more than 100 different countries. The Microsoft Business Certification Program is the only Microsoft-approved certification program of its kind.

What Is the Microsoft Certified Application Specialist Certification?

The Microsoft Certified Application Specialist certification exams focus on validating specific skill sets within each of the Microsoft Office system programs. Candidates can choose which exam(s) they want to take according to which skills they want to validate. The available Application Specialist exams include:

- Using Microsoft® Windows Vista™
- Using Microsoft® Office Word 2007
- Using Microsoft® Office Excel® 2007
- Using Microsoft® Office PowerPoint® 2007
- Using Microsoft® Office Access 2007
- Using Microsoft® Office Outlook® 2007

> For more information and details on how Shelly Cashman Series textbooks map to Microsoft Certified Application Specialist certification, visit scsite.com/off2007/cert.

What Is the Microsoft Certified Application Professional Certification?

The Microsoft Certified Application Professional certification exams focus on a candidate's ability to use the 2007 Microsoft® Office system to accomplish industry-agnostic functions, for example Budget Analysis and Forecasting, or Content Management and Collaboration. The available Application Professional exams currently include:

- Organizational Support
- Creating and Managing Presentations
- Content Management and Collaboration
- Budget Analysis and Forecasting

Index

Quick Reference Summary

In the Microsoft Office Excel 2007 program, you can accomplish a task in a number of ways. The following table provides a quick reference to each task presented in this textbook. The first column identifies the task. The second column indicates the page number on which the task is discussed in the book. The subsequent four columns list the different ways the task in column one can be carried out.

Microsoft Office Excel 2007 Quick Reference Summary

Task	Page Number	Mouse	Ribbon	Shortcut Menu	Keyboard Shortcut
AutoCalculate	EX 62	Select range | right-click AutoCalculate area | click calculation			
Bold	EX 38	Bold button on Mini toolbar	Bold button on Home tab or Font Dialog Box Launcher on Home tab | Font tab	Format Cells | Font tab | Bold in Font style list	CTRL+B
Borders	EX 111	Borders button on Mini toolbar	Borders button on Home tab or Alignment Dialog Box Launcher on Home tab | Border tab	Format Cells | Border tab	CTRL+1 | B
Cell Style, change	EX 35		Cell Styles button on Home tab		
Center	EX 113	Right-click cell | Center button on Mini toolbar	Center button on Home tab or Alignment Dialog Box Launcher on Home tab	Format Cells | Alignment tab	CTRL+1 | A
Center Across Columns	EX 40	Right-click selection | Merge & Center button on Mini toolbar	Merge & Center button on Home tab or Alignment Dialog Box Launcher on Home tab	Format Cells | Alignment tab	CTRL+1 | A
Chart, Add	EX 50, 205		Dialog Box Launcher in Charts group on Insert tab		F11
Clear Cell	EX 66	Drag fill handle back	Clear button on Home tab	Clear Contents	DELETE
Clear Worksheet	EX 66		Select All button on worksheet | Clear button on Home tab		
Close Workbook	EX 59		Close button on Ribbon or Office Button | Close		CTRL+W

Microsoft Office Excel 2007 Quick Reference Summary (continued)

Task	Page Number	Mouse	Ribbon	Shortcut Menu	Keyboard Shortcut
Color Background	EX 110		Fill Color button on Home tab or Font Dialog Box Launcher on Home tab	Format Cells | Fill tab	CTRL+1 | F
Color Tab	EX 216			Tab Color	
Column Width	EX 46, 122	Drag column heading boundary	Home tab | Format button | Column Width	Column Width	ALT+O | C | W
Comma Style Format	EX 44		Comma Style button on Home tab or Number Dialog Box Launcher on Home tab | Accounting	Format Cells | Number tab | Accounting	CTRL+1 | N
Conditional Formatting	EX 119		Conditional Formatting button on Home tab		ALT+O | D
Copy and Paste	EX 175		Copy button and Paste button on Home tab	Copy to copy; Paste to paste	CTRL+C; CTRL+V
Copy to adjacent cells	EX 27	Select source area | drag fill handle through destination cells	Select source area | click Copy button on Home tab | select destination area | click Paste button on Home tab	Right-click source area | click Copy | right-click destination area | click Paste	
Currency Style Format	EX 116		Currency Style button on Home tab or Format Cells | Number | Currency	Format Cells | Number | Currency	CTRL+1 | N
Cut	EX 64		Cut button on Home tab	Cut	CTRL+X
Date	EX 184	Insert Function button in formula bar | Date & Time | NOW	Date & Time button on Formulas tab | NOW		CTRL+SEMICOLON
Date, Format	EX 113		Font Dialog Box Launcher on Home tab | Number tab | Date	Format Cells | Number tab | Date	
Decimal Place, Decrease	EX 115		Decrease Decimal button on Home tab or Number Dialog Box Launcher on Home tab | Number tab | Currency	Format Cells | Number tab | Currency	CTRL+1 | N
Decimal Place, Increase	EX 118		Increase Decimal button on Home tab or Number Dialog Box Launcher on Home tab | Number tab | Currency	Format Cells | Number tab | Currency	CTRL+1 | N
Delete Rows or Columns	EX 180		Home tab | Delete button arrow | Delete Sheet Rows or Home tab | Delete button arrow | Delete Sheet Columns	Delete | Entire row or Delete | Entire column	
Document Properties, Set or View	EX 55	Office Button | Prepare | Properties			ALT+F | E | P

Microsoft Office Excel 2007 Quick Reference Summary (continued)

Task	Page Number	Mouse	Ribbon	Shortcut Menu	Keyboard Shortcut
E-Mail from Excel	EX 142	Office Button | Send | E-Mail			ALT+F | D | E
Embedded Chart, Delete	EX 67				Select chart, press DELETE
File Management	EX 259		Office Button | Save As | right-click file name		ALT+F | A | right-click file name
Fit to Print	EX 156		Page Setup Dialog Box Launcher on Page Layout tab		ALT+P | SP
Folder, New	EX 259		Office Button | Save As | Create New Folder button		ALT+F | A
Font Color	EX 39	Font Color box arrow on Mini toolbar	Font Color button arrow on Home tab or Font Dialog Box Launcher on Home tab	Format Cells | Font tab	CTRL+1 | F
Font Size, Change	EX 38	Font Size box arrow on Mini toolbar	Font Size box arrow on Home tab or Font Dialog Box Launcher on Home tab	Format Cells | Font tab	CTRL+1 | F
Font Size, Increase	EX 39	Increase Font Size button on Mini toolbar	Increase Font Size button on Home tab		
Font Type	EX 36	Font box arrow on Mini toolbar	Font box arrow on Home tab or Font Dialog Box Launcher on Home tab	Format Cells | Font tab	CTRL+1 | F
Formula Assistance	EX 101	Insert Function button in formula bar	Insert Function button on Formulas tab		CTRL+A after you type function name
Formulas Version	EX 136				CTRL+ACCENT MARK
Freeze Worksheet Titles	EX 182		Freeze Panes button on the View tab | Freeze Panes		ALT+W | F
Full Screen	EX 9		Full Screen button on View tab		ALT+V | U
Function	EX 101	Insert Function button in formula bar	Insert Function button on Formulas tab		SHIFT+F3
Go To	EX 48	Click cell	Find & Select button on Home tab		F5
Goal Seek	EX 225		What-If Analysis button on Data tab | Goal Seek		ALT+T | G
Help	EX 67 and Appendix C		Microsoft Office Excel Help button on Ribbon		F1
Hide Column	EX 122	Drag column heading boundary	Format button on Home tab | Hide & Unhide or Hide & Unhide button on View tab	Hide	CTRL+0 (zero) to hide CTRL+SHIFT+) to display
Hide Row	EX 126	Drag row heading boundary		Hide	CTRL+9 to hide CTRL+SHIFT+(to display
In-Cell Editing	EX 63	Double-click cell			F2

Microsoft Office Excel 2007 Quick Reference Summary (*continued*)

Task	Page Number	Mouse	Ribbon	Shortcut Menu	Keyboard Shortcut
Insert Rows or Columns	EX 178		Home tab | Insert button arrow | Insert Sheet Rows or Home tab | Insert button arrow | Insert Sheet Columns	Insert	ALT+I | R or C
Insert Single Cell or Range of Cells	EX 179		Home | Insert button arrow | Insert Cells		
Italicize	EX 203		Italic button on Home tab or Font Dialog Box Launcher on Home tab | Font tab	Format Cells | Font tab	CTRL+I
Margins, Change	EX 130		Margins button on Page Layout tab		
Merge Cells	EX 41		Merge & Center button on Home tab or Alignment Dialog Box Launcher on Home tab	Format Cells | Alignment tab	ALT+O | E | A
Move Cells	EX 177	Point to border and drag	Cut button on Home tab; Paste button on Home tab	Cut; Paste	CTRL+X; CTRL+V
Move Sheet	EX 217	Drag sheet tab to desired location		Move or Copy	
New Workbook	EX 67	Office Button | New			CTRL+N
Open Workbook	EX 61	Office Button | Open			CTRL+O
Paste Options	EX 176		Paste button arrow on Home tab		
Percent Style Format	EX 118		Percent Style button on Home tab or Number Dialog Box Launcher on Home tab | Percentage	Format Cells | Number tab | Percentage	CTRL+1 | N or CTRL+SHIFT+%.
Preview Worksheet	EX 132	Office Button | Print | Print Preview			ALT+F | W | V
Print Worksheet	EX 132	Office Button | Print			CTRL+P
Quit Excel	EX 59	Close button on title bar Office Button | Exit Excel			ALT+F4
Range Finder	EX 106	Double-click cell			
Redo	EX 65	Redo button on Quick Access Toolbar			ALT+3 or CTRL+Y
Remove Splits	EX 223	Double-click split bar	Split button on View tab		ALT+W | S
Rename Sheet tab	EX 217	Double-click sheet tab | type sheet name		Rename	
Rotate Text	EX 169		Alignment Dialog Box Launcher on Home tab	Format Cells | Alignment tab	ALT+O | E | A
Row Height	EX 125	Drag row heading boundary	Format button on Home tab | Row Height	Row Height	ALT+O | R | E
Save Workbook, New Name	EX 57		Office Button | Save As		ALT+F | A
Save Workbook, Same Name	EX 57	Save button on Quick Access Toolbar	Office Button | Save		CTRL+S

Microsoft Office Excel 2007 Quick Reference Summary (continued)

Task	Page Number	Mouse	Ribbon	Shortcut Menu	Keyboard Shortcut
Select All of Worksheet	EX 67	Select All button on worksheet			CTRL+A
Select Cell	EX 15	Click cell or click Name box, type cell reference, press ENTER			Use arrow keys
Select Multiple Sheets	EX 218	CTRL+click tab or SHIFT+click tab		Select All Sheets	
Series	EX 169	Drag fill handle			ALT+E | I | S
Shortcut Menu	EX 12	Right-click object			SHIFT+F10
Spell Check	EX 127	Spelling button on Review tab			F7
Split Cell	EX 41		Merge & Center button on Home tab or Alignment Dialog Box Launcher on Home tab | click Merge cells to deselect	Format Cells | Alignment tab | click Merge cells to deselect	ALT+O | E | A
Split Window into Panes	EX 222	Drag vertical or horizontal split box	Split button on View tab		ALT+W | S
Stock Quotes	EX 138		Existing Connections button on Data tab		ALT+D | D | D
Sum	EX 25	Function Wizard button in formula bar | SUM	Sum button on Home tab	Insert Function button on Formulas tab	ALT+=
Underline	EX 203		Underline button on Home tab or Font Dialog Box Launcher on Home tab	Format Cells | Font tab	CTRL+U
Undo	EX 65	Undo button on Quick Access Toolbar			ALT+2, CTRL+Z
Unfreeze Worksheet Titles	EX 194		Freeze Panes button on View tab | Unfreeze Panes		ALT+W | F
Unhide Column	EX 122	Drag hidden column heading boundary to right	Unhide button on View tab	Unhide	ALT+O | C | U
Unhide Row	EX 127	Drag hidden row heading boundary down	Unhide button on View tab	Unhide	ALT+O | R | U
Web Page, Save Workbook As	EX 256	Office button | Save As | Save as type: arrow | Single File Web Page or Office button | Save As | Save as type: arrow | Web Page			
Worksheet Name, Change	EX 141	Double-click sheet tab, type new name		Rename	
Workbook Theme, Change	EX 109		Themes button on Page Layout tab		
Zoom	EX 220	Zoom box on status bar or Zoom In and Zoom Out buttons on status bar	Zoom button on View tab		ALT+V | Z